The Political Economy of International Economic Organization

By the Same Author

With H. W. Singer, *Rich and Poor Countries,* Allen and Unwin 1982 (3rd edition)
With R. B. Ballance and H. W. Singer, *The International Economy and Industrial Development*, Wheatsheaf 1982

The Political Economy of International Economic Organization

Javed A. Ansari
Lecturer in International Economics
City University London

RIENNER   Boulder, Colorado

First published in Great Britain in 1986 by
WHEATSHEAF BOOKS LTD
A MEMBER OF THE HARVESTER PRESS PUBLISHING GROUP
Publisher: John Spiers
Director of Publications: Edward Elgar
16 Ship Street, Brighton, Sussex
and in the United States of America by
LYNNE RIENNER PUBLISHERS, INC.
948 North Street, Boulder, Colorado 80302

© Javed A. Ansari, 1986

British Library Cataloguing in Publication Data
Ansari, Javed A.
    The political economy of international economic
    organization.
    1. International economic relations
    2. International economic integration
    3. International agencies
    I. Title
    337'.06   HF1411
    ISBN 0-7450-0001-0   1508564

Library of Congress Cataloging in Publication Data
Ansari, Javed A.
    The political economy of international economic
    organization.
    Bibliography: p.
    Includes index.
        1. International economic relations. 2. International
    agencies. 3. United Nations Conference on Trade and
    Development. I. Title.
    I. Title.
    HF1411.A55 1986   337   85-10773
    ISBN 0-931477-42-5 (Rienner)

Typeset in 11pt. Times Roman by Gilbert Composing Services
Printed and bound in Great Britain by
Anchor Brendon Ltd, Tiptree, Essex

For
Anjum and Hussain

Contents

List of Tables

ix

Preface

International economic organizations have been widely studied since at least the end of the Second World War. Much of the writing has been the work of international historians, lawyers and political scientists. Paradoxically, contributions by economists have been relatively rare and this has hindered a wider appreciation of the substantive content of the work of the EIOs.

In this book I have sought to integrate the writings of authors from different disciplines in order to understand the process of international economic organization and the impact of this process on the world economy. It must be stressed that no attempt has been made to develop a general theory of international organization. This task has been addressed by several writers in the field of international political economy. My more modest concern has been to produce a practical book; a book which can be used by students, international civil servants and national policy makers in government and business, to assess the performance of specific EIOs, evaluate the appropriateness of negotiating techniques and decision-making procedures used by these organizations, and appreciate opportunities for improving organizational performance in specific issue areas. This is the *raison d'être* for the extended UNCTAD case study in Part II.

It is hoped that the book may be useful to advanced undergraduate and post-graduate students of international economic relations, development economics, public policy and political science.

A large number of people helped at various stages during the course of this work. Above all, without the help and advice of Roderick Ogley this work could not have been written. Nishat Akhtar also provided invaluable research support and was co-author of Chapter 7. Hans Singer, Robert Rhodes James, Mary Kaldor, Nicole Ball, Marc Williams, Raphael Kaplinsky, Susan Joekes, Dick Esimatoje, Geoff Kay, Jonathan Court,

Ehsan Rashid, Prof. Jack Spence, Margarida Santos and
Torbin Roepstorff, looked at various parts of this book. Some
sections were also presented as seminar papers and I benefited
from the ensuing discussion. My wife Anjum was also a great
help. Section 6.1 appeared in a longer version as an article in
the *British Journal of International Studies*, July 1978 (Vol. 4,
No. 2). Figure 5.1 is taken from A. Breton and R. Wintrobe,
*The Logic of Bureaucratic Conduct: An economic theory of
competition, exchange and efficiency in private and public
organisations*, Cambridge University Press, London 1982.
Permission to reproduce is gratefully acknowledged. During
the period this book was written I was employed by the United
Nations Industrial Organization. I have written this book in
my personal capacity and views expressed here do not reflect
the thinking of that organization in any way whatsoever.

Javed Ansari
Vienna

Abbreviations

ACABQ	Advisory Committee on Administrative and Budgetary Questions
ACAST	Advisory Committee on the Application of Science and Technology Development
ACC	Administrative Committee on Coordination
BTN	Brussels Tariff Nomenclature
CECLA	Special Commission on Latin American Coordination
CENSA	Committee of the European National Shipowners' Association
CIAP	Committee on the Alliance for Progress
CICT	Commission on International Commodity Trade
CMEA	Council for Mutual Economic Assistance
CPC	Committee on Program and Coordination
DAC	Development Assistance Committee
ECA	Economic Commission for Africa
ESCAP	Economic and Social Commission for Asia and the Pacific
ECE	Economic Commission for Europe
ECLAC	Economic Commission for Latin America and the Caribbean
ECOSOC	Economic and Social Council
EEC	European Economic Community
EFTA	European Free Trade Association
EIO	International Economic Organization
EPTA	Expanded Program of Technical Assistance
ESA	Department of Economic and Social Affairs of the UN Secretariat
FAO	Food and Agriculture Organization
GA	General Assembly
GATT	General Agreement on Tariffs and Trade
GNP	Gross national product
GSP	General system (scheme) of preferences
IACB	Inter-Agency Consultative Board

IAEA	International Atomic Energy Agency
IATA	International Air Transport Association
IBRD	International Bank for Reconstruction and Development
ICFTU	International Confederation of Free Trade Unions
IO	*International Organization*
ICC	International Coffee Council
ICCICA	Interim Coordinating Committee for International Commodity Agreements
ICITO	Interim Commission of the International Trade Organization
IDA	International Development Association
IEA	International Energy Agency
IFC	International Finance Corporation
ILO	International Labour Organization
IMO	International Marine Organization
IMF	International Monetary Fund
ITC	International Trade Center
ITO	International Trade Organization
ITU	International Telecommunication Union
IWC	International Wheat Council
LAFTA	Latin American Free Trade Association
LDDCs	Least developed among developing countries
MFN	Most favoured nation
OAU	Organization of African Unity
OECD	Organization for Economic Cooperation and Development
OEEC	Organization for European Economic Cooperation
OPEC	Organization of Petroleum Exporting Countries
OTC	Organization for Trade Cooperation
SDR	Special drawing rights
SITC	Standard International Trade Classification
SUNFED	Special United Nations Fund for Economic Development
TARS	Technical Association Recruitment Service
TDB	Trade and Development Board
TNC	Trade Negotiations Committee
UNCITRAL	United Nations Commission on International Trade Law

UNCLOS	United Nations Conference on the Law of the Sea
UNCTAD	United Nations Conference on Trade and Development
UNDP	United Nations Development Programme
UNESCO	United Nations Educational, Scientific and Cultural Organization
UNESOB	United Nations Economic and Social Office in Beirut
UNIDO	United Nations Industrial Development Organization
WFTU	World Federation of Trade Unions

PART I: Conceptual Approaches

International economic organizations (EIOs) have been in existence for at least a century and a half. They provide a wide range of functions within the world economy. Part one is concerned with assessing the role of the EIOs within the existing international economic system. It discusses a number of approaches currently in use for evaluating the environmental impact of EIOs. It focusses on the determinants of EIO organizational structure and on the process of decision making within EIOs. It evaluates the role of the secretariat in shaping organizational processes and determining environmental impact.

Addressing these questions does not lead to the development of a grand general theory, with prescriptive implications—that is a task which can only be addressed by developing a theory of the role of the state in the social formations characteristic of late capitalism. Part I should, hopefully, provide a basis for understanding the functional scope of existing EIOs and the environmental constraints on their effectiveness. It should enable us to evaluate the extent to which a given EIO has realised its environmental potential and also to identify the factors which account for its successes and failures. In order to test this conviction I utilized some of the 'middle level' theories and hypotheses outlined in the different chapters of Part I to study the environmental impact and the organizational structures of UNCTAD in Part II. I believe that other EIOs can also be studied on the basis of some of the approaches outlined in Part I.

1 The Nature of International Economic Organization

1.1 INTRODUCTION

This is a book about some of the process by which public goods and services are produced and distributed at the international level. The need for international public services, policies and goods has expanded in response to the growth in communications and economic transactions. The process by which these needs are met—the process of international organization—has become more complex and has involved a wider range of issues and areas since the Second World War.

The process of international economic organization is concerned with the regulation of the international economy. It involves the establishment and implementation of rules and procedures for the pursuit of internationally agreed upon objectives and norms. Often the instruments by which these objectives are defined and pursued are international organizations (IOs) which are charged with the responsibility of giving both stability and cohesiveness to a given structure of international economic relations.

International economic organizations (EIOs) may thus be conceived as instruments for the execution of the international economic policy of national governments. They may be considered to be similar in their relationship *vis-à-vis* national legislatures to the Treasury, the Department of Trade, the Federal Reserve Bank and the Ministry of Environment. They are in other words the constituent parts of an international public sector.

But is there such a thing as the international public sector? At one level it is undeniable that the provision of international public goods and services requires at least some organization that is fundamentally different in kind from the type of organization that ensures the production of public goods within nation states. The latter process is sanctioned and sustained by legitimate political authority. Although there

3

exists at the international level an elaborate administrative structure and a growing range of political institutions, EIOs do not possess the ability of the national treasury and the central bank to impose their decisions upon their membership. Similarly, individual national governments are less able to influence the production and distribution of the output of the EIOs than of national public agencies.

Despite these differences it must be noted that over a wide range of issue areas and in a wide variety of economic and political circumstances EIOs have succeeded in inducing member states to execute commonly agreed policies. There is a realization that the effective functioning of the international economy requires the imposition of certain limits on national sovereignty and adherence to procedures and norms of international co-operation. This is the reason why states rarely contemplate cessation from the EIOs to which they belong (the present US threat to the UN system notwithstanding) and, those which can afford to do so, usually pay their dues.

EIOs have developed a range of techniques for policy formulation and implementation.[1] The older IOs relied principally on the technique of rule-making. Rules could be formulated on the basis of unanimity, consensus or voting majorities. This may, of course, not coincide with the majority of the EIO membership for in many important EIOs, such as the IMF and the IBRD, votes are distributed in accordance with financial commitments. Rules made by EIOs vary in terms of their binding quality, ranging from general recommendations of the type made every year by the UN General Assembly—which exert only moral pressure—to totally binding conventions implying invariable obligations. Rule making is usually followed by attempts at monitoring compliance. The IMF uses surveillance and cross-questioning of government officials to determine whether its guidelines are being adhered to in the making and implementation of national policy. The International Telecommunication Union uses independent experts to monitor national compliance with its decision. A well-developed monitoring procedure can go a long way in enhancing the organizational influence of EIOs.

Other methods for increasing EIO authority are systematic co-ordination of national policies, provision of common

services, development of a research and information infrastructure, etc. All these are typically public-sector activities,
and it has been argued that 'the main difference between the
two systems is not in the degree of compliance, nor even in the
sense of community (but) in the scale of activity'.[2] The annual
expenditure of the EIOs is extremely small in comparison with
the budgets and resources of national public-sector authorities.
Nevertheless, the EIOs constitute an embryonic public sector.

This is a contentious view. Although the growing entangle-
ment of international production and exchange structure is
widely recognized there is no consensus on the implications of
this for the role of the EIOs. In the 1970s the interdependence
school had argued that a growing role for the EIOs in the
management of the world economy was necessarily implied by
the rising volume of international economic transactions.
Today, the economists and political scientists of the New Right
deny that thre is a growing need for the provision of public
goods and services. They argue for a contraction of the public
sector. They believe that international law rather than
international organization is an appropriate mechanism for
dealing with the problem of interdependence.[3]

Another objection to the perception of the EIOs as an
embryonic public sector is raised by the realist school—which
has seen a revival in the 1980s.[4] The brunt of the argument is
that EIOs, being instruments of national government, cannot
be viewed as independent makers and implementors of policy.
They lack autonomy and cannot transcend the existing state
system. They cannot be precursors of a new system of world
government.

Deferring an examination of these claims and accepting
them at their face value cannot lead to the conclusion that
international public goods and services do not exist. They do
exist and are in the main provided by EIOs. Even if EIOs are
creatures of national government, they represent a specific
pattern of interaction among the delegates of these states and
the civil servants appointed to execute mutually agreed
policies. They represent 'a focus of decision making and a
nodal point in a network of transactions'.[5] It is, of course,
possible to analyse a pattern of interaction on the basis of the
behaviour of its constituents. But social science has long

recognized that the whole may be greater than the sum of its parts. The institutional form which regulates this interaction may contribute a 'systemic' input to both the structure and substance of decision-making which is the outcome of this interaction. The institutional setting provided by EIOs is, therefore, a factor affecting the behaviour of those involved in the process of the production and distribution of public goods and services. Like other organizations EIOs may be conceived of as concerned with pattern maintenance, integration, goal attainment, adaptation to changes in environmental circumstances and orderly systemic transformation. These concerns affect both the volume and quality of public policies, goods and services generated within the international system.

Historically, EIOs have emerged in response to pressures created by the industrial revolution, which contributed to an integration of European trade and financial structures on the one hand, and stimulated the formation of nation states and the assumption by these states of an economic gate-keeping role on the other. Groom has argued that 'The effect of the French and industrial revolutions were reconciled by the development of international institutions to bring about controlled integration. As the eurocentric world became both more integrated, nationalistic international organization became more evident'.[6]

The earliest IOs concerned with international economic regulation were the European River Commissions. The Central Commission on the Navigation of the Rhine was established by the Congress of Vienna in 1815. The nineteenth century also saw agreements among European powers to administer public health and taxation jointly in certain areas of China and the Ottoman Empire. Similar international unions for the administration of telegraph, posts and telephone also appeared at about this time. EIOs emerged in America after 1889 under the auspices of the Conference of American States, which enacted numerous economic conventions and in 1901 established a Commercial Bureau, which nine years later became the Panamerican Union.[7] It is thus evident that 'international organization is a characteristic phenomenon of the modern state system . . . It has become a necessary part of the system for dealing with international problems. To organize or not to organize is no longer an open question for statesmen of our time. International organization is not an isolated phenomenon but part of a general context: its foundations are embedded in the same theoretical stratum which supports other modern economic, social and political developments'.[8]

The study of international organization has traditionally been the concern of diplomatic historians, international lawyers and political scientists. It is my contention that an economic—particularly a political economic—approach is also not irrelevant. It can be a basis for understanding the role of the EIOs within the world economy, for evaluating their impact and distinguishing the salient characteristics of the output mix they are likely to generate. EIOs are likely to play a significant role in the management of the international economy because the need (also the effective demand) for internationally produced and distributed public goods and policies is unlikely to contract significantly, and because individual national governments have a declining capacity to produce and distribute them. In the nineteenth century Britain undertook the role of the guarantor of international monetary stability. After 1945 the United States was the main provider and distributor of international financial assistance. But the relative decline of the USA as an international economic hegemon—the US share of the combined gross domestic product of the OECD group of countries fell from 50.55 per cent in 1960 to only 39.4 per cent in 1982[9]—has meant that the search for agreement and consensus among the rich OECD countries has become an indispensable basis for defining the mix of public goods and services that the international economy currently produces and the manner in which these goods are distributed. The Bretton Woods Agreement laid down the fundamental rules for the production and distribution of international public goods and gave the newly created EIOs an important role in the management of the international economy. This book hopes to provide a framework for assessing the policy contributions of the EIOs in the past forty years.

EIOs are a subset of IOs. The Yearbook of International Organization lays down a set of criteria for defining IOs. They must be genuinely international in scope and intention. Membership must be open to all appropriately qualified states. The IO must not be controlled by a single state. There must be clear procedures for the election of governing bodies and the constitution of a permanent secretariat which should consist of officers of different nationalities. Budget contributions should be distributed among the membership, and the aim must not be the making of profits.[10]

It is clear from this definition that all IOs produce public goods and policies, and at one level the theory to be evaluated in Part I is thus generally useful for understanding the behaviour and evaluating the impact of all IOs. However, the focus of the analysis has been narrowed down to concentrate on those IOs which operate in sectors traditionally recognized as having a direct impact on the organization of economic life. The provision of public goods by IOs within these sectors— called EIOs throughout this book—has a bearing on the management of the international economy.

From the main categories identified in the YIO 1983–4, the following have been selected as being principally relevant to the management of international economic life: 1. Transportation (YIO Classification No. 25); 2. Commerce (YIO No. 27); 3. Industry (YIO NO. 28); 4. Agriculture (YIO No. 38); 5. Management (YIO No. 42); 6. Economics (YIO No. 47); 7. Technology (YIO No. 48); 8. Environment (YIO No. 49); 9. Development (YIO No. 60).

There is a total of 6,814 entries within these categories— representing about 37 per cent of the total entries within the YIO. As many as 1,392 of these (6,814) entries represent processes of intergovernmental economic organization—they constitute about 26 per cent of the total intergovernmental entries recorded in the YIO. Entries representing non-governmental economic organization at the international level number 5,422 (21.2 per cent of the total).[11]

This book is principally concerned with intergovernmental EIOs involved in the regulation of the flow of goods, money and factors of production across national boundaries and in the making of international policies which aim to regulate these movements. It is recognized that intergovernmental EIOs are linked in a variety of ways with non-governmental EIOs and transnational corporations. Some of the work reviewed in the following pages may be of relevance to students of these entities.

EIOs—both governmental and intergovernmental—range from specialized consultative committees of experts to large highly politicized bodies with very broad operational mandates and a quasi-universal membership. It is not surprising therefore that there are a number of different theoretical approaches to a study of the EIOs. These are reviewed in the next section.

1.2 APPROACHES TO INTERNATIONAL ECONOMIC ORGANIZATION: AN OVERVIEW

International economic organization has been studied from a wide range of perspectives. In this section I will review the major conceptual approaches which have attempted to make sense of the phenomenon of international organization and to assess their usefulness for identifying the character, and evaluating the performance of intergovernmental economic agencies.

1.2.1 Association
Association has been described as 'a form of institutionalized relationship established between one or more states and international organizations'.[12] 'Association' permits the establishment of a system in which states integrate some aspects of their international behaviour while agreeing to keep other areas of policy making under national jurisdiction. Within an association system, the IO represents the main force which seeks to transcend the nation state level of decision-making in a gradually expanding policy area.

Typically, association systems are bilateral in character. Even when there are a number of associated members, the IO, which is the nucleus of the system, deals with each of the member states on essentially a bilateral basis. Some scholars believe that this bilateral character of association systems blunts their political impact and induces associated members to concentrate on economic and technical policies. However, political factors are of significance in both a negative and a positive sense. Political factors are of particular salience in relation to decisions concerning the desirability of 'upgrading' an associated member, as evident for example in the admission of Greece as a full member within the EEC.

Some European members of the EEC see it as a transitional association system. This transitional characteristic is almost certainly a function of the regional proximity of countries such as Spain, Portugal and perhaps even Turkey to the EEC. The non-regional association systems—such as that envisaged in for example the Lome Convention—are almost never transitional arrangements. On the other hand, association systems, whether regional or non-regional, are almost always functional in character. A growth in transactions between states and a strengthening of functionalist ties stimulate the development of association ties, although they are in themselves incapable of achieving the transformation of an association system into a system with a higher level of political integration.

The level of transactions within most association systems is high, as is the mobility of labour and capital. However, most members participate in bilateral economic and technical arrangements, and the IO becomes a natural focus for mediating these bilateral ties. The overall links of the association system may remain relatively undeveloped despite a high growth of bilateral ties within the system. The emphasis on utilizing a bilateral mechanism for the regulation of systemic transactions illustrates that association systems are constructed with an intention of avoiding supranationalism.

Association systems come into existence to regularize a growth in transactions of essentially a technical and functional nature. The process of regulation of these transactions can create momentum for upgrading an association system into a partially or wholly integrated system. Whether or not this is probable depends upon the level of systemic transaction, the reaction to its operation by powerful outside actors, the decision-making and executive institutions established as part of the association systems and the 'elite socialization' achieved as a result of the strengthening of links between the system members. There have been cases of the upgrading of association systems but virtually no incident of their ultimate disintegration.

Many intergovernmental economic organizations are part of association systems. The European Community has associates in Europe, Africa and the Caribbean. GATT has also sponsored a number of association agreements. GATT's predecessor, the still-born International Trade Organization, was also envisaged to take the form of an association system.[13] The United Nations Economic Commission for Europe can also be seen as an organization of this form. The OECD and the CMEA have associated members, as had OPEC until Gambia became a full member in 1976. OPEC has introduced association status for any potential member.

1.2.2 Harmonization

Harmonization is an attempt at avoiding discord between separate policies conceived and implemented by sovereign states. Harmonization involves the establishment of conventions defining policy principles in a diverse range of issue areas. Typically, these conventions are negotiated through the aegis of an IO.

Attempts at the harmonization of international economic policies are often based on Benthamite assumption about the nature of state policies and relations. The state—like the individuals of which it is composed—is here viewed as a 'utility maximizer', and there is assumed to exist a natural economic harmony of interests between states, similar to the natural harmony characteristic of national markets. States should co-operate to promote free trade, free movement of factors of production and the growth of international economic interdependence. This is necessary for the emergence of an efficient international division of labour, and such a harmonization of national policies would not necessarily imply an erosion of the political sovereignty of states.[14]

EIOs conceived as agents of policy harmonization are generally 'forum' rather than 'service' oriented organizations. The main concern of the secretariat is the collection, analysis and distribution of information necessary for the drawing of conventions and charters of principles. Successful harmonization of economic policies requires the existence of a common set of values and a common framework of interpretation. It also requires an awareness of the dimensions of economic interdependence and an acceptance of the need for harmonization of policies conceived and executed by national states and not by supernational agencies. Harmonization preserves national sovereignty and is a means to check the growth of supernational foci of decision making. Harmonizing agencies concentrate on the safeguarding of national interests and are rarely challenged by their clientele on questions of legitimacy or upgrading of the organizational mandate. The efficiency of such EIOs can be judged by the extent to which they succeed in expanding the area over which national decision makers find it desirable to seek to avoid policy discord. Success in harmonization usually depends upon a growing coincidence in the operational goals of national governments.

A harmonizing EIO may over a period of time abandon its original mandate and through elite socialization and bureaucratic initiatives seek a transforming role within its environment. Thus, in the early 1920s, the ILO was primarily a harmonizing EIO. Its main concern was the framing of international labour standards. These 'standards' were supposed to be incorporated in national policies in a form and at a pace determined by the nation states themselves. After 1948 the ILO became essentially a service organization subordinating its concern about international conventions to a greater involvement in the provision of technical assistance to the Third World.

There are, of course, many harmonizing EIOs which have not undergone such a transformation. The OECD is a relevant example. The OECD is concerned with harmonizing the economic policies of the major Western countries. These countries share a large store of common economic values and interests. The OECD's purpose is strictly non-contentious. The main techniques used by the OECD for harmonization are research, review of national policies, mutual cross-examination between high national officials and declaration of principles of intent. The OECD—and other harmonizing EIOs—are relatively toothless in that they cannot ensure implementation of recommendations. However, the increasing legitimacy of such agencies, a function of their non-controversial character and largely apolitical stance, enables them to play an important part in heightening their potential impact on economic policy-making processes because of the growing interdependence of markets and national economies.

1.2.3 Co-ordination

Co-ordination implies the construction of common policies by nation states which agree to modify their national policies in specified issue areas. The common policies are usually integrated into a joint programme for the achievement of mutually agreed objectives. The common policies and programmes are arrived at through a process of negotiation and compromise (not through the exercise of force), and members retain their right to reorder policy priorities. Co-ordinating IOs rely on the extensive use of experts to influence states to adopt common policies. The IO acts as a mediating agent with access to relevant specialized information which can facilitate the development of a common programme. The execution of the programme usually remains the responsibility of the member states.

Co-ordination involves a transfer of resources among member states. The transfer is usually a two-way process, and the co-ordinating agency has to convince member states that outflows and inflows are broadly balanced.

Co-ordinating IOs are involved in a perpetual process of adjustment in national policies which tend to diverge from the common programme. Co-ordination systems are subject to both centrifugal and centripetal forces. The IO attempts to strike a balance by a continuous process of examining national policies and assessing the extent to which they adhere to the objectives and methods identified in the common programme.

Many EIOs—particularly regional ones—are absorbed in policy co-ordination. The EEC has become a focus for the co-ordination of a very wide range of economic and social policies of the member countries. The commissions' initial proposals for policy changes are based upon consultations with non-governmental interest groups and governmental representatives based at Brussels. These proposals are considered by the Committee of Permanent Representatives in the light of national policies. Usually a number of commission proposals are modified and organically related to each other, forming a 'package deal'. Once agreement is reached, implementation is generally left to the discretion of individual governments, most of whom determine the pace of this implementation by making a selective use of the 'safeguard procedures' that are deliberately introduced into the original legislation for this precise purpose. The EEC thus represents a distinctive style of intergovernmental co-operating which consists of a systematic search for the co-ordination of national policies in a widening area of interests and influence.

1.2.4 Supranationalism
The European Community was not originally conceived to be merely a co-ordinating agency. The drafters of the Treaty of Rome dreamt of a federal Europe and were attempting to create a network of—at least potentially—supranational IOs.

A supranational IO is one in which the secretariat enjoys financial independence and is not under the control of national delegates. Voting decisions are made by changing simple majorities, and there is a strong *esprit de corps* among the employees of the IO. The IO should become increasingly capable of penetrating national legal systems and of creating a legal system which is common to its members. Nation states should become increasingly reluctant to apply available safeguards for opting out of compliance with the laws established by the IO.

The European Communities had during the 1960s taken some steps towards carving out for themselves a supranational role in the field of economic policy, but most observers believe that this tendency has been checked, particularly since the appearance of a regular summit as a focus of decision making. The IMF was also seen as a supranational institution by Keynes and White—the authors of the Bretton Woods agreement of 1944. Since the collapse of the Bretton Woods system in 1971 it has lost what little ability it had to act as a regulator of developed-country money and capital markets. It owes its increasing supervisory role in the Third World to the support it enjoys among the governmental and financial communities in the West, who have tended to tailor their aid and investment support programmes to the advice given by the IMF experts. The Third World countries regard the IMF not as a supernational EIO independent of the control of nation states, but as an instrument of the international economic policy of the Western countries. This is because decisions taken by the IMF are on the basis of a constant—not fluid—majority guaranteed by the larger share of quotas and votes allocated to these countries. Potentially, however, the IMF and EIOs entrusted with the task of maintaining an international financial or trade regime are supernational agencies. This potential, however, has as yet rarely been realized.

1.2.5 Functionalism and neo-functionalism

The functionalist approach to international organization is associated with the name of David Mitrany, who wrote his seminal work forty years ago.[15] Mitrany argued that 'form follows function'—tasks and functions naturally lead to evolution of forms of national and international organization which facilitate their accomplishment. In order to maximize welfare in international society it is required that we determine the geographical scope and the administrative structure of IOs so as to enable them to perform the organizational task entrusted to them effectively and efficiently. The functionalist approach is welfare-oriented and gradualist. It rejects adherence to any idealized set of political and social relations and regards the intrusion of 'high politics' as an impediment to the orderly pursuit of welfare in international society. Functionalist IOs would not be political assemblies but representative groupings of technical experts in areas such as health, energy, transport or trade. Mitrany used the example of the Tennessee Valley Authority to demonstrate how a self-evident task forced states to accept federal initiatives limiting their sovereignties. In other cases tasks could be introduced into social settings and could be capable of generating creative functional and political responses. Mitrany believed that this was, for example, possible in India. The addressing of technical issues involves people in processes of organization and decision making which gradually circumvent political barriers and facilitate the achievement of welfare goals.

The organizational process of functionalist IOs should have an impact on the attitude of those involved with them—elite socialization. It should also lead to a continuing expansion in transactions between states. This will increase interdependence and enmesh government in processes of exchange from which extraction becomes progressively costly. This is the essence of 'functionalist integration' as conceived by Mitrany. Functionalist IOs spur international integration by 'creating a sociopsychological community reflecting a co-operative ethos which helps form to follow function across national frontiers.'[16]

Functionalism envisages increasing international integration. It does not envisage 'a withering away of the state'. Integration leads to 'spillover' involving a change in popular attitudes. This stimulates a reordering of policy priorities— issues once thought to be of high political salience are no longer considered to be so. State decision makers become more involved in welfare issues. The substance of high politics changes, and there is no pressure to set up supranational foci for decision making in the 'high politics' areas of foreign policy and defence. Functionalism is not concerned with the possession or recomposition of national sovereignty.

Many EIOs can be approached from a functionalist perspective, but the pursuit of economic objectives has not made them apolitical. The process of economic integration— functionally conceived—has not made high politics issues irrelevant at either a regional or a universal level. However, these EIOs have played a part in increasing interstate transactions, promoting 'elite socialization' and, at least in the case of the EEC, inducing a broad-based change in popular attitudes which has facilitated the legitimization of a gradual restriction of national sovereignties and an increasing use of international rule making on the basis of recommendations of technical experts and specialists as a means for promoting welfares.

Ernst Haas and his associates have attempted to sharpen and refocus fundamental functionalist concepts.[17] Haas was also concerned about international integration, but in this conception integration leads to the emergency of a supranational framework of decision making and an eventual subordination of the nation state. This supersession of the nation state is to be brought about by the pooling of national resources for the joint performance of social, economic and technical functions. Haas stressed in particular the need for a gradual fusion of national economic interests as a means for integration. This fusion is to find its practical expression in the increasing authority and political salience of international central institutions, which become major decision makers within the integrated community. In this view 'elite socialization' is a more important integrative factor than are changes in popular attitudes.

Neo-functionalism assumes that 'the ends of foreign policy are qualitatively similar to ends implicit in any other field of politics. Whatever "laws" of political behaviour . . . can be . . . identified in the domestic field are therefore considered applicable to the international field as well . . . (it) attempts to synthesize the study of political behaviour . . . with an analysis of international relations as one manifestation of group aspirations'.[18] The 'laws of political behaviour' that neo-functionalism takes as given are derived from the processes of Western pluralist systems characterized by highly developed party and interest group structures. Neo-functionalist IOs are assumed to be able to penetrate such political structures and 'integrate' them at an international level by incremental economic achievements.

Neo-functionalist EIOs must formulate programmes which attract the attention and sympathy of domestic economic interest groups, which will in turn press for task expansion by the EIO. The task expansion should be so conceived and executed that it contributes towards further economic enmeshment and 'upgrades' the integrative role of the EIO. The EIOs will play a central directive role. Their political life is broadly similar to that of national decision-making institutions in the Western countries. Neo-functionalist EIOs are thus most effective in playing an integrative role when their members are mainly from this part of the world.

In the neo-functionalist conception, integration also involves 'spillover'. But 'spillover' does not mean a reordering of policy preferences or a change in popular attitudes, as is the case with the functionalists. The neo-functionalists define spillover as 'a given action related to a given goal which creates a situation in which the original goal can be achieved only by taking further actions which in turn create a further condition and a need for more action'.[19] Thus, spillover may occur when an action of an IO alters conditions of competition among its members, or in response to alterations and distortions occasioned by integrative policies both within and between states. Spillover is a consequence of the desire of IO members to arrive at a series of 'package deals' which seek to balance losses and gains for particular national groups and for the states as a whole. Spillover is thus sustained by the interaction of interest groups which increasingly politicize the operational processes of the neo-functionalist EIO and bring to it the traditional concerns and pressures of national decision-making forums. This politicization of the EIO leads to a continuous process of interpenetration of decision-making elites. National elites gradually acquire an interest in taking decisions in accordance with the norms, policy priorities and organizational procedures of the neo-functionalist EIOs.

It has been argued that the European Community was conceived of a a typical neo-functionalist form of international organizations.[20] But national interest groups and the central EC institutions have not lived up to the expectations of the neo-functionalists. The council—not the commission—is the main decision-making body. It makes its decisions on the basis of national give and take. The commission has been effectively subordinated by the Committee of Permanent Representatives, which vets commission proposals. Administrative policy leadership has, within the community, not overcome political instincts and perspectives. The formal legal powers of the nation state were not substantially eroded by pressures generated by the regional institutions.

Neo-functionalism does not identify the processes by which consensus formation associated with the growth of international organization affect the legal and formal power and mandate of the state institutions. It also does not recognize the fact that interest group leaders are not representative of their members in any direct sense—they are part of the national leadership and cannot play a particularly unique role as 'significant carriers' of an integrative ideology.

This is not to deny that international organization can play a significant role in redefining the context and content of national policies. Clearly the EC has played such a role in specific issue areas.[21] Non-regional EIO's such as ILO[22] and

UNCTAD[23] have also had a similar, although much more modest, impact. Neo-functionalism provides useful insights into the working of such IOs. Neo-functionalism needs to be complemented, however, by other approaches in order to develop a comprehensive appreciation of the policies and performance of EIOs.

There are, of course, other approaches to the processes of international economic organization.[24] Some are concerned with analysing its integrative impact, defining 'integration' diversely, but generally envisaging it to imply movement towards collective action in one or several policy dimensions. Others conceive of international organization as an aspect of the profusion of systemic ties that structure modern international relations, but do not create a comprehensible whole representing any 'grand design'. Still others are content to view international economic organization on an individual case-by-case basis. One approach that is relatively unexplored, but of particular interest to the mainstream neo-classical economists, is that which focuses upon the role of EIOs as producers and distributors of collective goods

1.2.6 The public choice approach
Public choice theory utilizes the standard tools of neo-classical analysis to study political processes. It claims to develop a 'positive' approach for understanding the behaviour of politicians, voters and bureaucrats, but it also seeks to establish 'efficient' political institutions which can contribute towards a maximization of welfare.

The three major characteristics of public choice theory are: (a) it regards the individual as the basic unit of analysis. The individual is assumed to be rational and to behave consistently on the basis of known and well-ordered preferences. He chooses a course of action which yields the highest benefit according to his own utility function. (b) Individual behaviour is explained by studying changes in the constraints upon the individual's ability for increasing his welfare. Preferences are assumed to remain constant. Marginal adjustments and perception of substitution possibilities are the standard responses to changes in constraints. (c) Finally, the main concern is with the generation of hypotheses that are, at least in principle, testable. Econometric procedures are widely used for such 'tests'.

Perhaps the most widely used concept in political analysis of economic behaviour emanating from this approach is that of public goods. A public good is one the production of which entails jointness of supply and non-excludability. Its supply cannot be restricted to those who bear the costs of its production, and hence there exists the possibility of 'free riding'. International law, international monetary agreements and international tariff conventions are all public goods. International rules and regulations have to be devised to limit the scope for 'free riding' within the system. The drawing up of such rules and ensuring that nations adhere to them is a very complex task. Rules devised must not only be 'Pareto optimal' for the system as a whole but also be such that their violation will entail a relatively high cost for the individual participating nations. Many EIOs—the IMF, GATT, the United Nations Conference on the Law of the Sea (UNCLOS)—are involved in the construction and enforcement of such rules, and often with very limited success.

EIOs are suppliers of public goods and services. Their operation creates an incentive for nations to act as free riders. Public choice theory postulates that EIOs will be effective if high costs can be imposed on free riders, and private goods—such as organizational and secretariat posts, decision-making power, concessional aid, lucrative business contracts, etc.—can be given to states which comply by the rules established by the EIO. Small (perhaps regional) EIOs are more likely to be effective than large global ones in this perspective. Moreover, the theory would lead us to expect that EIO secretariats would spend a significant proportion of resources in converting 'public' goods into 'private' ones if they are interested in enhancing organizational effectiveness. Alternatively, free riding may be discouraged by education and propaganda.

Fratianni and Pattison have presented a public choice based model of the formation of IOs.[25] Each state (i) which is a potential member of the IO is assumed to be concerned with the maximization of its own gain (G_i)

where $$g_i = b_i - c_i \tag{1}$$

and b_i and c_i are the benefits and costs to i of participation in the IO. We define B as i's share in total organization benefits $= (b_i/b_t)$ and C as i's share in total organization cost $= (c_i/c_t)$. The total benefits (b_t) and total costs (c_t) generated by the IO are assumed to be a function of its output Q.

$$\text{then} \quad g_i = b_i\,(Q) - c_i\,(Q) \tag{2}$$

and to maximize G_i implies

$$dg/dQ = db_i/dQ - dc_i/dQ = 0. \tag{3}$$

Assuming that policies adopted by the EIO will not alter the share of costs and benefits allocated to country i thus

$$db_i/dQ = B\,(db_t/dQ) \tag{4}$$

$$dg_i/dQ = B\,(db_t/dQ) = dc_t/dQ \tag{5}$$

indicates the optimum activity level of the IO from the point of view of country i. This level of activity is reached at the point where the share of the gains from the activity of the IO going to i times the marginal increase in the benefits for the entire membership of the IO is equal to the marginal costs for this membership. Note that this defines the optimum level of IO activity (Q) from the point of view of an individual member: for the entire membership the optimum level of Q is at the point when $db_t/dQ = dc_t/dQ$. There is no reason why dg_i/dQ should equal dg_t/dQ.

Fratianni and Pattison argue that increasing the size of membership leads to diminishing benefits but rising marginal costs (MC) for EIOs. Costs are a function of the level of organizational activity, the number of organizational partici-pants and the decision rules adopted by the EIO. The stricter the decision rules adopted by an EIO (consensus against voting majority) the higher the MC of its expansion. Furthermore, the larger the size of the EIO membership, the smaller the value of B, particularly for the powerful nations, hence the conclusion that smaller EIOs are likely to be more effective than large ones.[26]

A public choice approach has also been used to suggest the consequence of changing decision-making rules in EIOs.

Dreyer and Schotter have studied the consequence of the 1978 changes in the voting rules of the IMF. They found that four countries (Belgium, Japan, Netherlands, and West Germany) whose voting quota has been increased suffered a decline in influence within IMF, while thirty eight developing countries whose votes had actually been reduced experienced an increase in organizational influence.[27] This result was based on the observation that the four countries whose quotas had been increased obstructed each other from casting the 'pivotal vote' which could turn a non-winning coalition into a winning coalition, thus ensuring that the countries whose voting quota had been reduced had in fact an increased chance of casting the pivotal vote.

Other applications of the public choice approach to the study of EIOs can also be listed.[28] Its major limitation lies in the fact that it has nothing to say about the process and likelihood of changes in preferences and values—traditionally a central concern of political analysis.[29] Its main message is that IOs—and particularly EIOs—have acquired an unjustifiably large role in the management of international relations. Studies rooted in this tradition focus upon the weaknesses of the EIOs, and generally call for a reduction in their mandate and scope. This is consistent with the general predisposition of the public choice theorists towards a drastic curtailment of the role of government in society.

In sharp contrast to this type of analysis are the views of the authors associated with transnationalism. Transnationalism was particularly popular during the early 1970s. Nye and Keohane define 'transnational interaction as the movement of tangible and intangible items across state boundaries when at least one actor is not an agent of government or an intergovernmental organization'.[30] The transnationalism literature has mainly been concerned with documenting the extensive growth of transnational relations and interactions. The study of the impact of this growth on world politics has been undertaken within the interdependence paradigm, which may legitimately be considered as a natural descendant of the transnational approach. The main concern in the interdependence literature is with the location of EIOs within the international environment. It is, therefore, more appropriate to discuss this literature in Chapter 2. The one transnational organization, the activity of which was extensively analysed by the transnationalists is the multinational corporation. However, as explained in Section 1.1, this volume does not include an analysis of the role or policies of multinational business.

In this rapid overview of the major approaches to the study of EIOs I have so far made no reference to organization theory familiar to students of managerial and public-sector economics. There are important differences between governmental EIOs and public-sector bureaucracies. Governmental EIOs rarely influence individual behaviour in the societies of their member states. There bureaucracies are thus tenuously linked to this society. Their ability to coerce and discipline clients is heavily circumscribed. This would mean that much of the conventional writing of organizational theorists on the relationship of organizations to their environment would be of limited relevance as far as the study of international bureaucracy is concerned. However, in his pioneering study *Beyond the Nation State*, Ernst Haas has made an attempt to develop a model of the interaction of an IO with its environment on the basis of an eclectic reading of organization theory.[31] This is discussed in Chapter 2. Other authors have drawn on organizational theory to discuss the structures and functions of EIOs and interorganizational relations. Some have attempted to derive insights from this literature in the study of the strategy and impact of international secretariats and their leadership.[32]

However, in general, themes in conventional organization theory have been drawn on by a relatively small group of IO writers. This can in large part be explained by the fact that conventional organization theory essentially focuses upon four main organizational types: (a) the classical bureau, (b) the small group, (c) leadership, and (d) voting bodies. These organization types are derived from the world of business and government, with which the organizational theorists have remained largely preoccupied.

An IO can, of course, be decomposed in a way which can make possible an application of organizational theory relevant to one of these types. But like other social organisms an IO is more than a sum of its constituent parts. In order to understand the behaviour of the organization and assess its environmental impact, it is necessary to develop an insight into the processes whereby the parts of the IO interact with each other. The organization theory literature has little to say about how interaction occurs when the four organizational types are structured within different specific organizational forms.

Moreover, some IOs cannot be decomposed in a way suitable for the application of insights developed by orthodox organization theory. Thus, as Gordenker and Saunders have noted, international voting bodies differ from their counterpart in liberal democratic national politics in many fundamental aspects.[33] Organization theory postulates that the latter bodies consist of rational individuals with ordered preference lists seeking a maximization—or optimization—of utility or power or profits. But in IO voting forums voters represent not themselves but their states. In order to apply classical theory to voting in IOs it is necessary to assume that the states are rational individuals which is not only unrealistic but, as Graham Allison has shown, it is not a particularly useful basis for attempting to understand their behaviour.[34]

The variety of approaches outlined here permit us to study the international organization process in its multi-faceted dimensions. They will be explored throughout this book. Before we proceed to do this, it is useful to spend some time describing the salient features of EIOs in order to understand the role they can play in determining the level and form of economic transactions within the international system.

1.3 CHARACTERISTICS OF EIOS

There exists a great variety of EIOs and many authors believe their number will increase in the years ahead. Before attempting to assess their effectiveness and analyse their organizational process, it is necessary to highlight their main characteristics. This will enable us to develop an overview of the nature of these organizations and to situate them in the context of the international economic and political system. Identifying the main characteristics of the EIOs will, in other words, enable us to undertstand the role these organizations can play in the management of the world economy.

IOs are usually categorized in terms of membership, structure and function. IOs are commonly divided into:

(a)   those which have an exclusive governmental member-ship, usually called intergovernmental organizations (IGOs),

(b)   those with an exclusive non-governmental membership (NGOs), and

(c)   those whose members include governmental and non-governmental bodies. These have been described as transnational IOs (TNOs).

These three categories are, of course, subject to further subdivisions. Thus, the IGOs can be divided into those established by a treaty, involving all the institutions of the member states (executive, legislative and judicial), and those established only by the government;[35] those that permit membership by non-sovereign territories and those that do not; and those that limit membership to a specific region—however defined—and those that are potentially universal. A similar classification of NGOs and TNOs can also be attempted.

Distinction may also be made between IOs in terms of their functions. IOs can be classified into those that pursue 'general' aims—such as world peace, sanctity of universal human rights, economic development, etc.—and those whose objectives are more 'specific', such as undertaking research in biochemistry, facilitating exchange of legal information among parliament-arians, regulating air traffic, etc. IOs have also been classified as 'technical', 'political' and 'security'. A more comprehensive functional classification has been developed by Pentland, who distinguishes between organizations involved in 'high' and 'low' politics. IOs dealing with military security and diplomatic issues are classified as 'high' politics organizations. Those dealing with technical and economic matters are 'low' politics IOs in this scheme.[36] This approach does not, however, take account of the possibility that 'the security of a country may depend more on economic factors than on the immediate military and diplomatic ones'.[37] Technical and economic organizations may well be involved in the management of traditional 'high politics' issues.

Archer has suggested that this distinction between high and low politics can be avoided while retaining Pentland's focus on the activities of IOs. He categorized IOs as:

(a)   those that enhance co-operation between members who are not in conflict,
(b)   those that reduce conflict, and
(c)   those that produce and organize confrontation between members and outsiders, or among the members themselves.[38]

IOs may also be classified in terms of their organizational structure. Distinction may be made in terms of the relative power of 'plenary' bodies (on which usually all members are represented) and executive agencies, which usually have a more selective composition. Organizational structure is also influenced by the pattern of voting institutionalized (simple majority, weighted, etc.) This provides another category for distinguishing IOs. Finally, IOs may be categorized structurally by taking into account the extent to which their organs have the capacity to act independently within the international system.

Where do the EIOs fit into this picture? In Table 1.1 I have attempted to place a number of EIOs in accordance with the categories associated with membership and function. The first point to note is the arbitrary nature of this classification. Thus I have described the IMF as a specific function organization, although the First Article of Agreement of the IMF identifies the objectives of the IMF as 'the promotion of international monetary co-operation and the expansion of international trade'. However, as Meerhaeghe has noted 'these objectives are in the nature of general directives (and) the Fund's real task (is to) shorten the duration and to reduce the degree of disequilibrium in balance of payments'.[39] The main activities of the IMF have been the provision of short-term loans; and, particularly during 1947—71, the promotion of exchange stability. Hence I have classified the IMF as a specific function EIO.

On the other hand, Table 1.1 shows the EC and CMEA to be 'general' organizations despite the fact that they undertake a

Table 1.1: *Membership and Function Categorizations of EIOs*

Membership	Function					
	General			Specific		
	Co-operation	Conflict Reduction	Confrontation	Co-operation	Conflict Reduction	Confrontation
IGOs						
Universal		UN (ECOSOC)	UNCTAD	IMF, IBRD, ILO	Commodity Agreements	
Regional	OECD, CMEA, EC		OPEC	ECSC EFTA		
NGOs						
Universal				WFTU	IATA	
Regional				ICFTU		

host of specific trade, investment and production-related activities. However, it is my judgement that the overall orientation of EC and CMEA policy is determined by the general objectives of promoting economic integration, and the specific programmes are of a distinctly secondary character. There are many authors who would dispute this contention.

Similarly, the categorization of the IBRD as a 'co-operation promoting' EIO, of UNCTAD as a 'confrontation' EIO and of the Commodity Agreements as 'conflict reducing' are all problematic. This classification depends ultimately upon the author's interpretation of the policies and performance of the given EIO. Thus I classify the IBRD as a 'co-operative' agency because I consider that there is no conflict of national interests in undertaking 'the provision and guaranteeing of loans either from its own capital or from borrowed funds' (Article 1, ii of its charter) and the provision of technical services. These activities have constituted its main operational functions. Other authors (such as Teresa Hayter[40]) contend that the purpose of these activities is to strengthen the dependence of the poor countries on the West. In this view the IBRD can at best be described as an organization which aims to reduce the conflict that exists between Third World rulers and the West. The former accept increased dependence on the West because this is accompanied by financial resources which can be used to relieve poverty, foster industrial growth or strengthen their dictatorships. However, dependence on the West has both political and economic costs and the consolidation of dependency structures is at the expense of the poor countries.

It is thus necessary to provide arguable justifications for the categorization presented in Table 1.1. But despite the fact that there are many border-line cases, it does reveal some important characteristics of EIOs.

Firstly, important and influential EIOs are, in the main, intergovernmental agencies. It was decided to exclude the transnational corporations from the study on the grounds that their principal concern is the production and exchange of non-public goods. This has meant that I have chosen to bypass the most important NGOs in the economic field. The other NGOs identified in Table 1.1 clearly do not play an important decision-making role in the organization of international commodity, money or labour markets. The bulk of the following chapters will remain concerned with the organizational processes and the evaluation of IGOs.

Secondly, EIOs exist in both a regional and a global setting. At both levels there is a relatively small group of influential decision takers—and a large band of 'hopefuls'. At the global level, the influential EIOs are exclusively specific purpose. Conversely, the main influential regional EIOs are of a general-function character. One can, however, think of a small group of influential specific-function regional EIOs—EFTA being an important example. The specific-function character of the main influential EIOs implies that the theories of regional integration, policy harmonization and co-ordination are of as great relevance as are theories concerned with the maintenance or transition of global regimes.

Table 1.1 also shows that the major EIOs are instruments for co-operation and the reduction of conflict between members. Some EIOs have sought to foster confrontation between members. I have included UNCTAD in this category—once again an arguable classification; OPEC is perhaps the only EIO in this category which has achieved a significant level of success over a relatively extended period of time.

EIOs may also be categorized in terms of organizational structure. Here it is difficult to describe a 'typical' EIO. A variety of decision-making procedures and institutional arrangements exist. One may hazard the generalization that EIOs which 'realistically' reflect the environmental balance of economic development, etc.—and those whose objectives are their secretariats are regarded as neutral well-wishing brokers and experts by the clientele. On the other hand, EIOs such as UNCTAD, ILO, UNIDO, etc. do not have environmental influence of a similar level, despite the fact that organizational autonomy is not necessarily low. The secretariats of such EIOs do not have the image of neutrality that is portrayed by the mandarins of the EEC or the IMF. Moreover, use of the techniques of consensual decision making—has not enhanced the organizational effectiveness of these 'democratic' EIOs.

Finally, it may be noted that the few NGOs present in Table 1.1 are all of a specific functional character. Many ambiguities are involved in these classifications, particularly with respect to the universal regional dimension. I have classified the World Federation of Trade Unions as a universal EIO and the International Confederation of Free Trade Unions as a regional EIO. Both these associations limit membership on ideological grounds: the WTFU is a communist and the ICFTU is a social democratic liberal oriented body. However, in the judgement of this author the present membership of the WFTU is significantly less regionally concentrated than the present membership of the ICFTU.

Table 1.1 includes a small proportion of the universe of EIOs. I have concentrated on what I regard to be the 'best known' and 'influential' EIOs within the international economy. But this conception of 'influence' is no more than an intuitive one. The next chapter attempts to develop a more adequate concept of 'effectiveness' and 'influence' by focusing upon the role an EIO can play in the maintenance and/or transformation of different international systems.

NOTES

1. Detailed in Luard E. *International Agencies,* Royal Institute of International Affairs, Macmillan, London (1977) Ch. 17.
2. Luard, *op. cit.,* p. 2.
3. Both these views are discussed in detail in Ch. 3 and are also touched upon in Sect. 1.2.
4. *See* Ch. 3.
5. Groom, A.R. 'The advent of international institutions' in Groom, A.R. and Taylor, P. *International Organization: A Conceptual Approach,* Francis Pinter, London (1978) p. 12.
6. Groom, *op. cit.,* p. 17.
7. Reuter, P. *International Institutions,* Allen and Unwin, London (1958).
8. Claude, I. *Swords Into Plowshares,* Random House, New York (1964) pp. 5–6.
9. World Bank, *World Development Report 1984,* Washington (1984) Appendix Table 3, pp. 222–3.
10. Union of International Associations, *Yearbook of International Organizations 1983–84,* Sars, K.G., Munich (1984) 3 Vols., *passim.* The 1984–85 edition does include TNCs in a special Section 'M'.
11. The entries do not unambiguously represent the total number of IOs. Some IOs which have been included in the YIO have disappeared; others are relatively unknown. Moreover, the YIO includes both federations of

IOs and individual IOs as separate entries; there is therefore a possibility of double counting. Restricting ourselves to the relatively unambiguous categories (categories A–D), we find that intergovernmental EIOs number 181—31.6 per cent of the total entries. Non-governmental EIOs within these categories number 2,571—again 31.5 per cent of the total. If we exclude the 'federations' from these calculations, the number of governmental EIOs remains unchanged, but non-governmental EIOs number 2,381 and cosntitute 31.8 per cent of the total entries in categories B to D.

12. Kinnas, J.N. 'Association' in Taylor, P. and Groom, A.R.J. *International Organization: A Conceptual Approach*, Francis Pinter, London (1978) p. 155.
13. See *Final Act and the Havana Charter for an International Trade Organization*, HMSO Cmd 7375 (1948).
14. See *The Works of Heremy Bentham*, Vol. II, published under the supervision of his executor John Bowring, London (1938) pp. 541–62.
15. Mitrany, David *A Working Peace System*, Royal Institute of International Affairs, London (1943).
16. Taylor, P. 'Functionalism: the theory of David Mitrany' in Taylor and Groom, *op. cit.,* p. 243.
17. Haas, B. Ernst *Beyond the Nation State*, Stanford (1964).
18. Haas, E. and Whiting, A.S. *Dynamics of International Relations,* McGraw Hill, New York (1956) p. vii.
19. Lindberg, L. *The Political Dynamics of European Economic Integration,* Stanford University Press (1963) p. 10.
20. Harrison, R.J. 'Neofunctionalism' in Taylor and Groom, *op. cit.,* p. 53.
21. Detailed for example in Lindberg, L.N. and Scheingold, S.A., *Europe's Would Be Policy,* Prentice-Hall, Englewood Cliffs (1970).
22. Haas, E. *Beyond the Nation State,* Part II.
23. See Part II.
24. Reviewed extensively in Taylor and Groom, *op. cit.,* pp. 118–356.
25. Fratianni, M. and Pattison, J. 'The economics of international organizations', *Kyklos,* Vol. 35 No. 3 (1982) pp. 244–62.
26. Fratianni and Pattison, *op. cit.,* pp. 246–53.
27. Dreyer, J.S. and Schotter, A. 'Power relationship in the International Monetary Fund', *Review of Economics and Statistics,* Vol. 62 No. 1, (1980) pp. 97–106.
28. Ch. 5 utilizes this theory to study the behaviour of international bureaucracies. *See also* Frey, B.S. 'The public choice view of international political economy', *IO,* Vol. 38 No. 1 (1984) pp. 199–223.
29. Other limitations are discussed in Sect. 2.4 and Ch. 5.
30. Nye, J. and Keohane, R. 'Transnational relations and world politics', *IO,* Vol. 25 No. 3 (1971) p. 332.
31. Haas, E. *Beyond the Nation State,* Stanford University Press (1964) Chs. 2 and 3.
32. The following paragraphs rely heavily on Gordenker, L. and Saunders, P. 'Organization theory and international organization' in Taylor and Groom, *op. cit.,* pp. 101–5.

33. *Ibid.*, p. 104.
34. Allison G. *Essence of Decision,* Little Brown and Co., Boston (1971).
35. Jenks, C.W. 'Some constitutional problems of international organization', *British Yearbook of International Law,* Vol. 22 (1945) pp. 11–72.
36. Pentland, C. 'International organization' in Rosenua, J., Thompson, K. and Boyd, G. (eds.) *World Politics: An Introduction,* The Free Press, New York (1976) pp. 628–37.
37. Archer, G. *International Organization,* Allen and Unwin, London (1983) p. 52.
38. Archer, *op. cit.,* pp. 56–7.
39. Meerhaeghe, M.A.B. Van *International Economic Institutions*, Longman, London (1971) p. 23.
40. Hayter, T. *Aid as Imperialism*, Penguin, Harmondsworth (1971).

2 The International Environment

IOs function within an international context. The environment is both an influence upon the structure and performance of the IO and a target of organisational initiatives. In this chapter we will attempt to outline the major approaches which seek to describe the existing international political reality, as 'a system' or as 'a network'. Attention will also focus on works which seek to make sense of the existing pattern of international relationships by developing empirical or conceptual schemes. Such works have proliferated in the recent past and have been particularly useful for identifying the nature and character of international economic 'regimes'. In the final section of this chapter we will attempt to assess the impact that existing international economic regimes have on EIOs, as far as the definition of their organizational task is concerned and evaluate the role the EIOs can play in the existing international economic order.

2.1. CONCEPTIONS OF WORLD ORDER

Social scientists belonging to many disciplines—economists, sociologists, political scientists, lawyers—have attempted to understand the nature of the modern structure of international relationships. These attempts to 'make sense of the whole'—of how 'things hang together'—have been most rigorously formalized by the system theoretic applications to the study of international affairs. These approaches fall into three major categories.

Hoffman defines 'the concept of the international system as a construct for describing both the way in which the parts relate and the patterns of interaction change.'[1] He identifies different state systems on the basis of generalisations culled from a reading of international history. As against this the second major approach is explicitly scientific and involves a rigorous application of theorems of general systems theory to data generated from an investigation of international events. This approach is also prescriptive. Thus Singer's study of the correlates of war in a variety of international systems seeks both to verify relevant variables in a scientific manner and to suggest means for improving the conduct of international relations so as to reduce conflict.[2] Finally, efforts have been made to derive heuristic models of hypothetical international systems. The works of Kaplan and of Modelski are outstanding examples of studies of this nature.[3]

These approaches are of relatively limited use to students of the international economy. These studies are geared towards an analysis of the factors determining the political stability of given international systems, and argue that the configuration of political power is a crucial factor. Analysis thus remains firmly focused on political processes.

Moreover, as Yout has pointed out, 'these studies are vulnerable to the criticism of being debates about abstractions virtually divorced from empirical referents'.[4] In this they correspond to the vision of the world economy cherished by all neo-classical economists—and modelled by some—characterized by perfect competition, free trade and the universal prevalence of rational economic behaviour. Neither of these approaches facilitate an investigation of the role of the EIOs in the management of the world economy.

Many systems-based theories of international behaviour do, however, draw upon what might be described as the classical approach in international politics. This approach, familiar to most through the works of Morgenthau,[5] identifies political and military factors as the main determinants of the structure—and of change within the structure of international relations. Hedley Bull and Kenneth Waltz have sought to re-establish the continued relevance of this approach.[6]

Following Hugo Grotius, Bull argues that state behaviour and interaction patterns are constrained by the existence of international order. This is based on specific conceptions of international society shared by the states comprising the international system, and permits the development of legal and moral rules for regulating these interactions. Enforcement of these rules requires the operation of 'the institutions of international society', which Bull identifies as 'balance of power, international law, the diplomatic mechanism, the managerial system of the great powers and war'.[7] Bull ignores the role of the economic factors in the sustenance of international order on the basis of the assertion that 'the role of non state actors is less important today than it was in earlier days'.[8] However, he argues that a strengthening of international order requires the growth of a consensus on social and political objectives, and admits that 'a strengthening of consensus is unlikely to be achieved without a radical redistribution of resources in favour of the poor states of the Third World'.[9]

Waltz also ignores the importance of economic factors. This might seem paradoxical, for Waltz compares the international state system to the conduct of competition between domestic firms in a given industry. Each unit seeks to maximize power (profits). In multipolar state systems (oligopolistic markets) large states dominate: in bipolar systems (dupoly) access to power is monopolized by the superpowers. Balance of power theory is therefore both necessary and sufficient to explain state behaviour in this view.[10] Interdependence is particularly low in bipolar systems. Even in multipolar systems the large states—its main decision takers—are less dependent on others as they have a greater capacity to compensate for sectorial dependence—say in energy or natural resources—at the systemic level. Waltz argues that, as the size of the great powers has grown since the First World War, economic interdependence has declined. Moreover, there has been a concentration of military power, and the existing system of international relations is characterized by bipolarity. 'Economically America and Russia are markedly less interdependent and noticeably less dependent on others than earlier great powers were. Militarily the decrease of interdependence is more striking still for neither great power can be linked to any other great power in their mutually grasping ambitions.'[11]

Waltz's 'balance of power' model is as much an ideal type as is the 'theory of the firm' constructs on which it is based. This inevitably means that there are many crucial respects in which reality does not correspond to his 'vision'. There is, for example, an obstinate refusal to recognize the truly phenomenal growth of an international sector represented in the volume of world trade and financial flows, and to come to terms with the evident unwillingness of great powers to use military force for securing access to economic resources. Nor is any explanation offered for ignoring the multidimensional concerns of most states—including superpowers—in the conduct of modern diplomacy.

Waltz and Bull thus do not offer a satisfactory justification for ignoring economic factors in studies of the existing international order. The realist school had predominantly been concerned with territorial issues. They paid infrequent attention to economic issues but, unlike their modern followers, they acknowledged that in many situations force is an inadequate instrument for the pursuance of state objectives. Thus Morgenthau writes 'the means at the disposal of diplomacy are three: persuasion, compromise and the threat of force. No diplomacy relying only upon the threat of force can claim to be intelligent'.[12] It is, therefore, correct to argue that, unlike the new realists, Morgenthau and his colleagues did not present any cogently articulated theory of the relative importance of economic factors as determinants of system change. It has been argued that realists such as Morgenthau and Kenan adopted 'a rather naive non-political approach towards (international economic issues) such as the oceans, the seabed, energy and pollution'.[13] Their thinking thus does not provide an adequate reference point for investigation about the nature and structures of the international economy.

Attempts at integrating economic factors in theories about change and stability in the structure of international relations date back to the early 1940s. One pioneer in this field was David Mitrany, whose work has briefly been reviewed in Chapter 1. The Chicago school theorists—in particular Charles Merriam, Frederick Schuman and Quincy Wright—also made significant contributions. These scholars sought to understand international politics on the basis of the pluralist paradigm that had been developed to explain political decision making in the United States. The state was seen as a 'national association' of subnational groups, and was by no means the sole actor on the international level. 'Transnational relations' and 'political socialization' were significant aspects of international behaviour in this view. Central authority—in other words the 'state'—has a relatively limited role to play in the conduct of international relations because of the absence of a clearly recognized hierarchic order in the state system, and also because of the growth of 'modern methods of transportation and communication'.[14] Nor is the state the only entity to which individuals proffer loyalty. Transnational corporations, cartels and international labour confederations may play a similar role within the international system. Power within this system is distributed on the basis of national racial, religious and class conflicts and compromises. However, unlike the functionalists, the authors of the Chicago School regard political power as ethically neutral—'power politics' is not evil in itself—and therefore suggest no mechanisms for the depoliticization of international society. Quite the contrary, deliberate political planning could gradually accelerate mankind's historical progress. In this view this could ensure the transference of power from governments to large international economic units. Merriam comes close to advocating a functional dispersion of power at the international level. 'Power functionally fitted to life is not oppression but release'.[15]

As we have seen earlier the functionalists and neo-functionalists raised the level of analysis of international economic processes by developing a series of concepts and insights synthesized within the theory of political integration. Although the primary focus of this work was undoubtedly on regional integration it must not be forgotten that Haas's *Beyond The Nation State* studied the evolution and performance of the ILO within the context of this theory.[16] However, the study of international quasi-universal organizations was not particularly influenced by this approach.[17]

Neo-functionalism had its greatest impact in the area of the political analysis of regional IOs. However, as shown in Chapter 1, disappointment with the EEC led to disillusionment with the central postulates of integration theory. Haas himself developed a comprehensive critique of this approach arguing that 'theorising about regional integration as such is no longer profitable'.[18] The region undergoing 'integration' can no longer be regarded as a self-contained unit whose attempt at centralizing joint tasks can be viewed as autonomous. This has meant that the institutional outcomes of integration processes predicted by the neo-functionalists turned out with increasing frequency to be false. In general the incrementalist policy adaptations suggested by the integration theorist no longer reflects decision-making processes in national and international capitals, in Haas's view.

The obsolescence of regional integration arises from the fact that 'global politics and the search for a new world order are akin to what planners have called a "turbulent field . . . " Turbulence is the term we bestow on the confused and changing perceptions of organisational actors which find themselves in a setting of great social complexity. The number of actors is very large. Each actor is tied into a network of (confused) interdependence. Confusion dominates discussion and negotiation. A turbulent field can be substantial, national, regional, inter-regional and global—and all at the same time'.[19] In such a situation old values are discarded, and new rules and new institutions are created and discarded at a rapid rate. Technological advances are fragmentary and contribute to a blurring of how progress in one field of social endeavour is to be related to others. There is no shared consensus on how 'things hang together'. International order is sought primarily as a means for controlling turbulence.

In such an environment, decision making is undertaken not on the basis of 'the rationality of disjointed incrementalism' but on the basis of 'the rationality of fragmented issue linkage': incrementalist decision-making patterns exist under conditions of uncertainty, where bargaining takes place between participants whose goals sometimes conflict and sometimes converge. The objective of the bargainers is assumed to be constant, and they are expected to approach it by disjointed incremental policy initiatives: the disjointed and sometimes contradictory character of these policies is due to the prevailing uncertainty about their relative efficacy. 'Rational analytic' decision making attempts to reduce the uncertainty and routinize policy processes so as to optimize outcomes. 'Fragmented issue linkage' has been defined as a decision-making process in which 'actors who are really committed to the analytic style when faced with other actors still deciding according to incrementalist criteria are likely to settle for fragmented issue linkage . . . . Fragmented issue linkage occurs when older objectives are questioned, when new objectives clamour for satisfaction and when the rationality accepted as adequate in the past ceases to be a legitimate guide to future action'.[20]

Issue linkage remains fragmented because there is no shared vision of how an ultimate aggregation of diverse issue areas is to be achieved, as was the case as far as the integrationist theorists were concerned. In other words, international processes characterized by fragmented issue linkage need not lead to an upgrading of the scope and level of the IOs concerned. Issue linkage may lead to disillusionment, and pressures may build up within the system for a subsequent decomposition and disaggregation of issues; Haas cites many instances of how this occurred in the area of economic and monetary policy making by the EEC.[21] This has in effect meant an externalization of these issues and a diluting of regional organizational initiatives. The actors are anxious to 'keep all options open' and reluctant to proceed with the incrementalist logic which would increase the internal cohesion of the region, or to devise a new formula for a clearcut subdivision of regional and non-regional functions. Therefore many institutional focuses are devised and discarded and no overall pattern is consolidated. Haas argues that 'the future criterion of institutional legitimacy is the adequacy of the performance in maintaining a capability for action and in coping with the results of capabilities . . . the future of European institutions depends on adopting authority to the task of improving the performance of all kinds of public services which involve the active management of society and economy. But this does not mean that management must take the form of a European government'.[22] Institutional overlap—in terms of both structure and function—is likely to proliferate. The overlap will be asymmetrical. There will be no single co-ordinating centre or well-defined heirarchic layers of authority. Interdependence among the institutions and the decision makers will abound. It is, therefore, appropriate to subordinate the study of integration within the analysis of the changing patterns of interdependence.

Many authors have been concerned not so much with the presentation of a theory of interdependence as with the presentation of the extent of interdependence that characterizes the present world system; this brings the interdependence literature close to the work of the transnationalists, who also remained preoccupied with description.

Throughout the 1970s there was an animated debate between those who saw an increase in the interdependence of the countries of Western Europe and North America and those who argued that interdependence had in fact declined since the early 1950s.[23] Some authors have addressed the question of the impact of the growth of interdependence on the structure of international relations. Haas, for example, argues that 'the kinds of system change associated with interdependence imply a tendency towards strengthening of weaker actors as the web of relationship increases sensitivities, vulnerabilities and opportunity costs for the stronger'.[24] Scott predicts that increased interdependence will 'broaden the scope and linkage of international problem, render the international system fragile and inflate the cost of system maintenance. The vulnerabilities of the larger states will in particular grow rapidly as interdependencies proliferate'.[25] Morse argues that the growth of interdependence reduces governmental international policy choices and ability to control transnational actors. Interdependence thus gives birth to new types of negotiation and bargaining patterns.[26]

Keohane and Nye have developed some of the themes identified by Morse in an important study.[27] 'Complex interdependence' in their view is characterized by the simultaneous existence of multiple channels of diplomacy used by both state and non-state actors, an absence of hierarchy among international political, economic and social issues and the irrelevance of military force in determining bargaining outcomes. Crucial issue areas remain unconnected, and domestic pressure can be brought to bear on international bargaining processes. IOs—particularly EIOs—have the opportunity to play an important role in an environment characterized by rising interdependence. Unlike Scott, Keohane and Nye do not believe that the modern international system is an unstable one. They argue that the conditions of the further development of complex interdependence are good. The concern with demonstrating systemic stability naturally leads to a discourse centred on identifying conditions for 'regime change'.

Keohane and Nye take issue with both the realist school—discussed above—and the dependency theorists. In their view conditions of complex interdependence facilitate the emergence of weak states as influential actors on the international level. The weak states of the Third World find it possible to develop consistent and coherent international policies because of the underdevelopment of competing domestic interest group. Complex interdependence issues are typically negotiated within IO forums, the structures and processes of which enhance the power of the Third World countries.[28] This view is, of course, strongly contested by the dependency theorists who argue that the operation of the international political and economic system increases the disparity between the rich and poor countries. World capitalism is in this view so structured that the metropolitan centres extract economic surplus from the peripheries at an ever falling relative price. This is the essence of the 'theory of unequal exchange'[29], which seeks to demonstrate how market processes contribute to a perpetuation of international capitalist hierarchies. Other dependency theorists believe that there exists an alliance of the 'industrial capitalists' of the First and 'the comprador bourgeoisie' of the Third Worlds. The international division of labour between primary and manufacturing producers is sustained by this alliance and cannot be eroded by diplomacy.[30]

Like the dependency theorists, the world systems analysts also draw on many Marxist themes.[31] In this view the accumulation processes of international capitalism structures society. Capitalism is a 'mode of world wide exchange relations and production for profit. It has created a world wide division of labour, stratified into zones and fragmented into national units. Exploitation involves a relationship between nations or groups of nations, between a "world bourgeoisie" and a "world proletariat"'.[32] There is a clear hierarchy of core areas and periphery areas. The 'core' nations dominate 'peripheral' ones. Core areas have strong states capable of holding their own in international bargaining. Contradictions within the system emerge, due to a mismatch between aggregate demand and supply, centralization and concentration of power, and the appearance and consolidation of a 'disjuncture' between political form and economic content. 'One might say what the states try to unify the world economy tears asunder.'[33] This is reflected in increased conflict between rich and poor countries on the one hand, and public- and private-sector managerial elites in the metropolitan countries on the other.

An intensification of these contradictions will pave the way for system change: the possibilities of regime erosion are explored on the basis of historical analysis. Thus Bergesen and Schoenberg argue that colonial relational patterns depend on the degree of stability within the core areas of the world economy. Mercantalist regulation of the international economy is necessary at times when political instability predominates at the core; when stability returns to the core 'integration of the system resides with the economic linkages of the world economy and less with the more political linkages of colonialism'.[34] In other words, the economics and politics of free trade will dominate when the core areas enjoy stability.

Predictions of this nature remain vague and difficult to pin down. As Andrews has observed 'regardless of rhetorical verve or partisan compassion world systems analysis often seems driven perilously close to an immobilism laced with pessimism. Escape is impossible. In the end it can look like an updated version of those scientific laws of capitalist development that were once the stock in trade of orthodox Marxism'.[35]

Marxist authors have presented a well-established body of literature on the nature of the world economic and political system and on the pattern of international relations in the post Second World War era. These writings do not present a picture of the world order which assigns any particular significance to the role IOs can play in the management of the world economy.[36] IOs in this conception are instruments for the exercising of state power. The states themselves are dominated by specific classes or class alliances; in the case of the 'intermediate regimes' of the Third World IOs do, however, derive a certain level of autonomy from the fact that their membership contains 'bourgeoisie', 'proletarian' and intermediate 'states'. Relations among these states—within IOs and elsewhere—cannot be adequately theorized until the questions relating to the ability of capitalism to transcend the nation state are directly addressed. At the beginning of the twentieth century Lenin had argued that the nation state was the highest form of political organization that capitalism could achieve; Karl Kautsky had disputed this and predicted the development of supernational capitalist forms of political organization. But with the triumph of the Russian revolution, this debate was abandoned, with the result that most Marxist writing in the field 'excised of any reference to "capitalist interests" could well be written by any traditional commentator on government action within international organizations'.[37]

This rapid review has ranged from works which question the need for incorporating economic factors in a study of international relations to those which argue that economic variables are the primary determinants of the structures and processes of the existing world order. Other works have tried to study the interrelationship between economic and political factors in shaping international behaviour. They have provided a foundation for the study of decision making by intergovernmental agencies in areas such as international trade and finance. Impressive systematic work has been done by scholars who have focused on problems associated with 'regime maintenance and change'. I now turn to an examination of this work.

2.2. INTERNATIONAL REGIMES: NATURE, CHARACTERISTICS AND CHANGE

The interdependence school has argued that it is useful for students of international organization to situate their analysis within the context of international regimes.[38] Regimes may be defined as 'social institutions governing the action of those interested in specificable activities. As such they are recognized patterns of practice around which expectations converge. Regimes are social structures. It is important not to mistake them for functions. They may or may not be formally articulated and they may or may not be accompanied by explicit organizational arrangements'.[39] In Haas's view international regimes 'are increasingly designed to minimise the undesired consequences associated with the exploitation of scientific and technological capabilities'.[40] Regimes are thus devised to tackle problems of system maintenance or transformation. The nature of specific regimes reflects the perception of the system in the minds of those who construct the regime. The more holistic this perception, the more comprehensive the regime that is devised.

Most designers of international regimes use both entities—such as groups, states, regions—and relationships—such as activities, transactions and symmetries—as components. The regimes incorporate both social and physical processes. In Haas's words 'they seek to aggregate nature and society into a whole that permits projection into the future . . . combining factual with normative considerations and prescriptions'.[41]

Regime analysis may reflect two different perceptions of system operation. There is on the one hand an essentially biological approach, which views actor's motives as being subservient to the systematic rules. These rules determine the outcome of actor interaction. The object of such investigation is usually to show how equilibrium is to be maintained. Equilibrium states are 'the best of all possible worlds'. Much of neo-classical thinking, particularly in the field of pure trade theory, reflects such a view of the world economy.

Other system analysts focus on the behaviour of actors and argue that outcome is determined by these interaction patterns. In this view there is no inevitable final outcome against which performance is to be measured. Usually such authors do not claim an ability to present a holistic view of reality. They deliberately select certain isolated features of this reality, which they regard as crucial in determining specific outcomes. Since regimes necessarily reflect a commitment to the achievement of specific human purposes they must attempt a modification of system 'rules', as well as modification of human behaviour. Most regimes—particularly economic ones—incorporate an uneasy and changing balance of both holistic and heuristic perceptions of the international system. International regimes are devised—it bears repeating—to address problems emerging from growing interdependencies in an imperfectly perceived social and technological world environment. They may represent either incrementalist or holistic attempts at realizing actor objectives, either by modifying actor behaviour or by modifying the structure of the system itself.

Heuristic regimes do not usually represent comprehensive formulas or international reorganization because they do not admit a scientifically valid criteria for the ordering of actor objectives. They attempt to accommodate change in social values and political convictions. Holistic and deterministic regimes on the other hand claim to possess such a scientific basis for the ordering of actor objectives—usually summed up in some concept of 'the good for mankind'. Thus neo-classical economics believes that this 'good' is 'welfare', and 'welfare maximization' ought to be the ultimate rational objective of all domestic and international economic policy making.

Holistic regimes devote considerable attention to specifying the institutional framework for achieving the rationally valid objectives, but little effort is made to scrutinize the possibility of modifying actor behaviour for the achievement of the ultimate good. Actors are assumed to behave rationally. Thus the tasks assigned to a deterministic regime are grand and sweeping, but since they do not address the problems associated with behaviour modification they tend to be unspecific and rather vague. On the other hand, heuristic regimes typically are much more restricted in scope but attempt consciously to gear organizational tasks to the political and intellectual consensus among their clients. These tasks are thus usually concrete and specific, and reflect a changing and maleable consensus among those who sustain such a regime.

Having described the major differences between prevailing international regimes let us proceed to enumerate certain important similarities.

1. The formal members of international regimes are sovereign states, although action sanctioned or regulated by the regime may be undertaken by non-state actors.
2. The substantive component of a regime consists of a set of rights and rules defining actor obligations and oppor-

tunities. Obligations are defined by rules specifying subject group, behavioural prescription and operational scope. Rules may be divided into (a) use rules: generally specifying limitation on the exercise of rights, (b) liability rules specifying scope of obligation in case of violation of regime rules, and (c) procedural rules governing organizational behaviour and dispute settlement processes. Rules associated with international regimes are generally weaker than those operated by domestic regimes, owing to the non-existence of a powerful supranational rule enforcing body, but IOs' with substantial resources have the capacity to enforce rule compliance—as is evident in the case of the IMF's dealings with the poor countries of the Third World.

3. Regimes contain procedural arrangements for making collective choices about resource allocation and use.[42] This usually involves the establishment of institutional arrangements specific to the exercise of such choice in relation to given resources. Typically, international regimes employ unilateral claims, bargaining and coercion by individual powerful states as means for determining collective social choice. Other procedures such as voting systems, administrative decisions, markets and adjudication are somewhat less frequently employed.[43]

4. International regimes usually incorporate compliance mechanisms for rule implementation. Typically these are less formal than governmental agencies. Compliance mechanisms are in general underdeveloped, due to the high degree of power decentralization characteristic of the international system. They emphasize self-interest calculation and usually establish publicly recognized procedures for self-help to redress unilaterally violations of rights guaranteed by participation in a regime.

There is nothing inevitable about the existence of a regime.[44] They may not exist or may break down. Furthermore, in the real world, regimes are unsystematic and ambiguous incorporating contradictory concepts and interests; with the passage of time they tend to become less coherent. As we have seen, regimes may incorporate more or less formal organizational arrangements—indeed it is easy to think of heuristic regimes which exclude the establishment of institutions altogether. Inter-linkages between regimes are often tenuous, sometimes non-existent.

In part these 'deficiencies'[45] arise because of the wide variety of circumstances which lead to the formation of international regimes. They emerge from actions of groups of actors who may negotiate a 'constitutional contract' for establishing a regime or endorse existing practices and conventions. More frequently actors agree on some components of a regime without signing a comprehensive social contract. The initial agreements may have a 'spillover effect', and a relatively comprehensive regime may evolve over time. International regimes established by constitutional contract may also evolve as initial agreements are reinterpreted, explicated and modified. Typically most operational regimes generate pressure for their own transformation owing to changes in the nature of organizational tasks, distributive issues or the accumulation of knowledge. International regimes will usually incorporate transformation rules. They specify the skills—bargaining, coalition construction and maintenance, technical and legal expertise etc.—necessary for achieving regime transformation. Regime transformation at the international level is not easy to achieve because of the high level of decentralization of power in the international system.

Transformation is further complicated by the fact that international regimes exhibit the attributes of collective goods to a high degree (i.e. non-excludability and jointness of supply).[46] This implies that 'no markets will arise in international regimes per se though there may be markets in pollution rights, licences for deep sea mining'[47] and other subjects of international regimes. Actors will, therefore, compete with each other for 'appropriate' rules for regime maintenance. Conflicts of interests in the modern international system among major actor groups is severe, and there is a high level of unpredictability of the outcome of given institutional initiatives. In such an environment, regime transformation is a consequence of successful negotiation among a small group of 'market leaders'[48] or dramatic unilateral action by powerful actors capable of imposing their will upon 'the market'. As Young has observed 'the resultant dynamics are much like those occurring in oligopolistic industries. Where one actor is clearly dominant unilateral action is likely . . . Where several actors share power as well as a strong interest in the activity . . . bargains are likely to be struck among key groups of influential actors'.[49] Negotiated regime transformation is thus difficult to achieve in the modern international system.

Regime construction and transformation has been studied from a variety of perspectives. Structuralists argue that hegemonial powers are the primary sustainers of regimes. They explain regime change in terms of change in the international hierarchy of power.[50] Technological and scientific holists[51] believe that change in perception—expansion of the frontier of knowledge—can induce corresponding changes in regime structures even if the distribution of power remains largely unaltered. Interdependence theorists recognize the persistence of conflict among actors, but believe that, despite this, institutionalized collaboration can lead to the creation of new regimes or the modification of existing ones.[52] When collaboration becomes conflictual—when, that is, there are increasingly frequent and intense disputes about the distribution of the benefits of such collaboration—regime modification is both likely and appropriate. It reflects a specific perception of the sensitivity and vulnerability of the collaborating states in relevant issue areas. Issues are linked on the basis of perception about their relationship in the environment which a given policy seeks to influence. Thus the existing international monetary regime includes rules governing the size and type of reserves held at and by the IMF, conditions determining their accessibility to individual members, the rendering of balance of payments support, compensatory mechanisms and the guaranteeing of the maintenance of a certain level of international liquidity. These issues were not linked prior to the Bretton Woods agreement of 1944. These linkages became possible mainly because of the acceptance of Keynesianism as the new economic orthodoxy by the dominant powers in the West. It was a combination of a new intellectual breakthrough and a new commitment by a dominant hegemon to this breakthrough which led to the creation of a new monetary regime. In cases where one of these two vital ingredients is absent, in the case of the Law of the Sea and the New International Economic Order (NIEO) negoti-ations for example, regime transformation will not occur. The new intellectual consensus must be accompanied by a gradual convergence of the interests of dominant actors in order to ensure regime change. Issue linkage creates almost inevitably a redistribution of resources. It will be accepted if the hegemon within the system accepts that the cost of such a redistribution does not exceed the potential gains from regime transformation.

Regime transformation can be achieved by what has been described as the 'substantive linkage' of issues.[53] Here a new consensus on knowledge leads to the acceptance of new social goals by dominant actors. Contrast this with fragmented issue linkage,[54] which characterized the NIEO negotiations where Third World actors sought joint gains, but without agreement on how the gain would be distributed. Hence issues linkage represented bargaining on the basis of a maximum common denominator in order to preserve the Third World coalition. This attempt at adding on issues essentially for compensatory reasons reduced the coherence of the entire package in the eyes of the West, which found it increasingly difficult to believe that the transformation of the existing international trade and investment regime along the lines suggested by the NIEO advocates would be in its interest.

Perception of new interests leads to redefinition and expansion of goals. This also implies a reordering of objectives and priorities. This reordering is based upon consensual knowledge and is aimed at reducing environmental uncertain-ty. Styles adopted by negotiators for the construction and transformation of international regimes are discussed in Chapter 4. In general it may be argued that regime establishment or transformation will occur if negotiators share consensual knowledge and expanding goals. This implies a co-variation between knowledge and goals. In such circumstance the emergence of a new or substantially modified regime is the result of deliberate planning on the part of international negotiators. Such a regime will be comprehensive in scope and fairly stable. If, on the other hand, negotiators share consensual knowledge but goals are static and there is no co-variation between them and the expansion of knowledge, there will be instability and the regime will incorporate a smaller number of issues. It will, however, be fairly stable and capable of accommodating an expansion of goals. On the other hand if negotiators do not share consensual knowledge but have potentially expanding goals they will at best succeed in establishing an unstable and weak regime.[55] The norms and rules will be frequently challenged. Behaviour will not conform to regime procedures and expectations about efficiency and equity will not be realized. Such a regime is unlikely to be able to withstand changes in the political balance of power within the international system. It will disintegrate or undergo a process of imperceptible decay.[56]

Regime existence or transformation is not inevitable. The structuralists believe, however, that certain characteristics of the international system necessitate regime change. In this view, international regimes flourish when hegemons manage them. The regimes are nothing more or less than foreign policy instruments of the hegemons. Hegemons can modify regimes at will. Regime transformation or decay occurs when the supremacy of a hegemon is effectively challenged.

Cognitive explanations of regime change emphasize the growth of consensual knowledge for the 'upgrading' (strengthening and broadening) of regimes. Regime maintenance involves 'learning', that is realizing that existing knowledge can be utilized for joint gains. This generates an impetus for regime transformation and a redefinition of national interest in specific issue areas.[57] Whether or not such learning will occur and will ensure regime transformation will depend upon the negotiating style adopted in bargaining processes.[58]

An increase in knowledge may also contribute to regime decay. This is so if it leads to the realization that the costs of international collaboration outweigh its benefits. This may induce withdrawal or, as Haas has shown, there may be a decline 'in the coherence of norms, rules and procedures in relation to principles'.[59] Regime decay can occur without decomposition of a formal nature. Such decay is mainly a result of changes in the commitment of members to the rules, norms and procedures of a regime.

Regime decay or growth implies changes in the organizational structures defining it. Four distinct categories of institutional procedural mechanisms may characterize a regime:

1. A common framework geared to the organization and exchange of relevant information. Such a framework facilitates the pooling of existing capabilities, but may not be concerned with the creation or management of a new product.
2. A joint facility: here an explicit attempt is made to standardize policy-making and policy-scrutinizing routines.
3. A common policy involving the harmonizing of national policies in order to remove mutual contradictions and achieve a joint goal or purpose.
4. A single policy substituting and subordinating national policy objectives and procedures in given issue areas.

A regime concerned mainly with the exchange of information may have relatively few and relatively simple institutional arrangements. It may eschew the establishment of IOs altogether and function entirely through co-ordinating committees of national civil servants. If the establishment of a joint facility is envisaged, a relatively permanent international research staff is necessary to identify and suggest modification in the relevant standards. The construction of single-policy or joint-policy regimes usually involves elaborate international organization capable of continuous deliberation, policy making and policy implementation of a set of deliberately related issues.[60]

The procedures of international regimes will determine the rules that they have to devise. Regimes concerned merely with the pooling of information in a common framework need devise few rules for increasing this knowledge or determining its legitimate utilization by members. If a joint facility is to be established, pooled information has to be shaped and ordered for the development of standards and norms. If a common policy is envisaged, rules will also have to be formulated for closing the distance between the policies of member states. This must involve the making of policy outlining the process of convergence. This usually involves the setting of specific targets, which members are committed to achieve over a given time period. Finally if the regime aims at establishing a single policy it must establish rules for information sharing, information utilizing and policy convergence, and a framework for the ultimate supercession of national policies and the implementation of the single policy envisaged by the regime. This must involve the creation of a centralized IO.

It should be clear from this discussion that regimes are sets of norms, rules and procedures chosen by state actors to create order in the international system for the realization of specific objectives. There may be structuralist factors determining regime characteristics, and the scope and form of the regime change. But clearly the characteristics of the regime are hammered out in international negotiations. States can thus 'choose' the regime that is established as a consequence of intense political bargaining. What factors determine this choice?

Broadly speaking such choice reflects the competing cognitive stances at international sessions and the extent to which these stances can be reconciled within a comprehensive political strategy for the utilization of consensual knowledge. The greater the reconciliation of opposing consensual stances, the wider is the scope of consensual knowledge and the stronger the commitment to a fixed and relatively stable operational strategy based upon it. Regimes which are based upon wide consensual knowledge tend to 'freeze' norms, rules and procedures: those that lack such a base display a high level of flexibility and deliberately allow for the 'evolution' of norms, rules and procedures in order to avoid regime disintegration.[61] Here the emphasis is on decentralization and the addressing of specific problems rather than institutional coherence. Such a regime may well take the form of a system of closely co-ordinated arrangements in which differently situated states with different capacities and interests undertake diverse obligations but agree to maintain some form of regulated interchange. This is to be contrasted with a global regime making use of centralized IOs to develop uniform rules and procedures and to ensure compliance.

Considerations such as these have played an important part in negotiations leading to the construction and transformation of regimes in the international economy. I now turn to an examination of these regimes and an analysis of the factors determining their evolution and operation.

2.3 INTERNATIONAL ECONOMIC REGIMES IN THE MODERN WORLD

In this section I will begin by outlining the major characteristics of the international economic regime which developed in the non-communist world after the Second World War by contrasting it with its nineteenth century predecessor. I will attempt to describe the impact of this regime on the level and form of international economic transactions.[62] Finally I will investigate the process of regime transformation and attempt to identify the factors responsible for inducing regime transformation in the non-communist segment of the world economy.

Nineteenth century capitalism is generally interpreted as incorporating an international regime of free trade.[63] This emerged due to Britain's hegomonic role as an international economic manager, the gradual collapse of the manor and guild system, particularly in the Germanic states, the increased political influence of domestic interest groups which stood to gain from the removal of restrictions on the international flow of commodities and money, and the triumph of the ideology of free trade.[64] The restrictions on the role of the state as a manager of domestic markets were also incorporated in the international economic regimes. This can most clearly be seen in the case of the gold bullion standard which dominated Europe in pre First World War days. Adherence to this standard meant that the level of the domestic money supply was determined ultimately by the balance of payments. It was believed that the principal purpose of domestic monetary policy was the maintenance of gold parity. It was argued that states should not seek to undermine the equiliberating linkages in changes in gold reserves, the balance of payments and movements in the domestic money supply and income level.

The assumptions about the objectives of domestic economic policy which underlay the nineteenth century liberal international regimes were comprehensively abandoned in the inter-war period—particularly after the collapse of the gold exchange standard in 1931. Protectionism and state economic intervention proliferated throughout the system, leading to a disintegration of the international monetary regime and the emergence of distinct currency blocs in the world.[65]

The nineteenth century liberal international economic regime existed because of Britain's ability and willingness to act as the system's lender of last resort and to pursue a policy of free trade and investment. Sterling became the major international reserve asset. Most important was the fact that 'national monetary authorities were inclined to follow the market—and indirectly the Bank of England—rather than to assert independent national objectives of their own'.[66] The international gold standard system was thus based both on the actual supremacy of a hegemon and the dominance of an appropriate ideology among the group of national policy makers. In this sense it represented 'the best of all possible worlds'.

The international economic regime devised at the Bretton Woods conference was based on a different conception of the role of the state as a domestic and international economic manager. There were differences between the British and American position on the extent to which state regulation of economic life was desirable, but both sides accepted the Keynesian argument that the state had an important role to play in managing financial, commodity and labour markets. The commitment to multilateralism was part of a broader concern to ensure growth and full employment through using both domestic and international state policies. Indeed the purpose of multilateralism was the encouragement of domestic economic health. Institutions created under this regime were specifically mandated to waive general regulations if compliance with these created problems of economic insolvency or unemployment for the member countries. Thus despite the emphasis on free trade and investment the Bretton Woods regime was clearly an interventionist one which rejected the 'nightwatchman's role' for its members that had been a cornerstone of the international economic regime of the nineteenth century. Nor can it be argued that the regime which has emerged after the collapse of the Bretton Woods system represents a return to the orthodoxies of the nineteenth century. Despite the loudly proclaimed profession of belief in free markets, modern-day monetarists have shown no enthusiasm for signing a compact for the re-establishment of stable exchange rate linkages, and there is no hegomonic power which can act as an underwriter *à la* Britain. Governments are free to intervene, as much or as little as they choose, in the operation of the foreign exchange markets. This has in effect meant that the ability of the IMF to regulate the policies of the leading powers has dwindled substantially since 1972.[67] The United States continues to resist effectively the establishment of a dollar substitution account and to stall the expansion of the role of the SDR as an international reserve asset. Furthermore there is not likely to be any agreement on mechanisms for compelling surplus countries to accept a share of the burden of international adjustment—through, for example, comprehensive agreement on multilateral regulated revaluation of the currencies of the surplus countries—and adjustment within the system takes the form of the imposition of IMF conditionally on individual debtor countries of the Third World,[68] whose policies are scrutinized and evaluated by the IMF on a case-by-case basis.

The system of floating rates established in 1972 has many points of similarity with the dollar exchange standard. It has not led to competitive devaluation—the principal argument advanced in 1944 for the commitment to a fixed exchange rate regime.[69] There is no evidence to show that the volume of international trade has been significantly affected by the switch-over to the managed float system.[70] Finally this system has 'cushioned' domestic economic policy more effectively than its predecessor and reduced speculative pressure while facilitating a certain level of 'voluntary' adjustment, even on the part of surplus countries, particularly the United States and Japan, who have shown a willingness to accept currency revaluation occasionally. Thus the emergence of the managed float is best seen as a modification of the regime to achieve the objectives of the Bretton Woods regime—described by Ruggie as 'embedded liberalism'[71] It does not represent an abandonment of the objectives of the vision of the role of the state as a manager of domestic and international economic policy on which they are based.

As far as international trade is concerned it has been argued that it would be 'over simple to consider the modern regime a pale reflection of nineteenth century free trade since the basic principles differ'.[72] Today the commitment to free trade is not unconditional.[73] Trade is seen rather as a 'handmaiden of growth' and economic well–being. GATT rules accept this and permit contracting parties to take steps to reduce the domestic costs of trade liberalization. Moreover the modern international trade system relies much more heavily on regular consultations and periodic negotiations than did its nineteenth century predecessor. This has ensured that the escape clauses are not made use of indiscriminately, and member states have sought to strengthen the central core of the system.

The long recession which began in the West in the wake of oil price rises of 1973 and 1974 contributed towards an erosion of some of the gains that had been achieved by the reduction of tariffs during the 1950s and 1960s. Subsequently protection has increased in response to domestic pressure. However, the new trade restrictions are concentrated in a relatively small group of product areas: many of which are of primary interest to the newly industrializing developing countries.[74] Developed countries found it difficult to give adequate adjustment assistance to facilitate a flow of labour and capital from industries in which their international comparative advantage was declining, and generally found that the least expensive way of accommodating domestic interest groups that were exerting pressure in this area was by imposing selective import restraints.

Trade restrictions among the developed countries themselves have continued to be reduced. This is evident from the endorsement of the results of the Tokyo Round of GATT negotiations by all OECD countries in 1979. The negotiations were successful in that significant cuts in industrial tariffs were achieved; however, there are few substantive agreements on regulating non-tariff protectionist measures. The greater the reliance on non-tariff barriers, the greater is the erosion of GATT's ability to regulate international trade. As 'voluntary' trade restraints are usually achieved through bilateral bargaining their proliferation means a rejection of the principle of multilateralism and non-discrimination.

The sector-specific protectionism, characteristic of the modern international trade regime, reflects essentially the limitations of state policy as an instrument for economic regulation. It has been argued that state intervention is most successful in regulating the production and trade of standardized products, manufactured in the main by national firms employing a relatively constant and unchanging production technology.[75] On the other hand, internationally integrated sectors using a rapidly changing technology offer considerably less scope for state regulation. In these sectors trade has continued to expand, and state intervention has been limited mainly to providing domestic initiatives for the development of the 'national champion' industries. The scope of this type of encouragement is a function of the extent to which economies of scale prevail in a given sector.

Concentration of state intervention in the declining industries and the emphasis on non-tariff interventionist measures has meant that many of the detailed and rigid GATT rules have become unoperational and have been frequently bypassed. During the 1950 these rules had been effectively used and GATT had 'developed from a document into a working organization'.[76] In that decade the emphasis was on the settlement of disputes and the regulation of commercial behaviour. In the early 1960s GATT's membership grew as many newly independent countries joined the organization. This meant a decline in cohesion as agreement on desired outcomes and even the scope of arbitration and other legal procedures declined. As a result, compliance with GATT rules have fallen to such an extent that doubts are being raised about the whole legal framework contained in GATT's Articles of Agreement.[77] Dispute settlement mechanisms have been abandoned. *Ad hoc* procedures have proliferated. However, as we have seen in the case of the international monetary regime, the decline in formal rule making and rule implementation of procedures has not been accompanied by a decline in the level of international transactions.

A wealth of evidence can be cited to illustrate the following facts:

(a) Both international trade and international investment have been rising rapidly since at the least the mid 1950s.

(b)   Growth has been highly concentrated in geographical,
       sectoral and institutional terms. Most-rapid growth
       has taken place in the technology intensive industries
       located in the West and dominated by the giant trans-
       nationals.
(c)   Much of the rise in foreign trade and investment has
       taken the form of mergers and increase in intra-firm
       transactions.[78]

After reviewing the evidence in both international trade and
investment, Ruggie concludes that 'international economic
transactions increasingly reflect the effect of marginal cost and
price differentials of similar activities and products, rather
than the mutual benefits of divergent investment, production
and export structures. Moreover within the division of labour
there is a critical shift in functional differentiation from the
level of country and sector to the level of product and firm'.[79]

Many explanations can be offered for this evolution and they
need not be mutually exclusive. It is clear, for example, that the
international trade and monetary regime that developed in the
wake of the Second World War has at least evolved rules,
norms and procedures that do not hinder the type of expansion
of international trade and investment that has taken place.
This regime has emphasized liberalization, but has recognized
as legitimate state intervention for preserving domestic
economic welfare. The regime has thus permitted—some
would argue facilitated—the concentration of the growth of
trade and investment in areas where adjustment costs and
political and economic vulnerabilities are low. Clearly other
factors—such as the national patterns of technological
development, the emergence of the transnational corporation,
and change in the political salience of domestic interest
groups—have also influenced the evolution of modern
international trade and investment structures. The political
economist must seek to understand the interplay of these
diverse forces when attempting to explain the outcome of their
interaction.

Finally we turn to the question of regime change. As we have
seen in Section 2.2., two major groups of explanations have
been offered in these areas. One school stresses the importance
of hegemons and asserts that regime change reflects change

in the international balance of power. The other emphasizes the impact of the advancement of scientific and technological knowledge, which when significant enough can induce large and small powers to perceive substantial joint gains through reformulating the norms, rules and procedures of international collaboration. Other theories of international regime have also been advanced.[80] The most frequent basis for evaluating international economic regime change has been the theory of hegemonic stability. In the rest of this section we will focus attention on this theory in the context of changes in the international trade and monetary regimes.

The changes in the international monetary and trade regimes since 1944 have been described above. Briefly they consist of:

(a) An end to dollar convertibility into gold.

(b) The adoption of the system of floating exchange rates.

(c) The proliferation of non-tariff barriers and voluntary export restraints as a means for the sectoral and geographic concentration of protectionist measures.

(d) A relative weakening of the IMF and GATT as regulators of economic activity within the West since the late 1950s.

We turn first to an examination of change in the international trade regime. The breakdown of the ITO-related agreements was primarily due to US refusal to accept them. Few would dispute that the US played a hegemonic role in the international economy in the post Second World War period. It possessed an enormous resource advantage and pursued an active foreign policy to ensure that the newly emerging EIOs carried an indelible stamp of US preferences and policy stances. This was clearly so in the case of GATT, the organizational ideology of which strongly emphasized the efficacy of open markets and the liberalization of trade.[81] Gerald Meyer has shown that American influence was decisive in early GATT tariff reductions.[82] However, it is noteworthy that tariff cutting in GATT has persisted despite a general weakening of US international economic hegemony. Moreover, GATT's trade dispute handling procedures had virtually collapsed by the beginning of the 1960s—a period when US international economic dominance was clearly not in doubt: there has undoubtedly been a weakening of GATT's role as a manager of the international trade system as the hegemonic role of the US has declined, but the form that this weakening has taken cannot be explained by relying solely upon the hegemonic stability model.

Erosion of the regime has taken the form of a proliferation of sector-specific trade discriminatory policies which GATT is increasingly unable to control. In Lipson's words 'not only is hegemony gone, so is the international consensus produced by American victory and reconstruction'.[83] But it would be clearly mistaken to generalize from the problems experienced in some sectors. In others the regime remains strong. Its most significant success is the drastic tariff reductions achieved even during the height of the 1970s recession. Thus assessing the outcome of the Tokyo Round Baldwin, Mutti and Richardson conclude that 'the US has just completed one of the most comprehensive rounds of unilateral tariff negotiations. Yet it is paradoxically facing stronger pressures for protection than at any time since the 1930s. Most other developed countries are in the same position'.[84]

The Tokyo MTN achieved tariff reductions on industrial products of 33 per cent. These results compare favourably with the achievements of the Kennedy Round of tariff negotiations which were concluded under GATT auspices in 1967.[85]

The hegemonic stability model with its emphasis on the role of hegemonic countries is thus not an entirely satisfactory basis for explaining the weakening of the international trade regime in some areas and its endurance in others. It also does not explain the breakdown of general dispute-settling procedures that often led to using bilateral-negotiated agreements as a substitute for multilateral conventions.

Regime change—or perhaps regime adjustment—is better understood if we focus upon the production and marketing characteristic specific to industrial subsectors. International trade has grown in sectors characterized by the production of differentiated goods with high research and development requirements, increasing returns to scale and dominated by the transnationals. Trade in these sectors consists of the export and import of very similar goods. It cannot easily be explained by relying exclusively on the old familiar Hecksher–Ohlin model. This trade reflects a highly fluid investment strategy with firms constantly on the move to carve out specialization 'niches', which are abandoned as rapidly as they are developed. Adjustment costs of moving capital and labour are relatively low. State intervention is not particularly effective. It is thus likely that the growth of intra-industry trade creates an impetus for trade liberalization. GATT has been acutely conscious of the link between sector characteristics and trade liberalization. As Hufbawer and Chilas show 'GATT negotiations very much favour intra industry over inter industry specialisations'.[86]

In the face of these trends it seems unwarranted to talk of a collapse of the international trade regime following the United States' declining international economic hegemony. There has rather been a modification of the regime: it has weakened in some sectors but strengthened in others. This reflects the fact that, whereas the distribution of international economic power has changed significantly since the late 1940s, the commitment of the leading Western countries to what Ruggie has called 'embedded liberalism' has not changed; whenever liberal-ization of trade does not pose a significant threat to domestic economic expansion and welfare it is encouraged and the institutional preferences of the late 1940s are retained. Where liberalization does create significant unemployment and distributional problems, however, the norms, rules and procedures devised in that period are largely ignored.

Broadly similar trends are perceivable when we turn to an analysis of changes in the international monetary regime. The United States played a major part in the institutionalization of the monetary agreement of 1944. The United States' interpretations of the original Articles of Agreement created what subsequently came to be known as 'the IMF orthodoxy'.[87] Throughout the 1960s the dollar continued to weaken, and its gold convertibility became something of a myth by the late 1960s. The formal delinking of the dollar from gold in 1971 led to the search for new instruments for the creation of international liquidity and the settlement of debts. There emerged a multiple currency reserve system and a managed float exchange rate regime, in which unilateral decisions often took the place of collective ones. It is generally acknowledged that these changes have not violated the norms of the regime established in the wake of the Bretton Woods agreement. Hence the continued growth of international lending and the ability to manage exchange markets without seriously disrupting international confidence. The essential durability of that regime can be seen from the fact that the major proposals for long-term reform of the existing international monetary system all envisage the creation of the kinds of international mechanisms envisaged by Keynes. Specifically they advocate a strengthening of the SDR and of the dollar stabilization account based at the IMF, and the consolidation of the multiple currency reserve system. These mechanisms represent a return to the Bretton Woods perspectives, and not a departure from them. It seems justifiable to conclude, therefore, that the decline of US hegemony in the world economy has not been accompanied by a collapse of the international monetary regime because—as in the case of trade—the major Western countries have remained committed to the social goals outlined by the victors at the end of the Second World War. Changes in the distribution of economic power may be necessary but not sufficient causes for the reordering of norms. Changes in rules and procedures may accommodate this changed power balance and permit a pursuit of the original social objectives.

In this section I have outlined the major characteristic of the existing international regimes in the field of trade and finance. In the concluding section of this chapter I will pose the question: what role can the EIOs be expected to play within such international regimes?

2.4. THE ROLE OF THE EIOs

EIOs have achieved a significant expansion in number as well as work programmes in comparatively recent times. There have been voices calling for both an expansion in their role[88] and a drastic curtailment of their organizational task.[89] The latter group of scholars have based their views on the literature produced by the new generation of political economists, who have been arguing for a general reduction in state intervention within society.

Neo-classical welfare economists have generally argued that government has a role to play in correcting market failure, particularly in situations where externalities exist. The existence of technical and ownership externalities justifies government intervention on strictly efficiency grounds in this view. Pigou argued that government intervention in such cases should mainly take the form of the development of an appropriate taxation and subsidization policy, which would induce private firms to 'internalize' the externalities by making these externality-creating firms liable for harmful effects.[90]

This view has been challenged by the modern political economists of the New Right, who contend that a market system can internalize its externalities if the government refrains from interference. Coase has shown that if transaction costs are zero the resource alteration pattern will remain unaffected by the way in which property rights in creating or preventing the externality are distributed.[91]

The Coase argument can be illustrated by a simple geometrical exercise (see Figure 2.1)

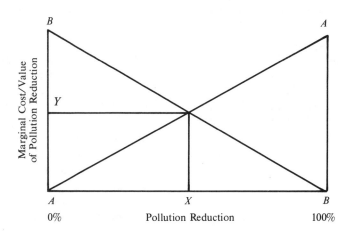

Figure 2.1

Here AA represents the marginal cost of pollution reduction to the polluter and BB the marginal value of pollution reduction to the pollutee. If the polluter can create pollution at will—if, that is, he has a property right in pollution creation—there will initially be zero pollution control. As long as the marginal value of pollution control (to the pollutee) is higher than the marginal cost of pollution, the pollutee will be willing to pay a price for pollution control to the polluter: equilibrium will be reached where marginal cost equals marginal value. In our case this is at a point where pollution creation is at X and the marginal cost is Y. If property rights in pollution control are vested in the pollutee, pollution control will be total—100 per cent: hence the polluter will pay the price as long as the marginal value of pollution creation is greater than the marginal cost of pollution control. Once again equilibrium will be at X and Y: hence the distribution of property rights does not affect the allocation of resources.

Where transaction costs such as detection, monitoring, negotiation, etc. related to pollution control are positive, Coase shows that welfare would be maximized if property rights were assigned to the party with the higher transaction costs. Government intervention should be limited to this function.[92]

This argument can be extended to determine the legitimate function of IOs. The existence of international externalities does not necessitate direct resource allocation by IOs. These externalities can be 'internalized' by an appropriate allocation of property rights.[93] This is the proper domain of international law which is concerned with the determination and protection of international entitlements, including property rights, liabilities and inalienable rights. Thus international environment law specifies liabilities for the creation of externalities and has well-defined principles for the apportioning of this liability.[94] Agreements on regulation of marine, resources, air, space and radioactivity externalities exist in the modern world, and in the view of the property rights school obviate the necessity for direct intervention by IOs to offset these externalities. This school thus emphasizes the importance of developing a system of international tort and property law for what in their view would be an equitable basis for dealing with international externalities.

In this view the primary task of IOs should be information gathering and providing a forum for legal agreements on the allocation of entitlements. It is argued that such a role has largely been accepted by the European Monetary System and GATT, which are concerned with the allocation of liabilities in case of violation of mutually agreed rules[95]—although GATT has, by accepting the principles of the legitimacy of customs union and positive discrimination in favour of the developing countries, tended to move away from this role.

A number of objections to the 'property rights' approach have of course been made. The most important from the perspective of the IO student is that the typical IO deals with the provision of 'public goods'—goods which are characterized by inappropriability and indivisibility. Public goods are usually supplied by the government. It has been argued that issue linkage, which is made possible by the existence of the conditions generally described as 'complex interdependence', enhances the need to increase the direct interventionist powers of IOs for the production of a growing volume of public goods, as interdependence generates a wide spectrum of problems which require international collaborative action.[96] The existence of public goods means that in many cases the market-regulated provision of this good will be suboptional and, although collaborative co-operation can to a certain extent offset this tendency, there is no guarantee that the existence of a 'norm of reciprocity' will ensure that co-operation will be extended to such a point that suboptimality will be entirely overcome. Thus in many cases the 'internalization' of externalities that exist at the international level through the privitization of public goods does not constitute an acceptable solution on the grounds of either efficiency or equity. Ruggie argues that pure international public goods require IOs for 'the introduction of elements of collective decision making and collective ownership into a particular activity'.[97] There is, of course, no guarantee that direct intervention by IOs—however necessary and justified—will actually result in an optimal provision of the public good concerned.

Conybeare argued that 'federalists, functionalists, neo-functionalists and pluralists all agree as to the inherent desirability of world government. The recent emphasis on "interdependence" in the IO literature has supported the traditional policy prescription.'[98] This is quite a misleading generalization. Its fallacy becomes evident if we examine the views of the functionalist and neo-functionalist authors, who developed integration theory with the interdependence school on the question of the role of IOs within the international system.

The integrationists clearly saw IOs as playing a key role. Their leaderships were charged with the responsibility of ensuring that the 'latent' spillover potential of an integration scheme was realized and institutionalized in a manner which effectively eroded national sovereignties. The integrationists were committed to an 'incrementalist' logic, which saw a gradual expansion of the possibilities of issue linkage leading to a politicization of hitherto technical venues of international collaboration. This politicization was seen as a process contributing to a sustained increase in the scope, level and authority of IOs and a subordination of national decision-making forums to this authority. Supranational institutions— for the example the European Community—were seen as advantageously placed to take the initiative in formulating package deals which would, by efficiently solving substantial problems of say trade and monetary management, generate systemic pressure for increasing the institutional mandate and authority of the Community EIOs.[99]

The interdependence school has found this perspective incomplete and an inadequate basis for analysing contemporary international reality. The most telling criticism of the integrationists is, of course, that European Community IOs have not developed in the way predicted by that theory. Within the context of the present system of international relations characterized by conditions of 'complex interdependence', the 'incrementalist' logic of decision making based upon a perception of automatic issue linkages and spillover has given way to the logic of what Haas has described as 'fragmented issue linkage'.[100] This may mean that domestic concerns and decision-making forums, again in importance relative to EIOs.[101] Pressure may mount for actively resisting the growth of the organizational mandate of the IOs. In the EC case it has been claimed that 'the integration theorists were . . . oversimplifying the common characteristics of pluralist industrialised countries as a basis for common policy making. In practice the dissimilarities of the different national systems are more marked than the similarities and effect every area of Community policy making'.[102] Hence in this view 'the European Community (institutions are) a set of instruments intermittently appropriate and intermittently used by national governments to seek and achieve essentially national goals.[103] This, of course, does not imply a necessary decline in the scope and authority of EIOs over time. Wallace and his collaborators, for example, argue that the EC institutions are increasing in authority in terms of scope but not in level.[104] Haas has argued that under conditions of complex interdependence all institutional outcomes are possible, and it is inappropriate to develop some general theory such as that of the integrations in such circumstances.[105] In the case of the EC institutions the overall pattern seems to be 'of something more than the pattern of intergovernmental co-operation contained within international organisation of the traditional type . . . (there is) growing decentralisation with power slipping from the grasp of government but not accumulating in any one place, certainly not totally in the hands of international organisations'.[106] Within such an international system EIOs will grow and decline rapidly. There will be no clearly determined and relatively stable hierarchy of issues and/or institutions. The future of IOs in such a system will in Hass's view depend on adopting authority to the task of 'improving the performance of all kinds of public services which involve the active management of society and economy'.[107]

It is thus clear that in relation to integration approaches 'interdependence themes de-emphasise centralised institutional processes. These studies are therefore in one sense less relevant to the study of international organisation than to the study of international politics as a whole'.[108] In another sense it may be argued that the interdependence view of the international organization process is radically different from that of the integrationists. In the former view, international bureaucracies interact through a network of horizontal leadership or programming within the system as a whole. External factors—such as strategic concerns leading to fragmented issue linkages in specific areas—may be more important than organizational leadership or ideology—in determining expansion or contraction of organizational task and authority. The interdependence school has been criticized for not indicating the relative importance of the many factors which in its view determine organizational and systemic outcomes.[109] Nevertheless, interdependence theorists have remained deeply interested in the work of EIOs.

The period of the growth of the interdependence school has been characterized by the emergence of a number of international organizations including since 1973 the UN Environment Programme, the World Food Council, the International Energy Agency, many producer's associations and the Conference on International Economic Co-operation, to name a few. These IOs have emerged in response to different needs but they have also served largely as a means for integrating newcomers into the existing structure of international relations. It has been argued that functionally specific EIOs with strong secretariat leadership can play a positive role in defusing conflict and realizing economic welfare objectives in a complex interdependence environment. IOs have gained in importance because 'the scope for "free riders" has been sharply reduced with the dispersion of economic wealth and power throughout the world. It is imperative at this point in history for the more important countries to join together to exercise systemic leadership'.[110] Since interdependence exists over a wide range of international issues, IOs must be deliberately devised to achieve 'fragmented issue linkage' in a way which makes the world 'safe for interdependence'. Interdependence implies that IOs should seek increased interaction with government bureaucrats. They should seek to reach beyond government into civil society and develop contacts with politicians, businessmen and domestic-interest groups, in order to protect the IOs organizational task and press for an extension of its mandate. It is precisely the inability of some EIOs such as UNCTAD to reach beyond government into society which characterised by complex interdependence. If a capacity of 'society penetration' can be developed EIOs have considerable scope for exercising leadership within the system.

Advocates of the 'interdependence' approach believe that increasing the effectiveness of EIOs is in the interests of national governments since the former address problems that cannot be tackled by unilateral initiatives. Governments can enhance IO effectiveness by a number of policy measures. Thus Bergsten argues that

> few governments are in fact effectively organised to backstop the international organisations of which they are members; most often there is a wide gap between people responsible for relations with the institutions and those responsible for the substance of these issues. The same government officials who are responsible for national decisions must participate directly in the international institutional process if that process is to succeed.[111]

Other authors generally accepting the interdependence thesis have suggested modifications of IO structure and government policy in order to increase the organizational efficiency of institutions such as the IMF, the IBRD, GATT and UNCTAD.

We have seen that the range of views on the role the EIOs can play is wide. There is general agreement however—with the possible exception of the 'property rights' type of scholars—that the nature of the international system is itself an important determinant of this role. Haas, in the days when he was an integrationist developed a view on the relationship between environment characteristics and organizational ideology which remains a useful perspective for circumscribing the role of EIOs within given international systems.[112] An international organization which seeks systemic transformation derives its ideology from its environment. At its inception, an international organization is almost inevitably merely one of a number of structures which may carry out functions determined by the actors—the nation states and the voluntary organizations. Some international organizations seek to become actors in their own right.

Whether or not an international organization succeeds in playing this role depends upon the ability of the organizational leadership to formulate an organizational ideology based upon the values and aspirations of the constituents, but combining these in such a way that task expansion is, on the one hand, possible and, on the other, leads to systemic transformation in the form desired by the leadership. This implies that the organizational ideology need not necessarily be the minimum common denominator of the demands of its constituents. Generally speaking an international organization and its leadership are not totally subservient to its constituents. After its formal establishment and the definition of its global task, the organization is free to select its social base. Its leadership can choose friends and enemies from the environment; it can orient its programmes to serve its friends; it can foster an elite within and without the organization infused with the organizational ideology; it can formulate its legal and administrative procedures or, what is more important, it can delay the progress of such formulation.

The organizational leadership is thus in charge of a structure which is potentially autonomous. The evolution of the organizational ideology and its articulation through the performance of specific tasks by the organization may, therefore, contribute towards strengthening certain relationships within the environment and weakening others. The organization is, moreover, concerned with the task of sustaining a dynamic balance of forces within a changing environment—a balance which permits the organization to articulate its ideology in the form of specific policies. It follows that the ideology and the specific functions which it entails are themselves responsive to changes in the environment. The leadership must endeavour to build viable interest coalitions within the environment whose interests are reflected in the organizational ideology and who identify themselves with the organization on this basis. These interest coalitions will then 'reward' the organization by arguing for greater organizational autonomy and for task expansion. The organizational leadership must be adept at recognizing which interest coalitions are viable on the one hand and desirable on the other. Attempts must be made to accommodate the interests of such groups in organizational programmes, and to reduce tension and antagonism within such coalitions.

The interplay between organizational ideology and environmental characteristics is complex. The environment constrains the evolution of the ideology in the form of specific programmes. Initially the ideology is based upon the shared objectives of constituents. The interpretation of the mandate received at formation and the articulation of the ideology in the shape of specific programmes are the responsibility of the organizational leadership. The leadership has to ensure that its interpretation of the ideology wins the support of viable interest groups who identify themselves with the organizational ideology, support the programmes and policies of the organization and argue for task expansion and organizational autonomy.

Different international environments thus provide different scope for EIO activity. However, the success of EIO programmes ought to be carefully scrutinized if their utility as instruments of international economic management is to be realistically assessed. This is a complex task. The next chapter discusses the major approaches to the evaluation of the performance of EIOs.

NOTES

1. Hoffman, S. 'An American social science: international relations', *Diedulus*, No. 106 (Summer 1977) p. 51.
2. Singer, D. 'Systems stability and transformation: a global systems approach', *British Journal of International Studies*, (1978) Vol. 4 No. 4, pp. 231–64.
3. Kaplan, M. *System and Process in International Politics*, Wiley, New York, (1956) and Modelski, B. 'Agraria and industria: two models of the international system' in Knoor, K. and Verba, S. (eds.) *The International System: Theoretical Essays*, Princeton University Press, Princeton (1961) pp. 124–61.
4. Yout, D. 'World order: the system's approach', *World Politics,* (1978) Vol. 32 No. 1, pp. 151–69.
5. Morgenthau, H. *Politics Among Nations*, Knopf, New York (1967).
6. Bull, H. *The Anarchical Society,* Columbia University Press, New York (1977) and Waltz, K.N. *Theory of International Politics*, Addison-Wesley, Reading, Mass. (1979).
7. Bull, *op. cit.,* p. 74.
8. Bull, *op. cit.,* p. 107.
9. Bull, *op. cit.,* p. 114.
10. Waltz, *op. cit.,* p. 117.
11. Waltz, *op. cit.,* p. 193.
12. Morgenthau, *op. cit.,* p. 157.
13. Michalak, S. 'Theoretical perspectives for understanding international

interdependence', *World Politics,* No. 2 (1979) p. 249.

14. Merriam, C. *Prologue to Politics*, Chicago University Press, Chicago (1939) p. 92.
15. Merriam, C. *Political Power,* Chicago University Press, Chicago (1934) p. 303.
16. Haas, E. *Beyond the Nation State,* Part II, Stanford University Press, Stanford (1964).
17. As an exception to this trend note Ansari, J.A. 'Environmental characteristics and organisational ideology: the case of UNCTAD', *British Journal of International Studies,* Vol. 4, No. 2 (1978) pp. 130–63.
18. Haas, E. 'Turbulent fields and the theory of regional integration' *IO,* Vol. 31 (1977) p. 174.
19. Haas, *op. cit.,* p. 179.
20. Haas, *op. cit.,* p. 184.
21. Haas, *op. cit.,* p. 194–6.
22. Haas, *op. cit.,* p. 204.
23. The debate is summarized in Rossecrance, R., Alexandroff, A., Hoehler, W., Kroll, J., Lacquer, S., and Stocker, J. 'Whither interdependence', *IO,* Vol. 31 No. 3 (1977) p. 425–72.
24. Haas, E. 'Is there a hole in the whole', *IO,* Vol. 29 No. 3 (1975) p. 860.
25. Scott, A.M. 'The logic of international interaction', *International Studies Quarterly,* Vol. 21 No. 4 (1977) pp. 429–60.
26. Morse, E. 'Crisis diplomacy, interdependence and the politics of international economic relations' in Tanter, R. and Ulman, H. *Theory and Policy in International Relations,* Princeton University Press, Princeton (1972) pp. 123–50.
27. Keohane, R. and Nye, J. *Power and Interdependence World Politics in Transition,* Little Brown and Co., Boston (1977).
28. However, the author recognize that the greater the salience of the issue and the smaller the number of domestic interest groups involved, as is for example the case in international monetary negotiations, the greater the likelihood that the larger Western states will dominate.
29. Pioneered by Emanuel, A. *Unequal Exchange,* Nex Left Books, London (1974).
30. Representative of this school is the work of Gulting, J. 'A structural theory of imperialism' *Journal of Peace Research,* 2 (1971) pp. 81—117.
31. *See* e.g. Wallerstein, I. *The Capitalist World Economy,* Cambridge University Press, Cambridge, (1979) and Bergesen, A. *Studies of the Modern World System,* Academic Press, New York (1980).
32. Andrews, B. 'The political economy of world capitalism: theory and practice', *IO,* Vol. 36 No. 1 (1982) p. 137.
33. Watkins, T. and Wallerstein, I. 'Patterns of world system development: a research proposal', *Review,* No. 1 (1977) pp. 111–45.
34. Quoted in Andrews, *op. cit.,* p. 144.
35. Andrews, *op. cit.,* p. 160.
36. For a review of Marxist writings on international organizations *see* Archer, C. *International Organisations,* George, Allen and Unwin,

London (1983) pp. 102–17.

37. Archer, *op. cit.*, p. 114.
38. *See* e.g. Keohane and Nye, *op. cit., passim.*
39. Young, O. 'International regimes: problems of concept formation' *World Politics*, Vol. 32 No. 3 (1980) p. 332.
40. Haas, E. 'On systems and international regimes', *World Politics*, (1974) Vol. 27 No. 2, p. 147.
41. Haas, *op. cit.*, p. 151.
42. Some regimes rely upon broader international arrangements for dealing with problems associated with the exercise of social choice, particularly with the adjudication of disputes about resource allocation.
43. For an elaboration of this *see* Young, O. 'Anarchy and social choice: reflections on the international policy', *World Politics*, Vol. 30 No. 3 (1978) pp. 241–63.
44. Although it is of course possible to describe any prevailing situation as a 'regime' such an approach is of little analytical value.
45. They may of course not be regarded as such.
46. On this Obson, M. *The Logic of Collective Action* Harvard University Press, Cambridge Mass. (1965).
47. Young 'International Regimes: Problem of Concept Formation', p. 353
48. For example, the existing regimes for Antarctica and for whaling in the North Eastern Atlantic are determined by the preferences of a small number of countries.
49. Young, *op. cit.*, p. 355.
50. Hirsch, F., Doyle, M. and Morse, E.L. *Alternatives to Monetary Disorder*, McGraw Hill, New York (1977).
51. *See* e.g. Falk, R.A. *A Study of Future Worlds*, Free Press, New York (1975).
52. Keohane and Nye, *op. cit., passim.*
53. On the difference between tactical and substantial linkages *see* Oye, K. 'The domain of choice: international constraints and the Carter administration' in Oye, K., Rothschild, D. and Leiber, R. (eds.) *Eagle Entangled* Longman, New York (1979) pp. 183–216.
54. *See* Sect. 2.1.
55. Or as in the case of the NIEO negoations they may fail to achieve regime transformation.
56. For a case study of the process of regime decay, *see* Haas, E. 'Regime decay, conflict management and international organisation 1945–1981' *IO*, Vol. 33 No. 2 (1981) pp. 189–256.
57. Cognitive explanations of regime change are typically presented in technological and scientific issue areas. *See* de Sola Price, D. and Speigel–Rosing, I. (eds.) *Science, Technology and Society*, Sage, Beverly Hills (1977).
58. This is discussed in Chapter 4.
59. Haas 'Regime decay, conflict management and international organisation: 1945–1981', p. 217.
60. This typology is based on Ruggie, J. 'Responses to technology: concept and trends', *IO*, Vol. 27 No. 2 (1975) pp. 568–84.

61. The leadership of the ILO adopted such an approach in the post Second World War period with some success. See Haas *Beyond the Nation State,* Part II.
62. In investigating these two questions we rely heavily on Ruggie, J. 'International regimes, transactions and change: embedded liberalism in the post war economic order', *IO*, Vol. 36 No. 2 (1982) pp. 379–415.
63. Gilpin, R. *War and Change in World Politics* Cambridge University Press, Cambridge (1981).
64. Kindleberger, C. 'The rise of free trade in western Europe 1820–1875', *Journal of Economic History*, Vol. 35 No. 1 (1975) pp. 20–55.
65. Briggs, A. 'The world economy, interdependence and planning', in Mouvat, C. (ed.) *The New Cambridge Modern History*, Vol. 12. Cambridge University Press, Cambridge (1968).
66. Cleveland, H. 'The international monetary system in the inter war period', in Rowland, B. *Balance of Power or Hegemony: the Inter War Monetary System*, University Press, New York (1976) p. 57.
67. For a discussion of the changes in the international monetary system since the collapse of the Bretton Woods arrangements *see* Singer, H.W. and Ansari, J.A. *Rich and Poor Countries* (3rd Edn), George Allen and Unwin, London (1982) Ch. 12.
68. Britain also experienced IMF 'conditionality' in 1976.
69. Singer and Ansari, *op. cit.,* p. 262.
70. This is discussed below.
71. Ruggie, *op. cit.,* pp. 393–8.
72. Lipson, C. 'The transformation of trade: the sources and effects of regime change', *IO*, Vol. 36 No. 2 (1982) p. 423.
73. Some authors contend that Britain's free trade commitment in the nineteenth century was not unconditional either, see Gallager, J. and Robinson, R. 'The imperialism of free trade', *Economic History Review* 2nd Series, Vol. 10 (1953–4) pp. 131–66, and Lawson, F. 'Hegemony an the structure of international trade: a view from Arabia', *IO*, Vol. 37 No. 2 (1983) pp. 317–37.
74. Nouzad, B. *The Rise in Protectionism,* IMF Pamphlet Series No. 24 Washington (1978).
75. Zysman, J. *Political Strategies for Industrial Order: State Market and Industry in France,* University of California Press, Berkeley (1978).
76. Lipson, *op. cit.,* p. 434.
77. Hudec, R. 'GATT dispute settlement after the Tokyo Round', *Cornell International Law Journal,* Summer 1980, pp. 141–67.
78. Evidence reviewed in Ruggie, *op. cit.,* pp. 398–404.
79. Ruggie, *op. cit.,* p. 402.
80. Thus Cowhey and Long have attributed a 'theory of surplus capacity' to Susan Strange. According to their version of this 'theory', regime change eroding liberal norms, rules and procedures in particular will occur 'when important nations face a sustained problem of large amounts of excess capacity for production' in some specific economic sectors (p. 162). Cowhey, P. and Long, E. 'Testing regime change: hegemonic decline or surplus capacity', *IO*, Vol. 37. No. 2 (1983)

pp. 165–88. Cowhey and Long test this theory with reference to the experience of the international automobile industry over the period 1950–80.

81. On this *see* Hirschman, A. *National Power and the Structure of Foreign Trade*, University of California Press, Berkeley (1945).

82. Meyer, G.M. *International Trade Policy* Macmillan, London (1975) p. 142.

83. Lipson, *op. cit.*, p. 441.

84. Baldwin, R., Mutti, J. and Richardson, D. 'Welfare effects on the United States of a significant multilateral tariff reduction', *Journal of International Economics*, Vol. 10 No. 3 (1980) p. 405.

85. GATT. *The Tokyo Round of Multilateral Negotiations*, Geneva (1979)

86. Quoted in Lipson, *op. cit.*, p. 445.

87. Which differed in many important respects—such as the role that was assigned to the dollar and the rejection of the multiple currency reserve system which Keynes strongly advocated—from the original Joint Statement of Principals signed by the UK and the US.

88. *See* e.g. Brown, S. and Fabian L. 'Towards mutual accountability in non terrestrial realms', *IO*, Vol. 29 No. 4 (1975) pp. 877–92.

89. *See* e.g. Conybeare, A.C. 'International organisation and the theory of property rights', *IO*, Vol. 34 No. 3 (1980) pp. 307–34.

90. Pigou, A.C. *The Economics of Welfare*, Macmillan, London (1920).

91. Coase, R.H. 'The problem of social cost' *Journal of Law and Economics* Vol. 3 No. 1 (1960) pp. 1–44.

92. Coase, *op. cit.*, pp. 10–14.

93. Since transaction costs are of course positive in this case.

94. Novak, J. (ed.) *Environmental Law: International and Comparative Aspects* Oceans, Dobbs Ferry NY (1976).

95. Conybeare, *op. cit.*, pp. 316–8.

96. Russett, B. and Sullivan, D. 'Collective goods and international organisations', *IO*, Vol. 25 No. 4 (1971) p. 849, Keohane and Nye *Power and Interdependence* pp. 30–2. The 'public goods' approach to IO is studied in Ch. 5.

97. Ruggie, J. 'Collective goods and future international collaboration', IO, Vol. 26 No. 4 (1972) p. 890.

98. Conybeare, *op. cit.*, p. 307.

99. *See* e.g. Haas, E. *Uniting Europe, passim*.

100. *See* Sects. 2.1 and 2.2.

101. Tsoukalis, L. *The Politics and Economics of European Monetary Integration*, George Allen and Unwin, London (1979) pp. 62–3, 110–24, documents this in the case of European monetary integration.

102. Wallace, H., Wallace, W. and Webb, C. (eds.) *Policy Making in the European Communities*, John Wiley, Chichester (1977), p. 46.

103. Wallace, *op. cit.*, p. 257.

104. Wallace, *op. cit.*, p. 321. The concept of 'scope' and 'level' are discussed in Ch. 4.

105. Haas, E. *The obsolescence of regional integration theory research* Study No. 25, University of California, Berkeley (1975) p. 62–3.

106. Wallace, *op. cit.* p. 316.
107. Haas, *op. cit.,* p. 80.
108. Nau, H. 'From integration to interdependence: gains, losses and continuing gaps', *IO*, Vol. 33 No. 1 (1979) p. 139.
109. Nau, *op. cit.,* p. 144–7.
110. Bergsten, F. 'Interdependence and the reform of international institutions', *IO*, Vol. 31 (1977) p. 73.
112. Haas, *Beyond the Nation State,* Part I.

3 Evaluating Impact

A study of the impact of an EIO is a study of its degree of success in modifying the structures of the international system, within which it is situated. A number of authors have studied the relation between effectiveness of IOs and the systemic characteristics of their environments.[1] Elaborate schemes for classification of environmental characteristics have been constructed.[2] Haas has studied the response of actors with different political, economic and geographic characteristics to decisions taken within the ILO.[3] Hoffman has found that a moderate international system—a system not racked by dominant power rivalries and ideological conflicts—enhances the effectiveness of international organizations. However, not every moderate international system need be one in which global international organizations play a major role.[4] For IOs to be effective the system within which they are situated must possess two characteristics.

In the first place, there should exist a broad procedural consensus among states which makes of multinational institutions the legitimate channels for the management of conflict and co-operation; in the second place, there should exist a preference for universal channels over regional ones.[5] EIOs, in particular, will enhance their effectiveness potential within moderate international systems, if they seek to prevent the occurrence of economic crises, if they promote patterns of associations between rich and poor countries which do not amount to neglect of the needs of the poorer nations or to a dangerous humiliation of the rich,[6] and if they develop new procedures for the institutionalization of changes within the international system.

An IO may be considered successful if it serves as a means for transcending those constraints which limit action by individual nation-states in a specific issue area. Such a transcending may be desired by the secretariat or by the member nations (or both). The initial step in this process is a pooling of national sovereignties, for the achievement of goals inaccessible to the individual nation-states. This initial pooling of national sovereignties may lead to what functionalists have called integration at a higher level, where nation-states will be willing to accept limitations placed by the IO on their national sovereignty.[7] Clearly, the crucial determinant of organizational success—as conceived of above—is the form and content of international bargaining which takes place within the IO. This bargaining process involves interaction between state representatives, who are influenced by the interests and orientation of national political economic and social groups. Thus the failure of an IO—at least of an IO involving bargaining between non-totalitarian polities—may be viewed as its inability to involve domestic economic or social groups in the formulation and implementation of its decisions. For if these groups do not perceive an interest in the process and outcome of an IO, its decisions are likely to remain formal agreements without the generation of domestic impetus which would make them effective instruments of substantive environmental transformation. This is a particularly useful way of looking at EIOs, for progress in economic relations within the capitalist system depends crucially on the attitudes and interests of private economic groups. EIOs may be described as successful if they generate policies supported by strong private economic groups, who perceive an advantage in the implementation of these policies, and who, therefore, press for an enhancement of the role of the organizations within the system.

Private economic groups within the capitalist system may need effective EIOs. Historically the modern nation-state has been an adequate instrument for the sustenance of national business enterprise. But it is clearly limited in its ability to provide the services necessary for the sustenance of the multinational corporation. Robin Murray has pointed out some of the major functions which a public sector has to perform in order to ensure the profitability of private capitalist enterprises. These include: the guaranteeing of property rights; the promotion of economic liberalism, i.e. acceptance of market criteria as a basis for economic decision-making; crisis control; and provision of key welfare services and development of a viable socio-economic infra-structure.[8]

Clearly the nation-state cannot at the international level undertake any of these functions without exercising political control over the areas where their domestic capital has established subsidiaries. Since the Second World War even the U.S. has not been able to play such a role, and this has undoubtedly been a major factor in the somewhat unsatisfactory relations between US-based multinational enterprises and the US Government.[9] In the main multinational enterprises have themselves evolved transnational structures capable of performing some of the functions outlined above. In general, area-based multinational corporations (i.e. organizations where management responsibility is delegated on the basis of geographical area coverage) have developed a significant level of autonomy, whereas product-based multinationals (i.e. where management responsibility is delegated on the basis of product coverage) rely primarily on states and groups of states to undertake these tasks.[10]

EIOs may play an important role in the provision of these services. There are strong pressures within Western polities which support some such organizations. We note, for example, the existence of an expanding area of coincidence between the policies of multinational firms, international commercial banks and the IMF. The IMF facilities the provision of international liquidity so that import restrictions are not imposed. It usually recommends devaluation and deflation to deal with balance of payments difficulties, and frowns upon exchange controls and the restriction of international capital movement. Devaluation policies adversely affect domestic business, whereas import liberalization is in the interest of area-based multinationals. The IMF also tries to ensure regular profit remittances from host countries to multinational headquarters by labelling investment income as a current account item on standard national balance sheets.[11] However, there are many groups within Western countries who do not see eye to eye with EIOs such as the IMF, the EEC, etc.[12] Prominent among them are domestic businessmen, trade union representatives and other groups adversely affected by the internalization of national economic structures on the basis of the market strategy of international corporations. These groups pressurize Western governments to resist international integration in this form, and the result is that Western governments vary in their response to IO initiatives for oligopolistic-style market integration. At times of economic crises, this resistance is most pronounced, but even during the boom 1950s and 1960s Western government proved reluctant to sacrifice national economic sovereignty by delegating authority to an international body for a gradual fusing of national fiscal, monetary and employment policies.

Thus a study of the impact of an EIO must attempt to answer the following questions:

(a) What are the targets set by the EIOs? What are their major environmental initiatives? To what extent are these initiatives relevant—that is, capable of inducing systemic transformation in accordance with the EIO's organizational ideology?

(b) To what extent have these targets been achieved?

(c) What is the impact of EIO policies on the attitude of governments, non-governmental groups and other IOs?

Assessing organizational effectiveness is a complex task. As Haas has reminded us, 'a given international organization may be ineffective with respect to the achievement of its explicit objectives but it is nevertheless effective if it contributes to the transformation of the international system'.[13] Organizational impact in a given case depends upon the ability of its leadership to redefine continuously the IO's objectives 'upwards', that is, it must seek to benefit from the systemic changes that it has created in the past. Organizational effectiveness thus implies a strengthening of the IO with respect to its environment.

Organizational effectiveness has been studied from a variety of perspectives. Many of the more behaviouralist scholars have used elements derived—often eclectically and somewhat informally—from the evaluation research approach. I turn to a description of this method for evaluating EIOs in the first section.

3.1 THE EVALUATION RESEARCH APPROACH[14]

Evaluation research has been defined as 'the application of the scientific method to experience with public programs to learn what happens as a result of program activities'.[15] Emphasis is placed on obtaining empirical evidence regarding the effectiveness of social intervention by IOs. A hypothesis-testing approach is used. Hypotheses are constructed on the basis of conjecture about the likely impact on the environment of a given programme undertaken by an IO. Hoole, for example, tests the hypothesis that WHO's smallpox eradication program led to a reduction in the international incidence of this disease.[16] The testing of the impact hypothesis involves the investigation of a relationship between a dependent variable— some environmental process—and a set of independent variables which includes some programme initiatives of an IO. The dependent variable is derived from a reading of the policy objectives and goals of an IO. The evaluation research methodology offers no guidance for identifying appropriate independent or impact variables or the form of the relationship—linear, non-linear, log linear etc.—between them. The hypothesis is sometimes derived from economic, political or social theory, but usually reflects the judgement of the IO scholar about the probable consequence of specific organizational initiatives. Thus a comprehensive evaluation of a programme will usually involve the testing of several impact hypotheses.

The results obtained from testing the impact hypotheses are subject to a number of explanations and interpretations, only one of which is that empirical evidence substantiates the existence of the kind of relationship between the dependent and the independent variables postulated by the hypothesis. Rival explanations may utilize the same dependent variable but add to or omit the independent variables contained in the impact hypothesis. Cook and Campbell have identified 35 possible rival explanations for the existence of a relationship.[17] These may be grouped into four categories:

    (a)   Internal validity: The relationship specified in the impact hypothesis can be challenged on the grounds that factors not included in the hypothesis actually determine the relationship observed. Changes in the dependent variable may occur simply due to 'maturation', that is, to the passage of time. The observed relationship may be a statistical illusion. It may have emerged because of differential selection of cases and control groups. There may be ambiguity about the 'line of causation' in, for example, the existence of a 'two-way relationship', etc.

(b)   Statistical conclusion validity: The relationship identified by the tests of the impact hypothesis may be due to the inappropriate use of statistical techniques. There may, for example, be small size, inappropriate setting of the level of significance, the selection of a one-sided hypothesis, unreliable estimators for measuring the relevant variables and heterogeneity. All these factors will cast doubt on whether good empirical results substantiate the existence of the type of relationship predicted by the impact hypothesis.

(c)   External validity: A relationship between variables discerned at one point of time or in one segment of the international environment may not exist universally over time. This is likely to be a consequence of unforeseen changes in the environment or in the structure, work program or ideology of the IO.

(d)   Construct validity category: It might not be justifiable to generalize from operational measures to theoretical constructs, for example owing to an initial inadequacy in the conceptualization of the theoretical construct.

This is likely to remain a strong possibility for a single operational measure, or if a single investigation procedure is adopted to validate a hypothesized theoretical relationship.

The evaluation research approach subjects impact hypotheses to a systematic series of tests by examining rival explanations for the existence of a relationship between organizational initiatives and environmental developments identified by the impact hypothesis. The evaluation research approach is concerned with controlling the effects of rival explanations in ascertaining the validity of impact hypotheses. The major research designs for controlling rival explanations have been presented by Campbell and Stanley.[18] Those of some relevance to the study of the impact of EIOs are discussed below.

1. One group post-test only design: This may be symbolised as:

$$[XO]$$

Where X is the measure of a change in an environmental characteristic induced by an organizational initiative O. For example, X may be change in the volume of machine tool exports following a liberalizing agreement in this industry worked out by GATT (O).

This is a weak research design. It does not allow an explicit comparison of the pretest situation with the post-test situation. It does not permit a comparison of the situation which would have been obtained had the IO not undertaken O with the situation created by the existence of O. It does not, therefore, control any of the rival explanations in the internal validity design.

2. One group pretest—post-test design: In symbols this is:

$$[X_1 \ O \ X_2]$$

Where X_1 is the measure of the environmental characteristic prior to the undertaking of a specific organizational initiative O, and X_2 is the measure after the IO initiative has been taken. Thus we may compare changes in the volume of machine tool exports before and after the GATT liberalization agreement. This test does not take into account the problem of the impact of the passage of time—the so-called 'maturation process'—and the interaction of other environmental policies with IO policies. It also does not deal with questions related to adequacy of statistical methods used in the measurement of the relevant variables and of the relationship between them.

3. Post-test only design with non-equivalent groups: This may be presented as:

$$\frac{OX_G}{XN_G}$$

Here X_G may be taken as the change in the level of machine tool exports of the countries which are members of GATT following a trade liberalization agreement and XN_G as the change in the level of machine tool exports among non-GATT-member countries over the same time period. XN_G thus represents a control group. Problems associated with an adequate selection of the control group in particular make this design somewhat weak.

4. Untreated control group design with pretest and post-test: this may be symbolized as:

$$\frac{X_{G1}\ O\ X_{G2}}{XN_{G_1}\ XN_{G_2}}$$

and compares changes in an environmental characteristic of a group affected by an initiative of an IO with that of a control group. Thus we may compared changes in machine tool exports on non GATT members who benefit from X—a liberalizing agreement—during a period extending from before to after the implementation of the agreement. This is clearly a superior test of the impact hypothesis than that represented by designs 1, 2 or 3, but problems of statistical appropriateness, selection bias and the influence of factors specific to particular observations still remain.

5. Interrupted time series design. In symbols

$$X_1\ X_2\ X_3\ X_4\ O\ X_5\ X_6\ X_7\ X_8$$

Here observations are taken of the environmental characteristic—the level of machine tool exports—at different points in time both before and after the organizational programme has been implemented. The interruption in the data pattern permits an identification and comparison of trends before and after the IO initiative. This design is, however, subject to all the other limitations discussed in relation to the one group pre-test post-test design.

6. Interrupted time series design with a non equivalent no treatment control group. This may be presented as:

$$\frac{X_{G_1}\ X_{G_2}\ X_{G_3}\ X_{G_4}\ O\ X_{G_5}\ X_{G_6}\ X_{G_7}\ X_{G_8}}{XN_{G_1}\ XN_{G_2}\ XN_{G_3}\ XN_{G_4}\ O\ XN_{G_5}\ XN_{G_6}\ XN_{G_7}\ XN_{G_8}}$$

This is a modification of design 4. It accounts for both changes in trends over time and the behaviour of groups not directly affected by the programmes of the IO. The groups are, however, not equated through the use of randomization techniques. It has been argued that this research design 'facilitates the control of all rival explanation challenging the internal validity of a study'.[19] The efficiency of this design can be improved by using appropriate randomization techniques.

Data availability is often a crucially important determinant of the choice of design by research evaluation investigators. Both the derivation of impact hypotheses and the collection of relevant data should prima facie be easier for students of EIOs than for those who investigate IOs dealing with peace keeping, human rights or cultural issues. The evaluation research approach should, therefore, be extensively used in the study of EIOs. This approach is difficult to employ when the impact of an EIO activity is seen to be indirect. This creates difficulties in the definition of relevant variables and of the form of the relationship that is presumed to exist between them. As we noted earlier, evaluation research provides no guidelines for tackling such questions. Moreover it must be emphasized that this approach is a limited guide to an assessment of changes in attitudes and transformation in the policy environment. This brings us back to the point that an IO may be regarded as successful even if its mandated objectives remain unachieved. The development of a consensus on relevant definitions within a research evaluation framework when considering the entire systemic impact of an EIO such as the IMF or UNCTAD, rather than that of a programme sponsored by these EIOs, remains a daunting task. IO scholars have recognized that the whole is always greater than a sum of the parts. The evaluation research approach can tell us how the parts of an IO—as represented by its programmes—are growing or stagnating. It cannot tell us how these processes of change relate to each other and whether success in achieving specific goals is contributing towards the type of environmental transformation envisaged in the EIO's organizational ideology.

3.2 PROJECT APPRAISAL

The evaluation research approach is particularly suitable for assessing the performance and impact of 'rule-setting' EIOs such as GATT and IMF. Other EIOs directly participate in the planning, execution and financing of particularly public-sector projects. Thus the World Bank dispenses about 14 billion dollars annually in the form of loans and investment commitments.[20] A large proportion of this is in the form of sector- and project-specific aid. Other international development banks also provide assistance of this nature. A large number of UN agencies provide technical assistance with the specific purpose of developing viable projects in Third World countries.[21] The impact of such EIOs can be evaluated by an application of the standard project evaluation techniques.

Neo-classical appraisal of public investment is firmly rooted to welfare theory and is concerned primarily with the 'optimum' provision of public goods, and with an analysis of government intervention in the natural monopolies. This theoretical perspective necessitates that public investment be regarded as one of several instruments that can be employed to attain at most a second-best social solution, in which the net gains from the removal of the initial divergence between marginal social value and marginal social cost are offset by the loss caused by the creation of some other divergence.[22] Investment is justified if it leads to a maximization of social welfare, where 'social welfare' is taken to be a function of the consumption level of the citizens of a country over time, and where the social value of commodities are measured in terms of border prices (prices of similar goods available outside the country). Non-traded and partially traded goods are also valued with reference to international price structures, and accounting prices of factors of productions are evaluated in terms of uncommitted public income valued in terms of foreign exchange as well. Substantial work has been done to develop appropriate criteria for evaluating the welfare impact of public investment.[23]

An appraisal of public investment requires that the impact be evaluated in terms of social opportunity costs. Social cost–benefit analysis retains the formal framework of present-value calculations, but recalculates factor prices (including the price of foreign exchange) in terms of the relative social scarcity of these factors. Public investment can thus be systematically geared to the task of correcting or offsetting market distortions and enhance both efficiency and equity.[24]

Extensive criticisms of this approach have been presented.[25] First, the derivation of shadow prices presupposes the simultaneous existence of an efficient output configuration. However, change in the output mix owing to the operation of projects selected on the basis of shadow prices that were correct for the original output programmes will imply that a different set of shadow prices is now required to achieve efficient resource allocation. Moreover, as Bhaduri argues, there is 'no guarantee that the national output configuration (on the basis of which "correct" shadow prices are being derived) has the required property of dynamic stability with respect to piecemeal use of shadow prices in selecting public projects'.[26] In other words the use of shadow prices, even when adequately corrected to take into account changing output mixes, does not guarantee that resource allocation patterns will gradually converge towards the (desired) efficient configuration of national output. Such a convergence can be shown to exist only if it is assumed that the problem of effective demand is of no consequence, that is, that government intervention through the systematic use of a given project selection criterion will not influence the level and composition of public investment, and this will not, in turn, have an impact on effective demand through the (Keynesian) multiplier mechanism.

Another important criticism of social cost–benefit analysis is that its use does not permit the analyst to take into account the qualitative differences in the output stream of different economic projects. Selection between a factory producing firearms and a factory producing wearing apparel in terms of the standard categories of social cost–benefit analysis obscures the profound qualitative difference in these two output streams. It also obscures the place each unit of production may have within a comprehensive integrated investment scheme. To integrate social cost–benefit analysis into a framework of national economic planning a deliberate choice as to the desired physical composition of national output must be made.

Social cost–benefit analysis relies on world market prices as indicators of the pattern of resource allocation that will permit a country to maximize the net flow of consumption from a given unit of investment over a specified period. The prices represent to the country concerned the opportunity cost of obtaining any given product. However, as Lall and Streeten have pointed out: 'The relative values of these products represent the demand patterns and preferences of the developed countries and the technological and marketing patterns of the large oligopolists which dominate production there'.[27] Since price formation in oligopolistic markets is strongly influenced by bargaining processes, there is a strong temptation to use policy mechanisms for exerting pressure to influence price formation. Moreover, articulation of preferences in developing countries is affected by forces at work in the international economy, and governments of developing countries are by sheer force of circumstance compelled to seek to modify the impact of these forces on the pattern of resource allocation within national economies. Thus, it is the desire to modify individual preferences—to make them conform to the government's own perception of the country's social needs—that lies at the root of most attempts at economic intervention by Third world Governments.

The problem of recording preference is not adequately addressed within the context of the neo-classical approach. This approach is based upon an ideological perspective that assumes that the individual's attempt at maximizing his own welfare provides the economist with a knowledge of correct social preferences. It is these preferences that 'ought' to be fulfilled. The optimization of social welfare can be achieved through the satisfaction of these preferences. The process of formation or articulation of these preferences is not regarded as an appropriate area for economic analysis.[28] Nor does economic analysis concern itself with assessing the extent to which the satisfaction of different preferences will increase social welfare. This liberal philosophy, and its implied theory of the state and of the role of the government in society which underlies welfare economics is thus an inadequate point of departure if one is concerned with explicating an economic strategy that attaches priority to satisfying basic needs, to achieving economic self-reliance or even to creating a better pattern of income distribution. In the neo-classical approach all these objectives may be regarded as economically irrational, since their pursuit may lead to a pattern of investment allocation that is 'suboptimal' in welfare terms in the sense that it does not maximize the flow of consumption over a given time period.

The neo-Kaleckian school formally dissociates itself from welfare analysis. It rejects the assumption that the individual consumer is a free and rational being who seeks utility maximization in perfectly competitive situations. It views society as an amalgam of conflicting forces. This would suggest that the neo-Kaleckian analysis of the impact of public industrial investment should concentrate on assessing its role in strengthening the political and economic dominance of a given interest group within a social formation. The economic strategies of different groups can be distinguished in terms of the desired changes in the composition of national output. Thus, emphasis on the restructuring of production in accordance with a country's international comparative advantage has traditionally been regarded as a development strategy that consolidates the position of private business and industry within the national economy. As against this, emphasis on the achievement of economic self-reliance has traditionally strengthened the hands of the public sector bureaucracy as an economic decision maker. It may, thus, be feasible to take the sectoral targets of a development plan as rough indicators of the group preferences of the dominant social forces within a country, and to ask which investment strategy is likely to lead to the achievement of these targets in the different production sectors at the minimum cost. Socialist economic analysis has popularized the use of the 'recoupment period criterion' as a means of evaluating different investment variants for producing a given output.[29] Assume two methods (technologies) of producing the same amount of steel. Method 1 involves the construction of a huge blast furnace. Method 2 requires the establishment of a number of 'backyard' operations of the type popular in China during the 1960s. Assume that the total capital cost of method 1 is $10 million and that of method 2 is $1 million. Furthermore, assume that the annual operating cost of method 1 is less by $0.2 million that that of method 2. Then it would take no less than 45 years to recoup the additional cost of $9 million in setting up the more investment intensive project. If, however, the difference in the annual operating cost of methods 1 and 2 were $2 million the required recoupment period would have been only 4.5 years. It is to be emphasized that the recoupment period criterion assesses the choice of an efficient (i.e.cost-minimizing) technology for producing a given output. Social cost–benefit analysis, on the other hand, uses international prices as a reference point for determining what bundle of output a country can most efficiently produce in order to maximize welfare.

The use of the recoupment period criterion is widespread in the analysis of public-sector investment in centrally planned economies. Neo-Kaleckian studies concerned with developing countries do not usually undertake detailed micro-level investigations and, therefore, the recoupment period criterion is less frequently employed.

The World Bank and most other international development-financing agencies employ the neo-classical project appraisal criteria in evaluating projects. EIOs such as the World Bank and UNIDO have remained concerned since the early 1970s with a refinement of these techniques. They provide a rough and ready guide for assessing the impact of both national and international public investment on the development of Third World countries. Problems associated with the use of these techniques have been briefly sketched in this section.

3.3 NETWORK ANALYSIS

We have so far been concerned with the evaluation of specific activities and projects undertaken by EIOs. Network analysis on the other hand focuses on the relationship between IOs and the problems they seek to address. A network may be defined as 'a group of elements which may be partially or completely interconnected. The interconnections termed branches or arches can represent roads, power lines, airline route, etc. . . The elements termed points or nodes can represent individuals, communities, organizations, etc., namely any point where a flow or relationship of some kind originates or terminates'.[29] An important difference between a systems and a network approach to international organization is that, whereas the former assumes the existence of an ultimate regulator of the relationships identified, the latter posits the existence of a plurality of relatively autonomous controllers. This means that it is difficult to associate a set of relatively stable goals to a network of perceived relationships.

Antony Judge has presented a lucid summary of network theory and its relevance to the study of international organization. He defines network as implying the existence of:

(a) relationships between a particular node and some central node (i.e. 'vertical' relationship);

(b) relationships between a node and less central nodes (i.e. a network of more than one level);

(c) relationships between nodes having a similar relationship to a more central node (i.e. 'horizontal' relationship).[31]

Many other forms of relationships may also be incorporated in a network. Networks may represent highly ordered structures displaying a stable and well-defined heirarchy of relationships, or they may be loose and informal. This is typically the case when environmental changes influence the relative salience of nodes—a node which is the least central under one set of environmental conditions any become of great importance with a change in environmental characteristics.

Network analysis proceeds by positing the existence of a pattern of structured relationships between IOs and the world problems they seek to address. World problems may be defined as 'conditions believed to threaten the balanced physical and psycho-social development of an individual in society whether the threat is directly to his well-being, to the values which he upholds or to a feature of the environment on which he is dependent'.[21] In this context the impact of an IO on its policy target may be mediated through several intermediaries. The IO might itself be the recipient of the impact of changes in the structuring of world problems and in the policies of other IOs. Moreover, there may be a loosely co-ordinated heirarchy of relationships between world problems on the one hand and IOs on the other. The impact pattern may thus take one of the

following forms:
  (a) directly from the IO to the policy target;
  (b) via a series of horizontal nodes to the policy target;
  (c) via a series of branches directly linked to the target;
  (d) via a series of branches linked to the target through intermediate nodes.
  (e) via a series of branches directly linked to the policy target and another series of branches linked to the target through several intermediate nodes, etc.

Network structures depict both a divergence and a convergence of impact. The greater the complexity of a given network pattern the more difficult is to identify the processes by which a particular initiative is likely to influence a given environmental characteristic, and also the extent to which it will do so.

The network structures linking economic sectors, world problems and EIOs are complex, and interlinkages are many and varied. Thus, according to the *Yearbook of World Problems*, linkages within the economic sectors categorized in that volume equal 157. These economic sectors are linked to 39 'world problems' and 109 IOs. Economic sectors have a totality of 766 relationships in the interlinked networld described in this work.[22] The volume presents separate lists for 'traded commodities' and products and for 'occupations'. Once again linkages are high. Commodities have totality of 235 relationships with world problems, 211 interlinkages with IOs, and a sum of 480 interseries relationships.[23] Interoccupation relationships amount to 243, and 1284 IOs have a link with these occupations.[24]

It is thus clear that assessing the impact of an EIO involves a careful sifting through of the intricate web of complex sequences through which this impact is mediated. Unfortunately:

'the social sciences are some way from being able to describe such sequences and track impact through them. It is even uncertain that there would be any consensus that such an approach is relevant to current preoccupations to render them communicable within the political arena . . . The meaning of impact may well be as elusive as that of electricity to whose movement through circuity (it) bears some resemblance'.[36]

It is not surprising that evaluation of EIOs undertaken purely on the basis of network analysis have been few and far between. Network analysis does, however, highlight the need to recognize the many different structures and levels through which the initiative of an EIO has to be mediated before it influences the behaviour or performance of the desired policy target.

3.4 SOME APPLICATIONS

The evaluation of EIOs has been undertaken from a wide variety of perspectives. Here we will review some of the major techniques and methodologies applied in these studies.

Many studies have focused on the role of the UN as an international actor.[37] From our perspective the most important studies are those which analyse programmes of specific agencies. Typically this involves testing hypotheses about the impact of programmes, budgeting procedures and leadership environmental initiatives. The influence of the United Nations is seen to be both direct and indirect, incorporating 'a refraction effect such that the United Nations setting may be said to influence the ways in which conflicts are conducted and justified'.[38] The impact of UN initiatives is evaluated using a wide range of exogenous and endogenous variables such as voting schemes, organizational roles (in particular office-holding patterns), socializing effects on delegate attitudes and perceptions, the level of economic development, the character of national political systems, the balance of international military capability, etc. In general, studies focusing on the specialized agencies and UN subunits—including EIOs—tend to attach relatively greater weight to endogenous variables than do studies focused upon the General Assembly. EIO studies assume a greater degree of organizational autonomy, and frequently employ concepts such as bureaucratic bargaining and incrementalism in explaining both the outcome of EIO decision-making processes and the subsequent impact of the policies executed on the basis of these decisions.

I will now summarize three approaches to EIO evaluation which I believe are typical of the literature in this field. Crane and Finkle's study assesses the population programme of the World Bank.[39] They attempt to explain organizational objectives in terms of the nature of the objective pursued,[40] organizational structure, organizational ideology and the attitude of secretariat officials responsible for programme execution. Crane and Finkle argue that the World Bank developed its population initiative largely in response in McNamara's personal interest in this field. He considered population growth to be 'the greatest single obstacle to economic development' even during the period when he was the US Secretary of Defence.[41] He prevailed upon his reluctant subordinates soon after joining the World Bank, and a Population Projects Department (PPD) was established in 1970. The rapid increase in Bank's resources ensured that the expansion of the population programme did not constrain the growth of other sectors.

This growth in funds allocated to the population programme did not lead to an increase in organizational effectiveness in this area. Moreover, the Bank's traditional clients in the poor countries are the ministries of finance and planning. The Bank has developed a close working relationship with these agencies. There has been a 'gradual convergence of organizational and professional interests. The Bank seeks to penetrate the inner circles of power in developing countries'.[42] The finance and planning ministries have seen the Bank as a major provider of concessional finance. The Bank is an ally of these ministries in their attempts to persuade other government departments to accept their preferred investment allocation strategies. The Bank relies upon these ministries as channels for exerting influence over LDC governments. The regional departments at the Bank's Washington quarters are responsible for liaising with the national planning and finance ministries, and 'unofficially represent client interests and priorities'.[43]

Crane and Finkle argue that 'because of the unusual political sensitivity and administrative complexity of population programmes ministries of finance and planning are generally less able to facilitate achievement of the Bank's population objectives than some of its other development aims. What is of equal importance, finance and planning ministries seem to rank population programmes low on the list of projects for which they would like the Bank's support—a ranking that is more or less reflected in the priorities of the Bank's regional offices'.[44] Moreover, finance and planning ministries are inept and inexperienced executors of population initiatives and programmes. The Bank's principal Third World clients represent distinctly unsuitable and ineffective instruments for executing its population projects. Nor are the regional offices adequately structured. The PPD is separated from these offices and usually finds it difficult to attract their attention and support.

The Bank's procedures for identifying appraising and supervising procedures are also unsuitable for effective participation in population control programmes. They involve detailed specification of project plans, centralization of decisions regarding project preparation and implementation, and identification of discreet opportunities for investment allocation. These procedures are patently unsuitable for evaluating and implementing population programmes where technical criteria for appraisal are not standardized, government policy preferences are subject to frequent changes and the period between initiation and implementation is relatively long. Furthermore, it is difficult to disaggregate a population control programme into discreet investment projects. Bank efficiency in this field has been restricted by the resistance of its own staff to a revision of its lending procedures and by the growth of rivalry with agencies such as the United States Agency for International Development (USAID), the UN Fund for Population Activities (UNFPA) and the World Health Organization (WHO): agencies relatively unencumbered by these procedures and apprehensive of an expansion of Bank activities in this field.

The Bank has been conscious of its ineffectiveness in the population field, according to Crane and Finkle,[45] and has made certain structural organizational changes to improve its performance—the most important of which is the decision taken in 1979 to incorporate the PPD into a new Population, Health and Nutrition Department and to begin lending directly for health services. No modification in project identification, evaluation and implementation are envisaged, however, and the impact of Bank initiatives in the population field is therefore likely to remain somewhat limited.

In their study of the World Bank's population programme, Crane and Finkle rely upon an evaluation of the history of the Bank's experiences in this field. Some macro-level data on bank allocations to specific countries is presented. But the suitability of specific projects and of levels of allocation is not evaluated. The authors do not go in for formal hypothesis testing, and their study represents a qualitative assessment of the Bank's population programme.

A broadly similar approach is adopted by Finlayson and Zacher in their paper on the role of GATT in the regulation of trade barriers.[46] They begin by identifying the 'central norms of the GATT trade barriers regime. The substantive norms concern non discrimination, liberalization, reciprocity, the right to take "safeguard action" and economic development. The procedural norms relate to multilateralism and the role of states with major interests in trade relations'.[47]

The principle of non-discrimination—once described by Wyndham White as 'the corner stone of GATT'[48]—has lost much of its earlier significance in GATT-sponsored negotiations. Currently GATT permits many exceptions to this principle. In 1955 over 90 per cent of trade within the context of the General Agreement took place at MFN tariff rates. In 1980 this proportion had fallen to 65 per cent.[49] It is likely that there will be further reduction in MFN-based trade. Finlayson and Zacher explain this development in terms of changes in environmental characteristics—the decline in US international hegemony, the appearance of strong regional groups, the emergence of the LDCs as an influential bargaining group in international trade negotiations etc.[50] Environmental developments are also seen as the main factors influencing the strength of the liberalization norm, weak in the early post-war years, significant during the late 1950s up to the middle 1960s, and declining since then owing to the downturn of economic activity and the proliferation of agreements such as Voluntary Export Restrictions (VERs) outside the GATT framework.[51] The importance of the reciprocity norm in the early years of GATT is explained with reference to the history of trade policy and legislation in the United States and its role as a factor creating a balance in the national interests of the major trading powers.[52] Members have deliberately sought to limit the growth of the organizational mandate by preferring to take action outside the regime framework, thus avoiding multilateral supervision.

GATT's operational procedures ensure that the Secretariat has relatively little room for taking initiatives. Bodies such as the panels of conciliation appointed by the Director General are less influential than the working parties, which are more political and contain national representatives. The permanent institutions established within the framework of the Secretariat are concerned with rule implementation, but it is not adherence to these rules (violations are increasingly being tolerated) which is the essence of the GATT system. GATT operates by its ability to foster the type of multilateral deals which balance effectively the national interests of a group of key trading nations.

Changes in GATT-related negotiating styles have been a consequence of environmental developments. Thus, in the view of Finlayson and Zacher, 'the development of linear tariff negotiations and even more so the growing importance of NTBs have introduced a stronger component of multilateralism into decision making in the GATT'.[53] This had led to the elaborate system of monitoring procedures which ensure compliance with GATT agreement. This has also facilitated rule interpretation in accordance with changing environmental characteristics and national policies.

Throughout the study the emphasis is on evaluating the regime. The conclusion that the regime has not broken down is explained almost entirely by 'the shifting power resources and policy objectives of the regime members'.[54] The role of GATT is an EIO in sustaining the regime is not systematically evaluated because 'it is the norms of a regime (established by negotiations among key states) and the importance the most influential members attach to them that largely determine the regime's rules and rule implementation as well as its decision making mechanism'.[55] This is in sharp contrast with Crane and Finkle's study of the World Bank population programme, where the focus is clearly on the role of the EIO, and environmental characteristics are considered only tangently. Methodologically the studies are similar in that both employ a historical analytic approach using macro-level data and the occasional interview with officials, delegates and 'informed' observers. Both eschew the formal testing of hypothesis.

In contrast, Auserbach and Yonekawa's study of the United Nations Development Programme does test two carefully developed hypotheses about the impact of the allocation of UNDP expenditures.[56] These are:

H1. The more UNDP project expenditure a recipient receives the more follow-up investment will be attracted.

H2. The larger the contribution to UNDP the more the contributor will receive in procurement awards for goods and services.

The independent and dependant variables are measured with precision. In HI the independent variable is UNDP expenditures (in current prices) in different developing countries in 1973. Dependant variables in HI are the follow up investment received by these countries (once again in current values) in 1974 and 1975. In H2 five dependant variables are specified. These are: (a) value of subcontracts awarded, (b) value of equipment orders, (c) follow-up investment for investor nationality, (d) number of experts per nationality and (e) fellowships per host country. These variables were measured for the year 1975. The independent variables were national contributions to UNDP for 1973, 1974 and 1975 implying different time lags between contributions and investment benefits. Standard regression and significant test techniques were employed to test the strength of the relationships specified in HI and H2. A relatively weak but significantly positive relationship was found to exist when HI was tested. The relationship between all dependant variables, except follow up investment per investor nationality 1975, was found to be significantly positive in the tests for H2. The relationship between UNDP contributions and the value of subcontracts and equipment orders was most strong. A two year time lag seemed to provide the best fit for these equations. These results are explained largely with reference to UNDP field and procurement activities. UNDP is seen as 'a multi-purpose and multifaceted entity'[57]—a system which benefits both developed and developing countries in diverse ways.

This review does not by any means exhaust the methods adopted for evaluating the impact of IOs. Another commonly used method for example involves asking concerned delegates or officials about their evaluation of the performance of an IO.[58] The review does show, however, that evaluation though problematical is possible and also necessary. Such an assessment must be based upon the environmental capability of an EIO and the suitability of its internal structure for an adequate performance of its organizational task. We will analyse these questions in Chapter 4.

NOTES

1. *See* e.g. Hoffman, S. 'International organization and the international system', *IO*, (1970) pp. 389–413, and Haas, E. 'Systems and process in the ILO', *World Politics*, (January 1962) pp. 322–52.
2. Haas, *op. cit.*; Deutsch, K. 'Towards an inventory of basic trends and patterns and international politics', *American Political Science Review*, (March 1960); Almond, G. and Coleman, J. *The Politics of the Developing Areas*, Princeton (1960); Cox and Jacobson, *The Anatomy of Influence*, Yale (1973). Haas and Cox and Jacobson attempt to describe environments specific to certain international organizations.
3. Haas, *ibid.*
4. Hoffman, *op. cit.*, p. 390.
5. Hoffman, *op. cit.*, p. 390.
6. Hoffman, *op. cit.*, p. 409.
7. *See* Haas, E. *Beyond the Nation State*, Stanford (1964) and Ogley, R.C. 'Towards a general theory of international organisation', *International Relations*, (1969) pp. 599–619. Ogley implies that the effectiveness of an international organization may be measured by its ability to create an institutional structure appropriately 'sharp/blunt' for the effective present pooling of national sovereignties for their future limitation.
8. Murray, R., 'The internationalization of capital and the nation state', in Radice, H. (ed.) *International Firms and Modern Imperialism*, Penguin, Harmondsworth (1975) pp. 107–34.
9. On this *see* Vernon, R. 'Multinational business and national economic goals', *IO*, (1971) pp. 693–704.
10. This difference originates from the difference in the needs of the international firms. The area-based firms, for example, are primarily concerned with the guaranteeing of free trade and free capital movements. As against this, product-based firms are mainly concerned with the provision of a healthy economic environment within most countries. *See* Wells, I.T. 'The Multinational Business Enterprise' *IO*

1971 p. 447–464.

11. *See* Fleming, I. *The IMF: Its Form and Function,* Washington (1964).

12. Payer, C. *The Debt Trap,* Penguin, Harmondsworth (1971) Ch. 3.

13. Haas, E. *Beyond the Nation State,* p. 126.

14. This section draws upon Hoole, F.W. 'Evaluating the impact of international organisations', *IO,* Vol. NO (1977) pp. 541–62.

15. Wholey, J., Scanlon, D., Duffy, H. Fukumoto, J. and Yogt, T. *Federal Evaluation Policy Analysing the Effects of Public Programs,* The Urban Institute, Washington DC, (1973) p. 19.

16. Hoole, *op. cit.,* p. 553–8.

17. Cook, T. and Campbell, D. 'The design and conduct of quasi experiments and true experiments in field settings', in Dunette (ed.) *Handbook of Industrial and Organisational Ideology,* Rand McNally, Chicago (1975) pp. 223–326.

18. Campbell, D. and Stanley, R. *Experimental and Quasi Experimental Design for Research,* Rand McNally, Chicago (1963) *passim.* This has been summarized in Hoole, *op. cit.,* pp. 549–52.

19. Hoole, *op. cit.,* p. 351.

20. Payer, C. *The World Bank: A Critical Analysis,* Monthly Review Press, London, (1982) p. 17.

21. e.g. UNDP and UNIDO.

22. Lal, D. 'Public enterprises', in Cody, J., Hughes, H. and Wall, D. *Policies for Industrial Progress in Developing Countries,* Oxford University Press, New York (1980) pp. 219–20.

23. Roemer, M. and Stern, J. *The Appraisal of Development Projects* Praeger, New York (1976) and Jenkins, G. *Performance evaluation and Public sector enterprise,* Development Discussion Paper No. 46, Harvard University, Cambridge (May 1978).

24. This approach is adopted by both UNIDO *Guidelines for Project Evaluation* United Nations Publication, Sales No. E.72.11.B.11, New York (1973) and Little, I.M.D. and Mirlees, J. *Project Appraisal for Developing Countries* Heinemann Educational Books, London (1974).

25. *See* e.g. Streeten, P. and Stewart, F. 'Little and Mirrlees methods and project appraisals', *Oxford Bulletin of Economics and Statistics,* Vol. 34 No. 1 (February 1972) pp. 75–91, and Bhaduri, A. 'Cost benefit analysis for project evaluation and structural changes in a developing country', paper prepared for the Global Preparatory Meeting for the First Consultation on Industrial Financing, Vienna, Austria, 23–5 March 1981 (ID/WG 334/3).

26. Bhaduri, *op. cit.,* p. 13.

27. Lall, S. and Streeten, P. *Foreign Investment, Transnationals and Developing Countries,* MacMilland, London (1977) p. 166.

28. For qualifications to this statement *see* Stilwell, F. *Normative Economics,* Pergamon Press, Oxford (1975).

29. Nove, A. and Zauberman, S. (eds.) *Studies in the Theory of Reproduction and Prices,* Polish Scientific Publishers, Warsaw (1964) pp. 73–89.

30. Judge, A.N. *'International organisation networks: a complementary*

perspective', in Taylor, P. and Groom, A. *International Organisation: A Conceptual Approach* Francis Pinter, London (1978) p. 388.
31. Judge, *op. cit.,* p. 397.
32. *Yearbook of World Problems and Human Potential 1976*, Union of International Associations and Mankind 2000, Brussels (1977) (Sect. R).
33. *Ibid.*, Sect. PE (Introduction).
34. *Ibid.*, Sect. PC (Introduction).
35. *Ibid.*, Sect. PJ (Introduction).
36. Judge, *op. cit.,* p. 405.
37. Summarized in Dixon, W. 'The emerging image of UN politics', *World Politics,* No. 1 (1981) pp. 47–61.
38. Falk, R. 'The United Nations: various systems of operation', in Gordenker, L. *The United Nations in International Politics,* Princeton University Press, Princeton (1971) p. 191.
39. Crane, B. and Finkle, J. 'Organisational impediments to development assistance: the World Bank's population program', *World Politics,* Vol. 3 (1981) pp. 516–53.
40. That is, the many complexities involved in achieving a reduction in the birth rate in Third World countries. The objective is such that international organization based in the West and reflecting Western attitudes, prejudices and styles of work can have only a limited impact in this area, argue Crane and Finkle, *op. cit.,* p. 517.
41. Crane and Finkle, *op. cit.,* p. 519.
42. *Ibid.* p. 523.
43. *Ibid.* p. 524.
44. *Ibid.,* p. 524.
45. *Ibid.,* p. 548.
46. Finlayson, J. and Zacher, M. 'The GATT and the regulation of trade barriers: regime dynamics and functions', *IO,* Vol. 35 No. 4 (1981) pp. 561–602.
47. *Ibid,* p. 566.
48. Wyndham White, E. 'Negotiations in prospect', in Bergsten, F. *Towards a New World Trade Policy,* Lexington, Mass. (1975) p. 321.
49. Finlayson and Zacher, *op. cit.,* p. 569.
50. *Ibid,* p. 566–70.
51. *Ibid.,* p. 570–4.
52. *Ibid.,* p. 574–8.
53. *Ibid.,* p. 586.
54. *Ibid.,* p. 593.
55. *Ibid.,* p. 593. The only point where Finlayson and Zacher acknowledge that GATT may have played a role in sustaining the regime is on pp. 588–9 where they argue that 'improving the quality and quantity of information about international trade policy has been one of (GAT's) major contributions'.
56. Auserbach, K. and Yonekawa, P. 'The United Nations Development Program: follow up investment and procurement benefits', *IO,* Vol. 33 No. 4 (1977) pp. 509–24.
57. *Ibid.,* p. 524.

58. *See* e.g. Ernst, H. 'Attitudes of diplomats at the UN: the effects of organisational participation on the evaluation of the organisation', *IO*, Vol. 32 No. 4 (1978) p. 1037–44.

4 Organizational Processes

In this chapter I will concentrate on describing the processes by which an IO generates agreements and consensus among its constituents. The focus here will be on assessing the capacity of IOs to effect their environment and on an analysis of the internal structure which institutionalizes continuous interaction among the delegates of the nations which are members of the IO. An 'effective' IO has an 'appropriate' 'scope and level', an 'appropriate' decision-making structure and an 'appropriate' distribution of influence in its decision-making forums. 'Appropriateness' may be conceived of as the ability of the organizational structure to generate the type of decisions most conductive for transforming the environment in accordance with the organizational ideology of the IO. In this chapter, the primary focus will be on an examination of the behaviour of the national delegates. The next chapter will address the questions related to the role of the Secretariat in the formulation and execution of organizational decisions.

4.1 SCOPE AND LEVEL

Organizational performance depends upon the initial 'scope' and 'level' of the organization concerned, and upon change in its 'scope' and 'level' over time. Schmitter has defined the scope of an international organization as a mixture of two dimensions: 'the *number* of social groups or policy sectors potentially involved (in making and elaborating the policy of the international organization) . . . and the *importance* of these policy sectors for the attainment of national sector-defined goals'.[1] The larger the number of groups involved in policy articulation, the greater is the likelihood that the IO will have an impact upon its environment.

The 'level' of the international organization refers to 'the extent of commitment to mutual decision-making both in

terms of *continuity*, i.e. the obligation to meet recurrently and
to re-evaluate periodically joint ventures, and in terms of
techniques, the nature of the policy-making process itself'.[2] The
greater the commitment to the institutionalization of decision-
making processes, subordinating national autonomy in
specific issue areas, the greater the likelihood that the
organization will transform the environment in accordance
with its ideology. Commitment may be said to be greatest when
member states are willing to devolve decision-making
authority to a supranational entity—the IO or its subunit—in a
particular issue area. Commitment may be said to be least
when member states take a 'once and for all' decision with
regard to a particular issue, and then formulate a policy to
share gains and losses, consequent upon the implementation of
this decision, without committing themselves to any further
action in the area concerned. The Generalized Scheme of
Preferences adopted by UNCTAD in 1970, for example,
represent a decision to grant preferences to LDC exports by
Group B countries, each of whom have drawn up a separate
'exceptions list', and there is nothing in the General Scheme of
References resolutions to permit the adoption of other
measures if the Preference Schemes fail to stimulate the export
earnings of the Third World.

If the initial scope and level of an IO is high, the organization
has a natural propensity towards task expansion. What
determines this initial scope and level? Haas and Schmitter
have listed a set of 'background conditions' which define the
initial level and scope of an IO, and are a determinant of an
eventual increase/decrease in this scope and level.[3] These
'background conditions' include:

   (a)   the functional similarity of member states;[4]
   (b)   level of transactional interchange (commodity and
         factor movements);
   (c)   degree of pluralism within each individual member of
         the international organization;[5] and
   (d)   complementarity of national elites.

An IO whose members are 'functionally' similar, with high
levels of pluralistic modes of conduct, and complementary
national elites, is likely to have a broad scope and a high level at
its inception. Furthermore, international organizations pos-

sessing these characteristics are likely to achieve rapid politicization,[6] which can potentially achieve an enchancement of their scope and level, provided that:

(a) members have 'identical' or 'convergent'[7] economic aims and strong political commitment;

(b) agreement is reached on a relatively fixed schedule for achieving objectives, thus setting in motion automatic processes to transform the environment.

Enhancement of scope and level depends also on actor adaptation during a learning period, when members of the organization learn to assimilate new (functionally relevant) information, accommodate new pressures, and reorganize administrative and political channels. Are decision-making processes widening and deepening the consensus between member states? Is the level of transaction rising? Is there a 'spillover' of involvement into areas which were initially beyond the operational scope of the organization?[8] It is generally believed that, if background conditions are favourable if the initial mandate of the organization promotes task expansion, and if the learning process proves fruitful, there is 'a high probability that spillover, externalization[9] and politicization will occur.[10] In other words, conflict between the members will be resolved by enhancement of the scope and level of the organization, and expansion in this scope and level will increase the impact of the organization of its environment. National groups likely to be affected by its policies will increase, and, as the number of the organization's clients grows, so will the controversiality of its decisions expand. Thus the 'technical' element will tend to become overshadowed by the political element in its decision-making processes.

In order to identify the scope of an EIO, we will have to identify the problems addressed by it and the issue areas with which it is concerned. It is also necessary to specify the different tasks—data collection, interest aggregation, providing a negotiating forum—that an EIO performs in each issue area. Broadly speaking, organizational tasks may be subdivided into two categories: macro and micro. 'Macro' tasks include functions such as information dissemination, research activities, hosting of official meetings, provision of technical assistance to member states and interagency co-ordination.

'Micro' tasks include budget approval, policy harmonization, the organization of a publications programme, etc. As has been pointed out earlier, the greater the diversity of organizational tasks and the greater the issue area spread, the wider is the scope of an EIO.

On the other hand, the concept of 'level' assesses essentially the degree of centralization at the international level in decision making procedures and processes—hence the concern with identifying the extent of supernationality in international decision making in, for example, the work of Haas and Schmitter and of scholars interested in the EEC.[11] If, as is more frequent, international decision making is entirely an inter-governmental affair,[12] the level might be measured by the extent to which members of an EIO are willing to abide by group decisions. The level of an EIO will rise when bilateral decision-making processes are substituted by procedures which require that decisions are taken on the basis of a consensus within the membership. It will rise further when decisions are made by majorities and the principle of consensus is abandoned.

Enhancement of the scope and level of an EIO usually leads to a corresponding increase in its environmental capability. This is reflected in an increase in its membership, budget and staff. However, a growth in resources and the spectrum of problems addressed does not of course guarantee that the resources are being effectively and efficiently deployed. An EIO well endowed with resources and addressing a broad range of problems may nevertheless be incapable of trans-forming the environment in accordance with its organizational ideology. To enhance environmental effectiveness, an EIO must develop an appropriate level of authority and autonomy within the international system.

4.2 AUTONOMY AND AUTHORITY

Functionalist and neo-functionalist writers have generally maintained that organizational characteristics can signifi-cantly influence the impact of an international organization on its environment.[12] The growth of organizational differentiation, durability, and autonomy does not necessarily enhance organizational effectiveness. It is relatively easy to conceive of 'over-institutionalization'. An IO may lose its effectiveness owing to its remoteness from environmental needs, or to the existence of rigid and cumbersome operational procedures. Different environmental actors may respond differently to various levels and types of organizational institutionalization. Moreover, in 'general-purpose' international organizations such as the UN General Assembly, differentiation, durability, and autonomy may vary over issue areas.

Measures for evaluating type and level of institutionalization attained by an international organization have been suggested by Keohane,[14] and by Volgy and Quistguard.[15] Indices measuring differentiation, that is, distinctiveness from environment, and indices measuring autonomy, that is, the ability of organizational norms and practices to influence significantly the outcome of its political processes, generally tend to be highly correlated. The purpose of seeking differentiation is to attain greater autonomy, and although greater autonomy does not, by any means, imply greater effectiveness, greater autonomy cannot be achieved in the absence of organizational distinctiveness. Autonomy and differentiation may be measured by estimation of the following indicators:

(a) length of service of delegates or officials;
(b) delegates/officials with experience;
      [total no. of officials]
(c) Officials promoted from within the organization;
      [total officials]
(d) distinctiveness of ideology from those of other international organizations;
(e) control over budgetary resources; and
(f) voting support for organizational values and norms.

Office-holding patterns in particular provide an important index for the measurement of organizational autonomy in particular, and of the internal structure of the organization in general. A study of office-holding patterns may allow us to answer questions such as: 'do members spend a significant amount of time and resources seeking organizational offices; does the organization 'reward' those members who adhere to its norms and contribute towards its development, or does the organizational office-holding pattern merely reflect the balance of environmental forces?'.[16] Answers to these questions will tell us a great deal about the internal functional processes of the organization, and about the relationship of the organization to its environment.

Distribution of offices within an international organization may be related to resource potential, regional representativeness, and alliance participation of the members. Weigart and Riggs suggest that 'development success' may be positively associated with office holding within the quasi-universal family of organizations. They also find a positive association between office holding and 'capability' indicators.[17] Other authors—notably Volgy—suggest that 'legislative' indicators may explain office-holding patterns. This assumes that the political process of quasi-universal international organizations resemble a quasi-legislative system.[18]

Durability of an international organization—that is, its ability to survive—may be assessed by estimating:

(a)   growth of membership;
(b)   rank and size of delegations;
(c)   challenge to the organization's right to exist;
(d)   growth in budget;
(e)   adaptability to new situations;
(f)   growth in number and type of organizational subunits;
(g)   diversification of functions;
(h)   change in level of agreement among members about task expansion; and
(i)   change in the stability of the environment.

A rapid rise in membership and budgetary resources, an increase in the rank and size of delegations, a reduction in challenges, an increase in organizational adaptability, diversification of organizational functions, and a growth in environmental stability are all likely to enhance durability. Environmental stability, may, however, reduce the need for the existence of an IO, and thus have a negative impact on its durability.

Changes within the internal structure of the oranization—involving a redefinition of the roles of its subunits—are also likely to have an impact on its durability, autonomy and distinctiveness. An enhancement of the role of the bureaucratic arm of the organization (the secretariat) over its political wing (the 'general assembly') may increase autonomy and distinctiveness, but will not necessarily promote the chances of organizational survival, nor will it necessarily enhance the effectiveness of the organization. It is, of course, true that the impact of internal restructuring on the organization's autonomy, durability and effectiveness depends significantly on the type of internal environment within which it is situated. Nevertheless, states attach considerable importance to the influence which they can exercise within IOs, as a general rule. Their attitude towards an organization—their willingness to subordinate their national policies to the outcome of its political processes—will depend significantly upon their success in influencing these political processes. Thus, a study of organizational development must make an attempt to evaluate the internal determinants of the effectiveness of the organization concerned.

The autonomy, differentiation and durability of an IO depends to an extent on its formal organizational structure. The range of viable organizational structures is impressively wide. There are EIOs such as UNCTAD with a quasi-universal 'legislative general assembly', an almost equally large supervisory executive board and a secretariat with more than 500 established posts. Decision making in such EIOs is usually on the basis of 'one nation one vote'. In the financial EIOs such as the Bank of International Settlements, the IMF and the World Bank the organizational structure reflects the dominance of the members who provide the bulk of the resources. Thus the IMF, for example, is headed by the Board of Governors, with each member country nominating a governor for a period of five years. The Board appoints the Executive Directors of the IMF. Countries with the highest quotas have the right to appoint Executive Directors. Voting rights within the Board of Governors are distributed in accordance with members' quotas. Regional grouping usually determines the composition of the elected part of the Board of Directors. Distribution of votes within the Executive Directors Board is also based on the quotas of the member states the individual directors represent. The Managing Director is appointed by the Board and is responsible for appointing the permanent Secretariat staff of the IMF.

These arrangements can be contrasted with those prevailing in regional EIOs such as the EC institutions. However, I will not attempt to do this.[19] Suffice it to say that EIOs vary greatly in terms of the powers of their constituent bodies and the inter-relationship between their bodies. The task of determining the autonomy enjoyed by an EIO and of ascertaining its 'appropriateness' in the context of the EIO's organizational mandate is a high complex one.

These difficulties become most clearly apparent when attention is focused on the rapidly expanding and increasingly varied international role of 'domestic' bureaucrats. Hopkins has argued that 'we should think of international organization as including those officials who are part of the organizational networks that perform international functions whether they are formally in international or domestic bureaucracies'.[20] The international role of domestic bureaucrats has been enhanced by the increased blurring between domestic and foreign policy, the growth of international interdependence, and the expanding role of technical experts in the making of economic policy decisions. The growth of the international functions of domestic bureaucrats—and of networks of co-ordination between national domestic bureaucrats—represents an alternative to the growth of conventional EIOs and expansion of their scope in areas such as food, energy, finance and technology.

Domestic bureaucrats not only participate in transgovernmental networks for the regulation of functional activities, they sometimes also play a distinctly managerial role. Collaboration between the domestic bureaucrats of western countries may be an alternative to the growth of the authority and effectiveness of EIOs in trade and in finance—EIOs which may be dominated by the voting majorities of the Third World countries.

Domestic officials involved in the management of international issue areas have many advantages over their IO or foreign service counterparts. Typically (particularly in Western countries) they have more secure budgets, greater legitimate authority, closer working relationships with relevant interest groups, etc. The US Department of Agriculture has played an important role in managing the international grain markets owing to its ability to affect the flow of resources to foreign markets. Hopkins argues that 'the management of global political problems, specially those of a non-military nature, resides primarily in decentralized, partially connected networks of executives in both national governments and private multinational business'.[21] He has documented the growth of the international involvement of US 'domestic' bureaucrats, that is, bureaucrats located in departments primarily involved in domestic activity, over the period 1962–74 and has found that growth has been impressive.[22]

Some indications of the opinions and attitudes of these bureaucrats has been reported by Hopkins,[23] but almost no work has been done to assess the relative influence and autonomy of the categories of domestic officials likely to be involved in the management of international markets and resources. Many important questions remain unanswered. What are the opportunities for officials in the agricultural, energy or transport ministeries of different types of states to develop the type of international contacts they desire? It is contended that 'domestic' bureaucrats of powerful Western states involved in international affairs are more resourceful, with greater scope of discretion and weight of influence, than the international bureaucrats working for the EIOs. Is there any empirical justification for this view, or is it the case that the relative influence and autonomy of domestic bureaucrats varies by issue areas? What are the major differences in the behaviour pattern of 'domestic' and international bureaucrats? Questions such as these will have to be addressed as the process of international organization penetrates domestic bureaucracies and the network of international economic relationships becomes increasingly complex. Assessing the autonomy and authority of 'domestic' bureaucrats is not an easy task.

The complexity involved in assessing organizational authority and autonomy is further underlined when we turn our attention to the activities of private-sector groups in the management of the international markets. EIOs in international finance act in close co-ordination with the private banks that dominate the Eurocurrency and Eurobond markets. The influence of these banks has increased dramatically since the early 1970s and they have become the principal lenders to some of the world's most rapidly-growing developing countries such as Brazil, Mexico and South Korea. Current outstanding debt in the Euromarkets is very considerable. They have responded commercial banks in the Eurocurrency markets have organized powerful lending syndicates which are 'virtually self-sufficient against default by solvent borrowers'.[25] The syndicates are well organized, with responsibility for loan collection resting with the agent bank and the institutionalization of extensive ties between major syndicates. The banks are in a position to cut off all international credit to a poor country which in their judgement has wilfully defaulted.

In the case of default arising from insolvency—Mexico in 1982, Bolivia in 1984—the banks apply sanctions and pressures within a policy framework developed by the IMF in the form of a stabilization programme involving a rescheduling of the outstanding debt. The IMF ensures that the renegotiation of debt is based on the acceptance of the 'stabilization and debt work-out' package by all parties concerned. Unilateral action by the debtor is firmly ruled out.

The management of the international debt of the Third World countries is the responsibility of the commercial banks, the IMF and the governments of the poor countries. Western governments and central banks have chosen to stand aside, and therefore the autonomy enjoyed by private West-based lenders in the Euromarkets is very considerable. They have responded by developing techniques of financial management such as credit syndicalization and the institutionalization of floating interest rates, which have secured them against the risk of international default while enabling them to offer attractive financial arrangements and terms to the newly industrialized countries of the Third World.

The commercial banks have, by acting in concert, succeeded in minimizing the impact of severe national debt crises—such as that of Mexico in 1982—on other debts within the international system. The Eurobanks have developed networks for co-operation during periods of crises, despite the fact that they compete intensively against each other and there are no 'term setters' in the Euroloan markets. Syndicate lending is deliberately designed to ensure increasing interdependence among the banks. Extensive cross-default clauses are written into most agreements. Elaborate procedures have been devised to reconcile differences in the treatment of debt in specific cases. 'Informal *ententes*' prevail among overlapping syndicates. The banks have succeeded in interlocking their relationships, and this has ensured that they can collectively impose extremely severe sanctions on poor-country debtors. Henry Wallich of the US Federal Reserve Board notes the power of the commercial banks to enforce repayment. The banks can ensure that a poor defaulting country 'will have to pay cash for every power station, every industrial project. That it can do so is beyond belief. Consequently these countries have to service their debts in whatever way they can'.[26]

The ability of the commercial banks to act in concert depends crucially upon the pivotal role the IMF plays in the system. The Fund has been described as playing 'the vital syndicate leadership role' in the management of Third World debt.[27] The IMF acts on behalf of the commercial creditors. It requires specific changes in the economic policies of the debtor governments to eliminate import controls, devalue the national currency and facilitate the transfer of capital abroad. The Fund provides credit in several stages as the debtor country adjusts to agreed stabilization guidelines. Accepting the terms the Fund sets, ensures that a poor debtor country will win a reprieve from the international banks. 'The Fund permits the banks to act in their collective self interest'.[28]

The Fund enjoys a relatively high level of organizational autonomy. Its working procedures are routinized. This is particularly so in the case of debt renegotiation procedures. IMF standby negotiations are paralleled by simultaneous meetings of the private and official creditors of the poor country which has requested an IMF standby loan. The outcome of the latter meetings depends upon progress in the IMF negotiations. IMF staff enjoy a high level of autonomy in the conduct of these negotiations. They play a crucial part in synchronizing the position of the official and private creditor clubs. Often the IMF succeeds in linking the rescheduling of public and private debt, the payments of the latter being a condition for concessions granted in public-debt rescheduling terms. Relations between the IMF and the private credit clubs remain highly informal, flexible and of an *ad hoc* uninstitutionalized form: the IMF has consistently resisted pressures to formalize these relationships. Lipson has identified the reasons the creditors prefer the status quo. 'Club arrangements isolate debtors while facilitating collective auction by creditors. Since they are convened only in payments crises, debt relief cannot even be discussed except under extreme conditions.'[29]

There have been many proposals for increasing the level of the IMF's resources. Western states reluctant to increase members' contributions due to the consequent increase in the political influence of the OPEC countries, have pushed for the establishment of 'special funds' within the IMF which do not involve an expansion of the voting rights of the creditors to these funds. The OPEC countries are, however, unlikely to increase IMF resources without a parallel growth in their political control. The IMF has also been reluctant to turn to the Euromarket for increasing its resources, as this would disrupt the existing links between quota payments, voting rights and access to credit.

Difficulties in expanding IMF resources represents one set of barriers to the growth of the IMF's organizational autonomy. Another set of barriers is constituted by the difficulties in retaining the allegiance of the debtors who fight shy of the Fund because of the extreme severity of its prescriptions. Modifying these terms would, however, erode the credibility of the Fund in the eyes of particularly private creditors, whose acceptance of the Fund's role as a syndicate leader is more important than the size of the Fund's financial resources in determining its authority and autonomy.

Assessing IMF organizational autonomy involves first of all an evaluation of the Articles of Agreement and of the revisions to these Articles enacted in 1969 and 1978. We can then document the interpretation of these Articles as evident in the policies of the Fund. We will find that some of the provisions of the Articles—those for example, that permit a regulation of the policies of the surplus countries—have remained non-operational. Others have been applied with varying degrees of stricture. Such an assessment will enable us to identify the

IMF's potential organizational autonomy and to measure the extent to which this potential has been realized.[30] Some of the discrepancy between realized and potential autonomy and some of the change in both can be explained by measuring changes in financial and manpower resources. However, these are ultimately dependent upon the role of the Fund as a manager of international financial flows. An assessment of the organizational autonomy of the Fund and of its systemic 'appropriateness' must, therefore, be based upon an essentially qualitative analysis of the changing pattern of relationships between the Fund, the international banks and the governments and monetary authorities of creditor and debtor nations. It must also involve an assessment of changes in the 'conventional wisdom' of modern international monetary theory, which reflects national interests in a diffused and highly aggregated manner, and is particularly important in determining the perception of problems by IMF staff, many of whom see themselves as intellectuals and theorists and not mere international administrators. In such a setting, adherence to a 'monetarist' or 'Keynesian' orthodoxy may be an important factor in determining organizational outcomes. The greater the relative importance of intellectual—as against national—interests, the greater is the autonomy of the EIO staff *vis-à-vis* its Board of Directors, which is usually controlled by the permanent representation of member states.

Ascher has enumerated a number of other factors determining the autonomy of an EIO's staff. These are:
1. Lack of clarity of organizational priorities and objectives.
2. Level of complexity in accomplishing the EIO's mandate.
3. Organizational size.
4. The number of 'boundary' personnel.
5. The number of decision points.
6. The reputation of personnel[31].

However, an EIO with a significantly autonomous staff may not enjoy a high level of organizational autonomy and authority *vis-à-vis* its environment. An enhancement of organizational authority and effectiveness requires the institutionalization of an appropriate pattern of decision-making procedures within the EIO.

4.3 ORGANIZATIONAL DECISION MAKING

Decision making within EIOs has been studied from both an economic and a political perspective. Since most EIOs represent an attempt at interest aggregation, those who have developed models of organizational behaviour have done so within the context of the theory of oligopoly. The basic assumption is that an attempt to maximize the economic self-interest of the members of the EIO provides the best predictor of the EIO's production and pricing decisions. This assumption is implicit in much of the analysis of the decision-making process of the rule-setting EIOs such as GATT and the IMF. It is explicitly stated in the many attempts at modelling the behaviour of OPEC and other Commodity Agreements. It is recognized that such organizations may make 'mistakes' and set the 'wrong' price for their product, but feedback from the international market will conclusively demonstrate the ir-rationality of such decisions, and the 'equilibrium price structure' will inevitably be restored.

OPEC behaviour is thus usually modelled on the assumption that it would choose a price path appropriate for a rational monopolist. The organizational task is to estimate correctly demand and supply elasticities, choose an appropriate discount rate and take into account the fact that oil is an exhaustable resource. OPEC seeks to regulate the rate of oil exploitation, and the choice of the price structure is a means for optimizing the rate of production of OPEC oil. Sweeney has shown that the price path of a monopolist producing an exhaustable resource will be initially higher and subsequently lower than in the competitive case.[32]

The 'economic optimizing' models can of course be disaggregated into subgroups containing countries with broadly similar discount rates for future versus present earnings and similar cost functions for postponing production. Hnyilicza and Pindyck use the theory of co-operative games to simulate interaction between the OPEC 'savers'—Saudi Arabia, Iraq, UAE, Bahrain,[33] Kuwait and Qatar—and the OPEC 'spenders'—Iran, Venezuela, Indonesia, Nigeria and Ecuador. Co-operation depends upon a willingness to accept a division of the incremental gains from co-operation in proportion to the losses the countries would have had to incur, had no agreement been reached.[34] However, an application of this formula for the resolution of interest conflict would be impractical, Hnyilicza and Pindyck admit, because the 'optimal' solution it identifies assigns zero output to 'savers' up to a point in time, and zero output to 'spenders' from thereon. The actual division of market shares is thus entirely arbitrary and the 'optimal' price varies widely with fluctuations in market shares, and welfare gains and losses to the 'saver' and 'spender' groups are considerable, consequent upon changes in market shares and the 'optimal' price structures they indicate. Hnyilicza and Pindyck have thus not succeeded in providing an analytical framework for the 'rational' reconciliation of member interests within OPEC. Other attempts at building such a model are no more successful. However, such analysis is useful in that it identifies two important facts 'first that within the optimization framework the actual price path for OPEC depends heavily on the relative balance in cartel policy formulation among the individual OPEC governments and second, that the stakes for these individual actors in approximating their optimal price and production policy are extremely large'.[35]

The economic optimization approach assumes that it is possible for each country to identify unambiguously its optimum price and production paths. This is, of course, not the case in the real world. OPEC pricing and production decisions have, for example, differed widely from the prediction and forecasts of econometricians, who saw their decision as being a prime example of the behaviour of a rational monopolist. This is particularly so in the case of decisions affecting production quotas and the distribution of market shares.[36]

Political scientists have also sought to explain decision-making processes within EIOs. Moran argues, for example, that 'an operational code of advancing Saudi political priorities while minimizing hostile external and internal pressures upon the Kingdom explains Saudi behaviour (within OPEC) better than the economic optimizing models'.[37] Saudi Arabia has sought to exercise price leadership when political stakes are low. They have allowed prices to rise when the oil market was relatively weak and restrained them when

the market was stronger. Complex political forces have
determined the Saudi response to changing economic opportunities in the oil market and have shaped the role they played
in the making of OPEC pricing and output decisions. In this
perspective, economic factors are not unimportant but
secondary to political considerations in the determination of
organizational outcomes.

Government decisions in the area of foreign economic policy
making have also been studied from the perspective of
'bureaucratic politics'. 'Bureaucratic politics' models of
decision making are based upon four major propositions:[38]

1. In every issue area governmental executive decision
    takers are dispersed within different branches and
    organizations with divergent goals and priorities.
2. Decision making is not usually dominated by a
    preponderant individual.
3. Decisions are the outcome of political bargaining and
    compromise among a large group of government
    officials.
4. Decision making and decision implementation are not
    continuous processes.

The 'bureaucratic politics' model identifies the structure of the
decision-making process in specific issue areas by identifying
the decision makers, their power, their vocational location and
the divergence in their priorities and perspectives. It also
identifies the decision-making process by describing the
conduct and outcome of transgovernmental negotiations
involved in the formulation and implementation of decisions in
specific fields. Sometimes the head of a bureaucracy deliberately seeks control over the decision-making process and
plays down the importance of achieving a consensus within the
administration. Typically governmental decisions in the area
of foreign economic policy making are likely to involve many
individuals and organizations, and political authorities are less
likely to play a dominating role in these areas than, for
example, in defence or the building of political ententes. At
times of crisis the involvement of politically dominant
leadership is likely to be high, but in the case of rule-setting
EIOs, where extensive prior planning for taking a decision is
usually done and the time available for the reconciliation of

different views is reasonable, bureaucratic politics are more likely to be prevalent. As Rosati points out 'the bureaucratic dominance structure of decision-making occurs when an issue is of moderate importance—not critical enough to attract the involvement of the President but important enough to involve a number of individuals and organizations'.[39] In such a situation, decision making results from compromise and negotiation. This negotiation can be in the form of a positive sum game if participants are willing to accumulate knowledge and display 'analytical thinking'. If participants are unwilling to accommodate and to learn they will bypass fruitful bargains, and negotiations will often result in impasses and stalemates.

'Fruitful' negotiations thus require that EIOs provide a framework for learning by national delegates. Such learning often results in the gradual development of extensive transgovernmental ties. Cox and Jacobson have identified the conditions necessary for the formation of transgovernmental coalitions.[40] Transgovernmental coalition building is likely to be particularly salient in areas where the centralization of decision making is required for efficiency reasons, but interests and resources are located in a wide range of governmental departments. Keohane has shown that 'decision-making in the International Energy Agency Governing Body is adequately described in interstate terms but the politics of policy implementation are only explicable by taking into account transgovernmental politics'.[41] The United States, West Germany and Britain were found to be the most influential states in the Governing Body of the IEA. The Secretariat is most successful when it acts as an ally of the US. However, Governing Body decisions are often vague and rather general. Implementation of these decisions involves collaboration between governmental officials, secretariat personnel and oil firm managers. Links develop between the secretariat and government bureaucrats because of the involvement of the secretariat in continuous training programmes. Opportunities for transgovernmental links also arise from the IEA's involvement in the periodic review of national energy policies. Keohane notes 'An IEA official commented that the national review process in effect puts the IEA into a coalition with the national energy agencies in competition for funds. The IEA provides bureaucratic ammunition for the National Agency'.[42] The IEA seeks to develop contacts with government departments and to construct a coalition which has the potential to challenge a similar coalition of Western government environment officials, who may be affected by the growth of IEA functions and activities.

Similar evidence on EIO attempts to build transgovernmental coalitions in the case of the IMF has been provided by Russell.[43] Meltzer documents how a senior US official used EIO machinery to achieve a reversal of US policy on the question of granting trade preferences to the LDCs.[44] Anthony M. Solomon, appointed US Assistant Secretary of State for Economic Affairs in March 1965, constructed an OECD 'wiseman group' containing senior trade officials from the US, UK, France and Germany to develop a common position on the question of trade preferences. It argued for accepting a modified version of UNCTAD's generalized preference scheme and strengthened the position of the US Economic Affairs bureau officials who held the same view. The Assistant Secretary used 'the wisemen' reports as a basis for building a coalition of officials in the State Department concerned about the need to appease Latin America, and some White House staff to overcome the resistance of the Department of Commerce to the granting of LDC preferences.

Anthony Solomon has been described as an 'entrepreneurial policy maker'.[45] The OECD provided mechanisms and opportunities to develop his political initiatives. Growing interdependence provides increasing opportunities for using IO mechanisms to influence government policy. IOs can thus provide a setting for and can participate in 'bureaucratic politics'. The 'bureaucratic politics' model explains how policy formulation and implementation takes place. It is perhaps more useful for analysing the role EIOs can play in international policy making, than is the 'rational actor' model,[46] which concentrates on the analysis of the 'efficiency' of such decisions in terms of their impact on welfare.

EIOs can play two important roles in international decision-making. Firstly they can as we have just pointed out provide adequate mechanisms appropriate to transgovernmental coalition building. Secondly, they can stimulate attitude change and promote a climate of international opinion conducive for systemic transformation in accordance with the IO's organizational ideology.

Many researchers have studied attitude change of national delegates within IOs. Some of these findings have been summarized by Peck.[47] Most of these studies showed that while there had been positive cognitive change (increase in knowledge) in delegate attitudes as a consequence of participation in IOs, affective change, that is, increasingly favourable or unfavourable attitudes, was minimal. Karns and Riggs, however, found significant positive change in the attitudes of US congressmen who participated in UN and interparliamentary sessions. Mathison found an increased willingness to avoid conflict among delegates at meetings organized by the Economic Commission for Latin America.

Peck himself examined attitudes of UN permanent delegates in terms of changes in general images of world politics, personal role orientation and the assimilation of super-nationalist attitudes. He found that long-tenured delegates from the LDCs were favourably inclined towards the UN, but they saw the UN forums as useful in that they strengthened the nation state. They were supporters of an expansion of UN-sponsored economic programmes, but strictly in accordance with government priorities. There was no commitment to supernationality. Participation in the UN will thus not induce the Third World delegate to argue for a reordering of the goal priorities of his government. He is likely, however, to argue for an increased use of UN machinery for pursuing national goals.

On the other hand, Peck found that long-tenured Western delegates acquire an appreciation of the value of a politically neutral UN Secretariat. They realize the limitations of the nation state as an instrument for the management of global problems. They therefore do increasingly subscribe to supernationalist ideas. But their growing dissatisfaction with the outcome of UN decision-making process leads them to seek a transfer from their jobs. This means that they lose considerable influence in attempts at reorienting their national policies in order to strengthen the hand of the UN Secretariat and enhance its organizational mandate. Thus Peck reached the conclusion that 'although there is some socialization of permanent representatives at the United Nations, it does not seem likely to give the UN much ability to change its environment'.[48] The problem of environmental ineffectiveness of the UN system as a whole is most dramatically illustrated by the increased inclination of the United States to play the role of an 'outsider' within the UN and its agencies.[49]

In order to increase the saliency and impact of IO decisions it is thus necessary to increase the commitment of the IO members to the decision-making processes of the organization. This must involve the evolution of an efficient pattern of influence distribution within the IO.

4.4 THE DISTRIBUTION OF INFLUENCE

Many national delegates have argued that restructuring IOs is necessary for both efficiency and equity reasons. Weighted voting at the UN has been suggested to counter the supposed anti-West bias and to satisfy the requirements of democratic justice, with the principle of 'one person one vote' replacing 'one nation one vote'. 'Population-accenting' and 'power-accenting' voting formulas have been devised. It has been shown that accepting the 'power-accenting'[50] voting formula would have reversed the outcome of UN deliberations on a wide range of North–South issues.[51] Western countries in particular have sought a restructuring of the UN system, to counteract both 'politicization' and a rapid proliferation of agencies and functions.

Restructuring IOs is of course no easy task. This is clearly evident from the opposition to a rationalization of UN structures put up by both national delegates and Secretariat officials. Institutional change is inextricably linked with change in the substantive content of the IOs programme—and hence likely to be resisted by those who would lose out. National delegates also act to protect their 'own' bureaucratic constituencies and protegés. The bureaucrats themselves resist encroachment upon their constitutional status and substantive responsibilities. International change usually takes place in a haphazard and tortuous manner.[52]

Nevertheless the need to relate organizational influence to

environmental capability cannot be denied.

The organizational influence distribution patterns may not correspond to the pattern of influence distribution within the environment of the organization concerned. Nation-states are related to international organizations in three ways. They are the sources of demands put before the organization, actors and decision takers within the organization, and polities which the organization seeks to influence. If states A and B are the most influential members within organization O, (and, therefore, most likely to influence its decisions), but nations C and D have the greatest influence within the environment of O (and thus action on their part is vital for the implementation of decisions taken in O), O is not likely to be a very effective international organization. This is because decisions taken in O will not reflect the interests of C and D, who will thus not act to transform the environment in accordance with O's ideology.

Cox and Jacobson have devised a useful framework for the measurement of the organizational influence of member states, and for relating the organizational influence pattern to the pattern of influence prevailing in the environment. They define influence as 'the modification of one actor's behavior by another'.[53] Actors may have overall or general influence within an organization, or their influence may be significant in specific issue areas. Influence may also vary by type of decision, and by the process of decision-making.[54]

Cox and Jacobson have devised a composite index of general environmental power. A state's general environmental power is a function of: (a) its GNP, (b) its GNP per capita, (c) its population, (d) its nuclear capability, and (e) its international prestige. 'Capability', within the environment specific to an international organization, may be estimated by measuring a state's performance on variables which assess the environmental characteristics of the organization concerned. Thus Nye ranks states, in UNCTAD's specific environment, on the basis of their position on two scales: (I) share of world exports, (II) amount of aid given. The influence of a state within an international organization may be estimated from the relationship:

$$C = Xc\,(G + S) + A$$

where C = organizational capability of a state,

Xc; $(G+S)$=the priority placed by the state's authorities to convert their general capability in the environment specific to the organization into influence within the organization,

A　= the personal attribute of the state's delegates in an IO,

and　l　= Xa $(C\ D)$,

where l is the influence of an individual actor in an IO:

Xa　= the decision of the individual actor to convert national power into organization influence,

D　= the distribution of all other individual influences within the organization on a particular issue.

None of the variables are directly quantifiable, and indices have been devised to estimate a state's position on scales of ordenal measurement by Cox and Jacobson.

It is, as I pointed out, of importance that states with environmental power should have organizational influence; if the environmentally powerful member states place a low priority on translating this power into organizational influence, or if the organizational influence of the environmentally weak members is high, the organization concerned is not likely to be a very effective one. The leadership of the organization faces a twofold task: on the one hand, it must ensure that there exists sufficient inducement for the environmentally powerful states to take the organization seriously, and to attempt to influence its decisions: on the other hand, it has to persuade these states to play a 'positive' role within the organization, that is, to exercise their influence in promoting a strategy which transforms the environment in accordance with the organization's ideology and objectives. Both these tasks can be successfully accomplished only if the internal structure of the organization facilitates the generation of conciliation between member states, and realistically reflects the distribution of environmental capabilities.

This consideration provides us with criteria to assess the usefulness of the organs of international organizations. We may ask: do these organs provided effective channels for the exercise of influence by the environmentally powerful states?

Do they facilitate consensus formation within the organization? This raises questions about the representativeness of these organs, their size, their functional differentiation, etc. It is held by some authors that an increased role for the smaller council-type organ, as against the conference-type organ, would tend to enhance the effectiveness of the international organization concerned.[55] It is also argued that 'because of the present structure of the world community an international organization may only be a form of co-operation between states. It may only act on the basis of their having come to an agreement for the purpose of satisfying their convergent interests and not the aims and interests of but a certain group of member states'.[56] Hence consensual decision-making procedures are likely to be more useful than majority voting. The voting mechanism ought to reflect the need to expand consensus when important decisions are made. Voting procedures—as indeed most other institutional mechanisms—are established at the time of the inception of an organization (though these procedures may, of course, change over time). The mechanisms should thus be established with the aim of ensuring the exercise of organizational influence by those who can contribute most to organizational effectiveness. This may imply the application of the principle of (an approximate) parity of representation of differing groups of states with similar interests. It must be remembered that the structuring of decision-making procedures within an organization is an important determinant of the type of decisions which this organization can make. If, for example, decision-making procedures permit a relatively permanent, but environmentally powerless, majority to impose its decisions on a relatively permanent environmentally powerful minority, the decisions of such an organization will mainly serve the purpose of articulating the views and perspectives of the majority. This is by no means an insignificant task. Interest articulation is an essential prerequisite for exercising systemic political influence. But organisations which merely serve the purpose of achieving interest articulation for the majority of their members cannot be expected to initiate large programmatic breakthroughs.

Institutional procedures also determine issue formation

within international organizations. Thus the acceptance of the group system as the basis of representation on all decision-making bodies within UNCTAD ensures that the North-South conflict provides the focus for all UNCTAD activities. This has the effect of leaving the Eastern bloc states 'out in the cold', and has thus restricted the number of actors whom the UNCTAD leadership seeks to influence, in its quest for a transformation of the international economic system. On the other hand, the evolution of the group system has permitted an aggregation of the Third World interests, which has transformed 'the style of LDC interest articulation, from latent, diffuse, particularistic and affective, to manifest, specific, general and instrumental'.[57] This, again, is an important achievement. However, the process of interest aggregation through the group system may introduce rigidities into the bargaining and negotiating processes, and the insistence on group cohesion may impede substantive progress. The question, therefore, arises: is the survival of the Group of 77 necessary? UNCTAD accepted the group system as the basis of its decision-making structure, at a time when decolonization had transformed the nature of centre–periphery relationships within the international system. There had been a 'process of fragmentation of the linkages of the centre of the system to its peripheries'.[58] For the period from the early 1950s to 1964, Dominquez found that 'Continent subsystems among the peripheries are relatively isolated from each other'.[59] The group system served as a useful mechanism for ending this isolation, aggregating and articulating the interests of the Third World within most international forums. But the international system of trade and finance of the 1980s may have reduced the need for group cohesion among Third World countries. If so, the group system is likely to become an inappropriate mechanism for the distribution of influence within EIOs seeking to foster dialogue between rich and poor countries

An appropriate pattern of influence distribution requires at least a rough and ready estimate of national influence within EIOs. Measuring influence within EIOs is a complex task, however. It is relatively easy to measure national control over resources, GNP, population, level of foreign trade, etc. The crucial question is 'how (will this) control over resources be converted into control over actors and events?[60] Some authors have argued that it is possible to identify a 'conversion process' by which control over resources is translated into control over events.[61] But in this perspective no provision is made for the fact that the GNP of a country may not be 'owned' by the government, and the mobilization of national resources involves an unpredictable political interaction between private and public agencies. A government is usually not in a position to mobilize all the economic resources of the nation. This limits the exercise of both coercive and non-coercive power in international forums.

Influence over other countries depends upon a state's ability to get them to do something by persuasion or coercion. Game theorists see influence as a function of bargaining. 'The outcome of bargaining depends on the expected utilities which the two actors assign to compliance and nonconformance outcome as well as their relative abilities to escalate threats or offer inducements'.[62] Rational' bargaining implies a search for utility maximization. The distribution of utilities as a consequence of bargaining reflects the degree of asymmetry of threat or influence among the bargainers. In the real world, since information about the initial distribution of 'utilities' is rarely available, such deductions can rarely be made with any degree of precision. Nevertheless 'it is possible to observe attempts to exercise economic power and to assess the success of these attempts if the initial goals of the actors can be ascertained and if negative, non coercive, unintentional and silent power are assumed to be unimportant'.[63]

This approach is essentially of relevance to situations of two-person bargaining. Usually in economic negotiations, control over events is shared among a number of actors who are interdependent. Hart uses Coleman's theory to assess the distribution of influence in a hypothetical example representing interdependence. One begins by identifying a set of actors and a set of events. Then two matrices are constructed: (a) the control matrix (C) whose entries C_{ki} represent the control of actor i over event k and (b) the influence matrix (X) whose entries X_{ik} represent the proportion of the total interest of actor i in event k. From these, it is possible to derive a bilateral power matrix which represents the pattern of interdependence among the collaborating power sharers.[64]

Variables in these matrices can be defined in a wide variety of ways, and the degree of precision in measuring influence is, in general, modest. One attempt at measuring the influence of delegates, at International Telecommunication Unions World Administration Radio Conference in 1979 by Codding, illustrates how to approach such questions.[65] General environmental influence was measured by GNP, GNP per capita and population. Influence in the field of tele-communication was measured by figures on the use and production of radios and television sets, and the national use of frequencies. Influence within the conference was measured by the size, composition and competence of national delegations. Delegates were also interviewed after the conference 'to identify the components of actual influence and to test them against the variables chosen earlier'.[66] Representational influence was measured in terms of delegates regarded as most influential by those interviewed. Positional influence was measured by computing office-holding scores. Behavioural influence was estimated as:

$$I = \frac{Y_i}{X_i} \times \frac{Y_i}{A} = \frac{Y_i z}{X_i A}$$

where I = influence, X = number of arguments in which delegation i was involved, A = the total number of arguments, Y = the number of arguments won by delegation i. Coleman found that correlation between actual influence and predicted influence[67] was positive but low.

Measuring organizational influence is a difficult task. It is nevertheless essential because influence distribution patterns have a direct impact on organizational performance. Krasner has studied this relationship. He measured national influence in regional development banks by indices such as 'the distribution of voting power, the geographical allocation of resources and the lending style of each of the banks, particularly their sensitivity to the desires of borrowing members'.[68] Krasner found that the development performance of the Inter American Bank was superior to that of the Asian Development Bank and the African Development Bank. In his view this is explained by the fact that the former is dominated by a hegemon—the United States—which is essentially concerned about maintaining its political interests and is willing to pay an economic price for this. The Asian Development Bank, which is dominated by Japan, offers less attractive loans to its developing country clients because Japan is less concerned with politics and zealously guards its economic interests. The African development Bank, in which the donor countries have little influence, is moribund and starved of funds. The moral, according to Krasner, is 'that the best structure for weak developing countries, is one in which there is a hegemon (which) may accept considerable loss of control over an international organization, provided that the state's basic long-term political objectives are not violated'.[69]

As the economic power and potential of the developing countries increase, the appropriate structure of international organization will change. The institutionalization of change in international organization forms, as well as in the substance of international economic transactions, usually depends upon successful multilateral negotiations. In the final section of this chapter, I will examine some of the problems associated with the conduct of negotiation as a means for organizational development within EIOs.

4.5 INTERNATIONAL NEGOTIATION PATTERNS AND PROBLEMS

Formal bargaining theory is useful in describing how rational deals can be struck between self-interested negotiators seeking policy changes in clearly defined issue areas. It identifies several principles which should in its view lay the basis for a successful outcome of negotiations.[70] Negotiations should be entered into by each side when the expected outcome is superior (generates more utility) than the expected outcome of refusing to negotiate. Negotiators should act on the basis of expectations of how the other side will respond if ideological conflicts are avoided, principles it adheres to are not questioned, and its power position within the international system is realistically appreciated. Negotiators should build on shared interests, avoid excessive initial demands and 'fractionalize' or divide problems so that incremental progress can accumulate and generate a momentum for escalation.

Much of international negotiation theory is implicitly based on the models of domestic bargaining in pluralist societies. There is thus a systematic bias to underemphasize several of the characteristics which distinguish domestic politics in Western capitalist countries from international political processes. There are no sovereign authoritative institutions for the implementation of collective decisions at the international level. Collective bargaining within pluralist societies is generally based upon an agreed set of rules, and within a relatively stable organizational context. Bargainers generally accept a dominance of 'expertise' over 'ideology', and bargaining is usually an attempt at discovering a politically relevant range of efficient solutions. Pluralist negotiating systems work best when resources are available to defuse crises. Incremental change is seen as the only realistic option by most bargainers because of the existence of the very large number of interest groups whose claims have to be continuously balanced against each other.

Many of these conditions do not characterize the context of international bargaining. Here, bargaining often takes place between 'mistrustful and unequal protagonists who pursue divergent goals by conflicting tactics'.[71] Rising international transaction levels have created an undoubted awareness of the need for international negotiation. But interdependence has been accompanied by conflicting and overlapping interests, rapid shifts in comparative advantage and technological developments. Growing international uncertainty has made national interventions in world forums, contradictory and indecisive.

There has been little convergence among the principal international actors on the ordering of economic priorities or on the mechanisms through which these should be pursued. Incremental change may continue to be negotiated within such a system but 'the international system has the elements of a failed incremental system in which the capacity for response and adaptation falls increasingly behind demands for change'.[72]

Successful international bargaining involves not a search for piece meal solutions, but an adroit and effective linkage of international issues. Such linkage can create a basis for both substantive change in the volume and composition of economic transactions and for organizational developments which can make EIOs more efficient instruments for the management of the world economy.

Tolinson and Willet have developed a theory of 'mutually advantageous linkages'.[73] The establishment of linkages is seen as a means for compensating countries who lose out when a welfare optimum solution is accepted in one issue area. Thus countries which lose because of a tariff dismantling international agreement, may be compensated if tariff dismantling is linked with increases in financial aid. Linkage of international negotiations is thus seen primarily as a distributional means for offsetting gains and losses arising from individual agreements.

The possibilities and problems associated with issue linkage are discussed in detail by Tomelson and Willet.[74] They study bargaining between two representative negotiators. They show that negotiators will prefer to link bargains—to negotiate simultaneously about the allocation of resources to produce different outputs—when there are substantial economies of scale in concentrating production in one country and direct side payments are difficult. An efficient linking of issues implies the deliberate relating of negotiations in areas in which the comparative advantages of the negotiating partners are widely different. This allows for an automatic distribution of side payments consequent on an efficient international allocation of resources. The linking of issues is unnecessary when a balanced distribution of benefits in given issue areas does not create significant diseconomies.

There are, of course, a number of qualifications to which this type of analysis is subject.[75] It is not easy to define 'national interests' unambiguously in international negotiations and to assess the true 'representatives' of negotiators with reference to these interests. In pluralist societies, interest groups compete to define 'national interests' continuously. Moreover, individual negotiators may become so committed to the successful conclusion of complex bargaining processes that they may downgrade the importance originally attached to the pursuit of national policy priorities. Moreover, genuine differences may exist in perception and measurement of economic costs and benefits, and on the weights to be placed on the protection of economic *vis-à-vis* strategic or foreign policy interests.

The fruitful outcome of complex negotiations depends at least as much as the context in which there negotiations are taking place as it does on a rational perception of policies and objectives and the methods for their reconciliation. If these perceptions are clear and unambiguous, the higher the level at which negotiations are conducted the better. Top-level negotiators will be able to combine considerations of a wide range of issue areas and to strike bargains involving many sets of complementary side payments. If on the other hand there is a difference of opinion on policies and objectives, issue linkage becomes problematic. Negotiations in such cases centre on a technical clarification of issues and are best handled by middle-level representatives.

Another important factor determining the extent to which issue linkage will be achieved is the number of bargainers involved in the negotiating process. 'The greater the number of actors the more difficult it should be to arrange linkages so that each negotiator should be willing to accept greater deviations from the efficiency frontier to achieve a more balanced distribution of benefits'.[76] Negotiations should be conducted between groups with clearly defined stakes. The voting rules of an EIO will influence both the pattern and outcome of negotiations. In particular, if voting powers differ substantially from the distribution of costs and benefits of voting outcomes, there is the likelihood that there will be a serious under-production of the collective good which is being negotiated within the EIO.[77] This is most clearly illustrated by the failure of the ill-fated NIEO negotiations, where the Third World's voting majority became a hindrance to substantive progress.

Issue linkages are thus a means for co-ordinating international economic policy. Such linkages imaginatively engineered, provide the best context for the restructuring of EIOs. For without institutional flexibility it is almost impossible to negotiate and implement international agreements in discrete and disparate issue areas. Institutional developments are most easily accommodated when nation-states perceive these developments to be a basis for achieving substantive policy breakthroughs which are in the interests of all bargaining partners. Successful issue linkage is, however, an exception rather than a norm of modern international politics. The extensive literature which lays down the prerequisites of such linkages offers many explanations of why this is so.[78]

Modern negotiation is distinguished from classical diplomacy by a number of characteristics. It is usually conducted in multilateral forums, is more usually susceptible to the influence of domestic interest groups and, even when overtly political, is much more influenced by technological developments. Modern negotiators are often involved in creating a system and structure out of a mass of information, and in this sense 'negotiation is now more akin to the art of management is practised in large bureaucracies than to the art of guile and concealment as practised by Count Mazarin'.[79]

Many of these characteristics become apparent from an analysis of the processes and content of the Kennedy Round negotiations which were held under GATT auspices over the latter half of the 1960s. [80] In these negotiations most national delegations had factions with different interests and perspectives, and a significant amount of time and resources had to be devoted to the 'internal' reconciliation of divergent points of view. Moreover, the delegations were under pressure from a wide range of domestic interest groups. At the Tokyo Round 'the US negotiating team (was) having to respond to 45 private sector committees composed of 900 knowledgeable people well aware of their own interests'.[81] This is because the negotiations cover vast areas—at both the Kennedy and the Tokyo Rounds, negotiations deliberated about removing restrictions on thousands of products, international trade of which was restricted by hundreds of different administrative and economic measures. It is thus inevitable that uncertainty characterizes the negotiator's response to all major initiatives. The purpose of negotiations is often not the resolution of specific disputes, but the creation of routines and procedures for reducing uncertainties and restricting the operation of unregulated market forces. It is always a matter of conjecture as to whether the 'optimum' level of restriction has been approached by a negotiated agreement.

The behaviour of international negotiators is often similar to that of business managers confronted by market uncertainties. Their concern also is with establishing common business practices rather than with fixing prices or market shares. The establishment of these conventions make rational economic planning possible within the individual firm.[82]

The implications of considering international negotiations in this light are important. First, it must be realized that international economic negotiators are more concerned with process than with outcome. Negotiators attempt to establish a 'bargaining' language to facilitate the emergence of common perceptions. This usually entails the bureaucratization of the negotiating process, with the establishment of working groups and the decomposition of the agenda. Progress is first achieved in these working groups, and an overall compromise is often constructed 'from the bottom'. The existence of uncertainty ensures that international economic negotiations are relatively unstructured and represent a 'trial and error search' for common perceptions. The discovery of 'common perceptions' leads to the emergence of negotiating rules, which make a trading of concessions possible. It also makes possible the creation of an issue-hierarchy—the acceptance of the relative importance of the many objectives being pursued by the negotiators. This involves an allocation of time available to the various stages of the negotiation. As the end approaches, precise calculations of costs and reciprocity become less relevant. The final agreement is a work of statemanship. Winham shows that at the Kennedy Round 'those who persisted in such calculations lost their grip on the overall developments in the negotiations usually to their own disadvantage'.[83]

International economic negotiations can best be understood with the help of 'concepts from the literature of decision-making, business management and organization theory and not necessarily from studies of bargaining theory'.[84] The irrelevance of formal bargaining theory to understanding the outcome of modern international negotiations is also illustrated by Winham,[85] who has reported the results of an exercise to elicit the views of senior US governmental negotiators on how they conceive the task of international negotiation. Negotiation is defined 'as a tool in the management of external relations',[86] not merely the extracting of asymmetric concessions. Negotiators see themselves as engaged in a two-way exchange—with both domestic lobbies and interest groups and representatives of other states—and emphasized the importance of domestic staff support in the capital and the establishment of a defining framework at the negotiating venue. In three important respects the practitioners dispute the findings of standard negotiation theory:

1. They regard relations with their own government at least of as great importance as those with the representatives of foreign governments, and explicitly reject the assumption that international negotiation is cut off from the domestic policy-making processes.
2. They view negotiations as managerial and policy rather than a strategic problem. Negotiations are seen as being concerned primarily with the elaboration of consensus and not merely with a narrow trading of concessions.
3. They emphasize the importance of substantive information and generally regard factors such as individual personality and sociological background as largely inconsequential.

In general, as Winham has argued 'practitioners emphasize flexibility over consistency, priority setting over calculations and the establishment of a definition of the situation over a strategy for the situation. In modern negotiations a premium is placed on the intellectual capacity to understand complex issues and the bureaucratic ability to organize a team to sell the government's position on these issues both at home and abroad'.[87] The conducting of modern negotiations provides ample opportunities for the redefinition and elaboration of the role of EIOs within the international economy so as to facilitate the transformation of the environment in accordance with the organizational ideology. It also provides political space for the systematic intervention of the secretariat of EIOs, which can play an important part in structuring these negotiations. The secretariat of EIOs attempt to develop a strategy based upon the resources of the organization to achieve specific goals. The next chapter assesses the role of the secretariat in enhancing organizational performance and capability.

NOTES

1. Schmitter, P.C. 'Three neo-functional hypotheses about international integration', *IO*, Vol. 23 No. 1 (1969) pp. 161–6 (Schmitter's emphasis).
2. *Ibid.*, p. 163 Schmitter's emphasis.
3. Haas, E.B. and Schmitter, P.C. 'Economics and differential patterns of political integration, projections about unity in Latin America', *IO*, Vol. 18 No. 4 (1964) pp. 705–37.
4. That is, their size and potential within the specific functional content of the international organization concerned (trade in the case of GATT, armed forces in the case of NATO).
5. Haas and Schmitter describe as pluralistic a 'prevalent mode of group conduct (which) . . . is functionally specific, universalistic, or achievement-oriented', Haas and Schmitter, 'Economics and differential patterns', p. 711.
6. For evidence on this point *see* Lindberg, N.N. *The Political Dynamics of European Economic Integration,* Stanford University Press, Stanford Cal., (1963), and Haas, *The Uniting of Europe,* Princeton (1956).
7. 'Identical (commitment) . . . can be said to prevail if the parties agree on the terms of the compact as well as on the paths of reasoning which led them to it. A mere convergence of aims takes place, however, when the negotiators agree on certain objectives even though they may have been led to them by quite different . . . paths of reasoning.' Haas and Schmitter, 'Economics and differential patterns', p. 713.
8. Haas and Schmitter's analytical framework (which I have utilized in this section) was designed to evaluate the integrative potential of economic union. It can be used to determine the 'scope' and 'level' of an international economic organization; e.g. UNCTAD surely aims to create institutional arrangements in the field of international trade (perhaps also in international finance)' under which . . . nation-states cease to act as autonomous decision-making units with respect to an important range of policies', *ibid.*, p. 709. This is the reason behind UNCTAD's insistence on a generalized approach on the question of the 1 per cent Aid Target, the GSP, the SDR Aid Link and the Common Fund. Group B countries have consistently resisted this attempt to reduce their ability to 'act as autonomous decision-making units with respect to an important range of policies', *ibid.*, p. 709, but the Group of 77 has generally endorsed the Secretariat's strategy.
9. By 'externalization', Schmitter means the adoption of a common policy, by the members of the organization *vis-à-vis* an outsider.
10. Schmitter, *ibid.,* p. 164.
11. *See*, for example, Lindberg, L. 'Political integration as a multi-dimensional phenomenon requiring multivariate measurement', *IO*, Vol. 24 No. 4 (1970) pp. 897–911.
12. As is the case with Asian regional EIOs documented by Schubert, J.N. 'Towards a working peace system in Asia: organizational growth and state participation in Asian regionalism', *IO*, Vol. 30 No. 2 (1977), p. 425–62.

13. *See* in particular, Haas, E. *Beyond the Nation*

14. Keohanne, R. 'Institutionalization in the C
Vol. 23, No. 4 (1969) pp. 859–96.

15. Volgy, T. and Quistguard, J. 'Correlates of orga
the United Nations', *IO*, Vo. 29 (1974) No. 1, pp.

16. Volgy and Quistguard, *op. cit.,* p. 185.

17. Weigart, K. and Riggs, R. 'Africa and the UN elect
analysis', *IO*, Vol. 23 No. 1, (1968) p. 14.

18. Volgy and Quistguard, *op. cit.,* pp. 184–5.

19. On this *see* Archer, C. *International Organizations, Ge*
Unwin, London (1983) Ch. 1.

20. Hopkins, R.F. 'The international role of "domestic" bure
Vol. 30 No. 2 (1977) p. 406.

21. Hopkins, *op. cit.,* p. 413.

22. Hopkins, *op. cit.,* pp. 418–24.

23. Hopkins, op. cit., pp. 428–30.

24. *Arabia: the Islamic World Review (London)* monthly (August 198₄

25. Lipson, C. 'The international organization of Third World deb
Vol. 35 No. 4 (1981) p. 606.

26. US Congress Senate Committee on Banking, Housing and Ur
Affairs *Hearings on International Debt* 95th Congress, 1st Session, 19
p. 88.

27. US Congress House Committee on Banking, Finance and Urban Affairs.
*Hearing on US Participation in the Supplementary Finance Facility of the
IMF.* (Statement by F. Heldring, President Philadelphia National Bank
95th Congress, 1st Session, 1977, p. 142.

28. Lipson, *op. cit.,* p. 619.

29. Lipson, *op. cit.,* p. 622.

30. For one attempt at relating organizational ideology to policy as a means
for assessing autonomy and authority *see* Roerseler, F. 'Pressures to
adjust balance of payments disequilibria: an analysis of the powers of
the IMF', *IO*, Vol. 30 No 3 (1977) pp. 433–52.

31. Ascher, W. 'New development approaches and the adapability of
international agencies: the case of the World Bank', *IO*, Vol. 37 No. 3
(1983) pp. 415–39.

32. Sweeney, J. 'Economics of dependable resources, market forces and
intertemporal bias', *Review of Economic Studies* (February 1977).

33. Bahrain is of course not an OPEC member. The authors do not offer
any explanation for including it among 'the OPEC savers'.

34. Hnyilicza, E. and Pindyck, R. 'Pricing policies for a two-part exhaustible
resource cartel, the case for OPEC', *European Economic Review,* Vol. 8
(1976) pp. 74–103.

35. Moran, T. 'Modelling OPEC behaviour, economic and political
alternatives', *IO*, Vol. 35 No. 2 (1981) p. 247.

36. Some of these findings are discussed in Moran, *op. cit.,* pp. 249–53.

37. Moran, *op. cit.,* p. 253.

38. Helpiron, R. *'Bureaucratic Politics and Foreign Policy',* Brookings,
Washington DC (1974).

39. R
P

40. (

41.

42

4?

4

)sati, J. 'Developing a systematic decision-making framework', *World olitics,* (1981) p. 249.

:ox, R. and Jacobson, H. *'The Anatomy of Influence',* Yale University ?ress, New Haven (1973).

Keohane, R. 'The International Energy Agency: state influence and transgovernmental politics', *IO,* Vol. 31 No. 4 (1978) p. 932.

Keohane, *op. cit.,* p. 949.

. Russell, R. 'Transgovernmental interaction in the international monetary system—1960—1972', *IO,* Vol. 27 No. 4 (1973) pp. 411–64.

4. Meltzer, R. 'The politics of policy reversal: the US response to granting trade preferences to developing countries and linkages between international organization and national policy making', *IO,* Vol. 30 No. 3 (1977) pp. 649–68.

45. Meltzer, *op. cit.,* p. 666.

46. Discussed in connection with OPEC's price and production decision making.

47. Peck, R. 'Socialization of permanent representatives in the United Nations: some evidence', *IO,* Vol. 32 No. 3 (1979) pp. 365–90.

48. Peck, *op. cit.,* p. 382.

49. For one analysis of the role of the 'outsider' within the UN system *see* Volgy, T. 'The role of the outsider in quasi legislative systems: the potential utility of a legislative model', *IO,* (1971), pp. 85–97.

50. As measured by GNP, UN assessment, energy consumption, defence expenditure, etc.

51. Newcombe, H., Young, C. and Sianiko, E. 'Alternative pasts: a study of weighted voting at the UN', *IO,* Vol. 31 No. 3 (1977) p. 583.

52. For one account of attitudes towards the restructuring of the UN system *see* Meltzer, R. 'Restructuring the United Nations system: institutional reform efforts in the context of North–South relations', *IO,* Vol. 32 No. 4 (1978) pp. 993–1018.

53. Cox, R. and Jacobson, H. *The Anatomy of Influence,* Yale University Press, New Haven (1973) p. 3.

54. According to Cox and Jacobson 'Government representatives would generally be most influential in representational, symbolic and rule-creating decisions. Executive heads would be most influential in pragmatic and boundary decisions', *op. cit.,* p. 45.

55. Moraweicki, W. 'Some problems connected with the organs of international organizations', *IO,* Vol. 19 No. 9 (1965) pp. 913–28.

56. Moraweicki, *op. cit.,* p. 921.

57. Walters, R. 'International organization and political communication', *IO,* Vol. 24 No. 4 (1969) p. 823.

58. Dominguez, R. 'Mice that do not roar: some aspects of international politics on the world's peripheries', *IO,* Vol. 24, No. 2, p. 208.

59. Dominguez, *op. cit.,* p. 208.

60. Hart, J. 'Three approaches to the measurement of power in international relations', *IO,* Vol. 31 No. 2 (1977) p. 290.

61. *See,* for example, Kno, K. *'The Power of Nations: The Political Economy of International Relations',* Basic Books, New York (1975) p. 9–10.

62. Harsanyi, J. 'The measurement of social power, opportunity costs and the theory of two person bargaining games', *Behavioural Science,* Vol. 7 No. 1 (1962) p. 72.
63. Hart, *op. cit.,* p. 295.
64. Hart, *op. cit.,* pp. 296–303.
65. Codding, G. 'Influence in international conferences', *IO,* Vol. 35 No. 4 (1981) pp. 715–24.
66. Codding, G. *op. cit.,* p. 718.
67. As measured by indicators such as GNP, technology indices, size and experience of delegations, etc.
68. Krasner, S.D. 'Power structures and regional development banks', *IO,* Vol. 35 No. 2 (1981) p. 304.
69. Krasner, *op. cit.,* p. 305.
70. On the principles of formal bargaining theory *see,* for example, Kelman, H.C. *International Behaviour,* Holt, Rinehart and Winston New York (1965), and Coddington, A. *Theories of the Bargaining Process,* George Allen and Unwin, London (1968).
71. Rothstein, R. *Global Bargaining: UNCTAD and the Quest for a New International Economic Order,* Princeton University Press, New Jersey (1979) p. 10.
72. Rothstein, *op. cit.,* p. 13.
73. Tolinson, R. and Willet, T. 'An economic theory of mutually advantageous issue linkage in international negotiations', *IO,* Vol. 33 No. 4 (1979) pp. 425–49. The following paragraphs are based upon this paper.
74. Tolinson and Willet, *op. cit.,* p. 428–434.
75. Noted by Tolinson and Willet, *op. cit.,* pp. 441–8.
76. Tolinson and Willet, *op. cit.,* p. 446.
77. This is clearly demonstrated in Olson, M. and Zeckhauser, R. 'An economic theory of alliances', *Review of Economics and Statistics,* Vol. 48 No. 3 (1966) pp. 266–79.
78. For an analysis of the preconditions of successful issue linkage *see* Stein, A. 'The politics of linkage', *World Politics,* Vol. 33 No. 1 (1980) pp. 62–81.
79. Winham, R. 'Negotiation as a management process', *World Politics'*, Vol. 32 No. 1 (1977) p. 89.
80. Discussed in Winham, *op. cit.,* pp. 90–110.
81. Winham *op. cit.,* p. 91.
82. Cyert, M. and March, J. '*A Behavioural Theory of the Firm'* Prentice-Hall Englewood Cliff (1963).
83. Winham, *op. cit.,* p. 109.
84. Winham, *op. cit.,* p. 99.
85. Winham, G. 'Practitioners' views of international negotiations', *World Politics,* Vol. 32 No. 1 (1979) pp. 111–35.
86. Winham, *op. cit.,* p. 113.
87. Winham, op. cit., pp. 129–30.

5 The Role of the Secretariat

In the previous chapter I concentrated upon an analysis of the behaviour of the national delegates who are the formal sources of rule setting within the international system. These national delegates are the sponsors of the EIOs and are responsible for defining the organizational mandate. The decisions taken by these sponsors are, however, executed by the EIOs permanent secretariat. The secretariat is most clearly identified with the IO and—as we will see in Section 3—the executive head of the secretariat is universally regarded as the leader of his organization. The secretariat is therefore not merely an implementor of the decisions taken by the sponsors of an EIO. It attempts to influence this decision-making process by determining conference agendas, constructing interest group alliances, mediating between rival groups and taking other systemic initiatives. In this chapter I will assess the role of the secretariat as on organizational actor within the international system.

5.1 BUREAUCRATIC BEHAVIOUR

A study of the international secretariat has to be situated within an analysis of the role of the bureaucracy in modern society. Max Weber, as is well known, made a distinction between 'bureaucratic' and 'patrimonial' administration[1]. In the latter, the inferior–superior relationship is determined on the basis of personal legality. Authority within such an administration is legitimized by tradition and custom. The recruitment and remuneration system reflects these characteristics.

As against this a 'bureaucratic' organization institutionalizes a highly developed division of labour. There is a precise and detailed description of the duties and responsibilities of each office. There is a 'rational' and impersonal regulation of superior–inferior relationships. Authority is legitimized by a belief in the correctness of the process by which administrative rules were enacted. Bureaucrats are recruited on the basis of possession of specialized knowledge. Emphasis on specialization is accentuated by the promotion and remuneration structure. The bureaucrat is a professional who does not bequeath his status or his authority to his offspring—unlike the employee of the patrimonial organization.

Weber believed that the 'ideal' bureaucrat would be politically neutral despite the relative autonomy which the growing professionalism of the bureaucrat ensures for him. The sponsors—that is, the political superior of the bureaucrat—can dominate this professionalism because of the intense competition among bureaucrats for position. Weber believed that the impersonality of the bureaucracy made it a tool which can be used by many different political groups.

This view has, of course, been widely challenged. Marx had argued before Weber that the bureaucracy is an instrument of class oppression, 'the greater the level of state bureaucratization, the higher the level of the exploitation of the proletariat and the peasantry'.[2] Other authors, such as Robert Michels, predicted the political dominance of the bureaucracy in both capitalist and socialist societies. In this view, increased social complexities and specialization facilitate the monopolization of power by organizational elites, who systematically exclude 'the rank and file' from all decision-making processes.[3] Some of these themes are echoed in the 'managerial revolution' literature which celebrates the 'separation of ownership from control' in mature capitalist economies, in the belief that the bureaucratic manager who supersedes the capitalist entrepreneur would be both more efficient and more capable of bridging the gap between the haves and the have-nots in modern society.[4]

The inclination to view bureaucracy in black-and-white terms has been somewhat modified by the work of authors of the decision-making school, foremost among them being Herbert Simon. Simon argues that an individual's behaviour as a decision maker is determined by both factual and value premises. The organization limits the decision-making environment of the individuals that belong to it. The organizational division of labour defines the need for decision making at different official levels. The organizational hierarchy structures the decision-makers' environment. Individuals within the organization seek to achieve 'satisfysing solutions, given the structuring of value and factual premises created by the organizational environment. In this perspective the organization as a whole is also seen as a 'profit satisfiser' which adapts its behaviour to market conditions. The 'organizational system' is presumed to 'tend towards equilibrium' because of information linkages between organizations. These linkages ensure that 'deviant' or 'irrational' decisions are controlled and eventually corrected. Organizations, thus conceived, are efficient decision takers to the extent that market imperfections do not constrain efficient organizational behaviour. The bureaucracy adheres to market rationality.[5]

These theories are thus in broad agreement with the Weberian view that modern bureaucratic organizations are 'formally the most rational means of carrying out imperative control over human beings'.[6] Such organizations are both efficient in terms of use of organizational resources and effective in the pursuit of organizational goals. The bureaucratic organization is technically superior to other organization forms. In the Weberian view—as we have seen above—the organizational goals are essentially set by sponsors and the bureaucrats themselves are politically neutral. The 'decision making' theorists—and the managerialists—regard organizational goals as being determined by 'the market'; the overriding goal being profit maximization/'satisfysation.' These schools down play the importance of the relationship between the environment, the sponsors and the bureaucrats as determinants of organizational goals, resources, structures and outcomes.

These views have been challenged by both 'revisionists' and 'rejectionists.' It has been argued that organizational effectiveness is determined by the extent of conflict of 'authority' and 'power' systems within the organization.[7] Organizational authority reflects adherence by bureaucrats to expectations associated with their formal roles. The motives and perspectives of some bureaucrats may not be congruent with the formal role expectations of the organizational system. In such a case the formal authoritative relationships that were established on the basis of the formal rationality that guided the establishment of the organization, are challenged by new power structures established by 'defiant' bureaucrats who attempt to realize goals and interests that conflict with organizational objectives. Such conflicts exist in both bureaucratic and patrimonial organizations. There is no a priori reason to expect conflict among functionaries to be more or less intense in a particular type of organization. Rudolph and Rudolph argue that most organizations combine bureaucratic and patrimonial characteristics and these characteristics can mitigate dysfunctional conflict within the organization. Thus the alienation created by the impersonality of bureaucratic structures may be offset by an assiduous cultivation of 'old boys' networks' and other forms of patronage.[8]

In order to determine the effectiveness of an organization we have to ascertain the internal distribution of authority and power. Authority is hierarchically distributed. Power, on the other hand, tends to flow from the bottom up. Those with authority have to struggle for power with their subordinates. This power struggle affects not merely the internal life of the organization, but also the relationship of the organization to its broader environment. 'Men in organizations sometimes rebel against the machine like expectations of formal rationality and differential distributions of benefit and authority . . . they pursue strategies and engage in behaviour that is from the perspective of organizational goals and procedures irrational and dysfunctional'.[9] Power struggles over organizational goals, resources, official roles and the distribution of costs and benefits thus challenge the formal rationality on which the original organizational mandate is based. In other words, an organization may not pursue the objective of maximising or 'satisfysing' profits because of the type and form of power struggle characteristic of the relationship between sponsors and bureaucrats and among the bureaucrats themselves. Thus, for bureaucrats to behave 'rationally'—for them to pursue growth maximization or satisfysing profits—there must be a complementarity between the values, interests and perception of the bureaucrats and the formal goals of the organization. This result can also be achieved if dissenting bureaucrats are rendered organization-

ally powerless and organizational power is monopolized by
those bureaucrats who possess legitimate authority within the
organization.

Bureaucrats resist the authority of sponsors in struggles over
job description, entitlement provisions, work procedures and
the structuring of intra-organization communication networks. In these struggles bureaucrats have an opportunity for
appropriating organizational resources and reinterpreting
organizational goals. Negotiating organizational routines
gives subordinates the chance to behave efficiently or
inefficiently in order to realize their personal goals and
objectives. Once this possibility is recognized there is no basis
for accepting the Weberian prediction that bureaucratic
administration is necessarily efficient and bureaucratic behaviour is politically neutral, and that organizational objectives are in themselves sacrosanct as far as the bureaucrats are
concerned.

We have seen that authors such as Michels have argued that
bureaucrats establish organizational oligarchies. It has been
argued that this must imply a distortion of rational
organizational goals. The emphasis on strict adherence to
organizational rules and procedures means that the preservation of conformity to this system become more important
than the achievement of the substantive organisational
objectives. Bureaucracies suffer from organizational rigidity
which inevitably constrain their ability to pursue rational
goals. Further complications are introduced by the fact that, as
tasks multiply, bureaucracies inevitably split up into subunits
with imperfect communications. The subunits then have a
tendency to emphasize the achievement of subgoals, and the
overall organizational objectives tend to become less operational are often ignored or thrust into the background. The
overall coherence and internal consistency of organizational
policy is reduced.[10]

The proliferation of subunits has led a group of theorists to
view organizations as configurations of conflicting groups.
Conflict between these groups for the appropriation of
resources and interpretation of goals is continuous and a
central feature of the life of the organizations. In such a
perspective the overshadowing of organizational interests by

the interests of particularly advantageously placed groups is seen as a likely outcome. Bureaucracies consist of both horizontally and vertically integrated cliques that use political strategies to pursue their particular interests and to camouflage this by an appropriate reinterpretation of the organization's overall goals and objectives.[11]

This rapid review of the vast range of writings on the bureaucracy points to the conclusion that bureaucrats can, if they choose, behave 'rationally', and pursue objectives such as 'satisfying' profits or optimum growth. They can also choose to do so and generate intra-organizational conflict, which reduces the environmental impact of this organization. Thus, Friedman's view, bureaucrats expand their organization while actually reducing the level of service they provide to the public.[12] Other forms of inefficiency have also been widely noted. The crucial question clearly is: under what conditions do bureaucrats choose to behave efficiently for the realization of 'rational' organizational objectives?

5.2 THE PRODUCTION OF PUBLIC POLICIES

This question has been recently addressed by the 'political economics' tradition within the resurgent New Right. The discussion is based on the neo-classical insights into the processes which determine the production of 'public' or 'collective' goods. 'Public' goods are defined as goods possessing the characteristics of 'non-exclusiveness' and 'jointness'. In other words, the consumption of public goods—such as pollution control or defense—cannot be limited to those who bear the cost of production of these goods. Secondly, the consumption of public goods by 'free riders' does not diminish the supply of the goods available to others.[13] Roberts and Sullivan have argued that 'one of the meanings of living in a smaller more interdependent world is that increasingly even the nation state can no longer provide desired benefits because more and more goods are becoming collective at the international level'.[14] These authors have shown that collective goods—such as joint defence and environmental protection—can be produced at the international level if the costs of production are equitably distributed, the number and impact of free riders is effectively limited, adequate compensation arrangements are made and knowledge of the benefits of collective goods production is widely disseminated.[15]

Neo-classical economists have attempted to identify the factors that determine the price and output level of collective goods under different market conditions. The general conclusion is that price and output levels are determined by the preferences of a median voter, consumer or citizen. Consumers whose preference schedules differ from that of the 'median' voter are 'coerced' into accepting a 'non-optimal' production of public goods, and consequently suffer an inevitable welfare loss. In this perception, welfare can always be enhanced if the proportion of 'private'[16] to 'public' goods in the national output rises.[17] Hence the current emphasis on the importance of reducing public expenditure.

It is clear that this approach does not permit an appreciation of the role of the organizational bureaucracy in determining the price and output level of public goods. These are set by political sponsors in line with the preferences of the 'median' consumer or voter revealed in election processes. The bureaucrat is a politically neutral executor of the decision taken by his superiors and sponsors. The neo-classical perception of the role of the bureaucrat is thus broadly similar to that of the sociologists within the Weberian tradition.

This view has been systematically challenged by economists belonging to the New Right. Authors such as Tulloch[18] and Niskamen[19] argue that bureaucrats play a crucial role in organizational decision making. Bureaucrats possess resources which enable them to achieve their ends and 'distort' production and price policies. They are able to achieve this 'distortion' because of the lack of competition in the markets for which they produce and their ability to act as pure discriminating monopolists. The bureaucrats can successfully defy their political sponsors because the allocation of resources among 'bureaus' is not determined by the efficiency of individual bureaus. The bureaucrats, therefore, have no inclination or incentive for efficient behaviour in modern capitalist economies.

Breton and Wintrobe have recently sought to bridge the gap between the Weberian and the 'Parkinsonian' analysis of bureaucratic behaviour.[20] They accept that bureaucrats do influence organizational decision making and, therefore, affect the production and prices of both public and private goods, but argue that the relationship between bureaucrats and their superiors is neither necessarily co-operative nor necessarily antagonistic. There relationships are seen as 'relationships of exchange' in which superiors 'trade' 'rewards' for 'obedience'. 'If the price is not right the subordinates will not obey'.[21] The bureaucrats have an ability to 'choose' efficient and inefficient behaviour and they exercise this choice in a systematic manner.

The main concern of bureaucrats in both domestic and international public organizations is the production of public policies. These are defined as policy and technical decisions for the production of 'price regulations, diplomacy, war censorship, family allowances' etc.[22] The concept of 'public policies' is thus significantly wider than that of 'public goods', although the former share the latter's twin distinguishing characteristics of non-exclusiveness and jointness. The essence of the policy-making process is, to determine the extent and the amount of a given good or services that is to be produced: in other words, to identify the degree of 'desired' product differentiation. It is assumed that rational bureaucrats will opt for the degree and type of product differentiation that maximizes the value of their objective function.

Product differentiation is achieved by defining the characteristics of a policy package. Some characteristics are essential. A national health policy must have something to say about doctors, medicines and hospitals. But which doctors and which hospitals and which forms of health services are emphasized is clearly optional. Policies differ from each other in terms of the specific combination of 'essential' and 'non-essential' characteristics they embody. Bureaucrats may play an important part in defining policy characteristics both because of their inherent complexity and because legislators may deliberately leave them vague and loosely specified. Much of the bureaucratic influence emanates from the fact that bureaucrats are the main instruments of policy implementation. Bureaucrats—as for example in the EC—may also play a role in the initial stages of policy formulation and conceptualization. Breton and Wintrobe emphasize that throughout the process of policy conception and implementation, bureaucrats and their sponsors are engaged in a constant exchange of 'favours' and 'services' which at least partly determines the characteristics of the policies that are produced.[23]

The principal commodity the bureaucrats have to offer their superiors in exchange for policy characteristics and direct benefits are 'informal services'—defined as work undertaken by subordinates not specified by the formal workload assigned to the jobs they occupy to achieve ends desired by their superiors. Bureaucrats seek to maximize 'well-behaved ordinal utility functions'[24] by balancing the undertaking of specific informal services against the receipt of direct rewards and the incorporation of desired characteristics in specific policy packages. Utility may, of course, be derived from a number of objectives such as growth in budgets, security, prestige, etc.[25] and specific policy characteristics may be associated with these goals.

Bureaucrats can choose to deliver or not to deliver the types of informal services desired by their sponsors. The provision and withholding of informal services can raise or lower the average cost curves and hence the efficiency of the bureau concerned. Bureaucrats can select co-operation or non-co-operation with sponsors because the bureaucratic environment makes it very costly to detect bureaucratic manipulation of the flow of intra-organizational information and the speed at which formal organizational tasks are accomplished. This manipulation requires the establishment of 'networks based on trust in which informal services of subordinates can be exchanged'.[26] This implies that the greater the trust between superiors and subordinates, the greater the propensity of the latter to provide 'efficient' informal services, that is, informal services which lower the average cost curves for achieving goals specified by sponsors. 'Inefficient' informal services are those which raise these cost curves. Superiors reward subordinates for efficient informal services. Inefficient informal services permit the bureaucrats to extract a higher real price for their work than is contained in their formal job contract. The ability of subordinates to raise this price can be reduced by effective monitoring of the inefficient services they choose to delivery to themselves.

The determination of the price and supply in informal services can be conceptualized in straightforward neo-classical terms. In Figure 5.1, D is the demand curve for informal services, D_e is the demand for efficient informal services. If there was perfect trust between superiors and subordinates, D would be identical with D_e, and the equilibrium price of informal services would be P_e at the point of intersection between D_e and S, the supply curve for efficient services. Because trust is imperfect—because subordinates do not have perfect confidence that they will be adequately reward-ed—there are positive transaction costs.

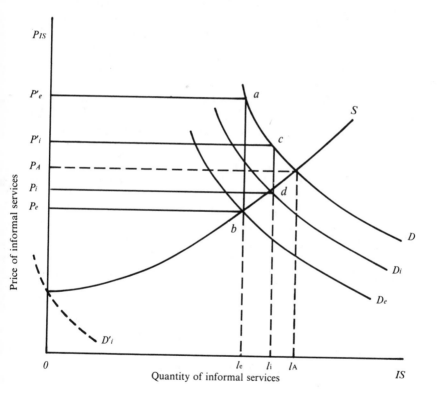

Figure 5.1

This implies that the price for efficient informal services is P_e, but bureaucrats receive only P_e. The area $P'eabP_e$ is the total cost of transacting these deals between bureaucrats and their superiors. As trust increases this area is reduced. The position of D_e is thus determined by trust between sponsors and bureaucrats.

D_i is the demand curve for inefficient services. It represents the amount of the price taken by bureaucrats at different volumes of inefficient services. The position of D_i is determined by the amount of trust among the bureaucrats themselves. Since this trust is also imperfect, there are positive transaction costs of P_i, cdP_i and the bureaucrats themselves receive P_i. D_i also depends on the costs and extent of the monitoring of bureaucrats undertaken by superiors. Thus we can see that:

(a)   the provision of efficient informal services depends upon trust between sponsors and bureaucrats;

(b)   the provision of informal inefficient services depends upon trust among bureaucrats and the extent of the policing of bureaucratic activities;

(c)   the demand for efficient informal services can be eliminated by sufficient lowering of trust between bureaucrats and sponsors: that of inefficient informal services can be eliminated by a sufficient increase in monitoring and a sufficient reduction in trust among bureaucrats. If both these conditions prevail, the demand for informal services will be zero and only formal services—those specified in the work contracts—will be supplied.

Depending on these conditions, it is possible to predict whether bureaucrats will behave efficiently, inefficiently or formally—that is, in strict approximate accordance with their job contracts—in the production of a particular public policy. If bureaucrats decide to render efficient informal services, this will lower the average cost curve associated with the production of a public policy. If inefficient informal services are supplied, the average cost curve will rise.

Sponsors are thus concerned about creating conditions to maximize the production of informal efficient services. This depends upon the volume of trust which exists between sponsors and bureaucrats. The existence of trust as a basis for transactions is essential when it is difficult to estimate accurately the value of the goods that are to be exchanged between the transactors and the time at which specific exchanges can take place. Objects traded in bureaucratic networks have these characteristics. Demanders have the means to 'reward' suppliers, but typically they do not know with certainty when they will be able to do so or the form the reward will take. Payments in the form of rewards are deferred and debts are allowed to accumulate over time. The greater the volume of trust, the longer is the period that the service debts will be allowed to accumulate. Trust increases when individuals agree to postpone the immediate use of resources and forego demanding payment for the informal services they render. Trust is a capital asset jointly produced and used by networks of bureaucrats and sponsors. The distribution of trust is, of course, not entirely symmetrical, but there must be at least an element of mutuality for trust to persist over protracted time periods.

Networks in which trusts accumulate can be both internal and external to an organization. External networks link the secretariat of an organization with other organizations in its environment. The size of networks depends on the intensity of trust in a relationship as well as the number of 'trust relationships' that an individual seeks to establish. 'In an open, mobile and relatively impersonal society large investments in trust in a small number of relationships—investments in intensive trust—are seldom observed, whereas the profitability of many contacts and relationships—investment in extensive trust—is usually the rule'.[27] The size of networks is determined by the amount of informal services, whether efficient or inefficient, required to achieve a given set of objectives. Expanding networks is, however, problematical. This is because the typical supply curve of informal services is 'truncated', as shown in Figure 5.2. Here the 'realistic' supply curve S_R is fractured at point f. It is greater than S, which is the supply curve of informal services if we assume that transaction costs are zero. The difference between S and S_R for the provision of 010 level of informal services has two components: fg that measures 'normal' transaction costs arising from the fact that trust is not perfect; and gh, which is

152 Conceptual Approaches

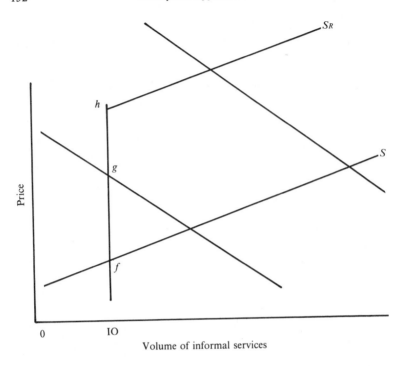

Figure 5.2

the 'abnormal' transaction costs that have to be borne because individuals who do not possess the 'right' social characteristics—such as race, school background, political views, etc.—have to be included in the network of relationships that is necessary for the production of OIO.[28] The limit on network expansion places a limit on the provision of informal services within bureaucracies.

Bureaucrats provide informal services in competition with each other. This competition is often structured in the form of rival networks relating the organizations with their environment. Substantial empirical work illustrates that competition characterizes bureaucratic behaviour in public organizations.[29] Bureaucrats compete against each other for jobs and for positions in networks which ensure access to organizational rewards and resources. This competition does reduce the rents or 'monopoly price' extracted by the bureaucrats, but it does not reduce their capacity for selective behaviour. This implies that competition increases the incentive for seeking network membership by individual bureaucrats—for membership ensures access to organizational rewards by being selectively efficient. Bureaucratic competition thus does not ensure that organizational efficiency will increase over the long run.

Competition exists not only among individual bureaucrats, but also among the organizations and networks they inhabit. Competition among organizations compensates bureaucrats for the 'barriers to entry' into bureaus and networks which restrict access to rewards. On the other hand, restrictions on the redistribution of resources among organizations increases the incentive for competition among bureaucrats in specific organizations. It is to be emphasized that in both inter- and intrabureaucratic competition, the concern of the individual bureaucrat is with increasing control over resources.

The control over resources by an organization depends crucially upon its 'capacity for selective behaviour'[30] and the networks which sustain its leadership. Competition for resources among organizations leads in equilibrium to the allocation of resources in proportion to their marginal capacity for 'selective behaviour'. The equilibrium price of informal services is equalized throughout the bureaucratic sector. In equilibrium, therefore, bureaucrats seek a resource allocation pattern which maximizes their value to the bureaucracy as a whole. 'If policing were costless, trust between sponsors and bureaucrats perfect, cost curves were directly observable, subordinates would always use their resource efficiently and the allocation of resources among bureaus would also optimize the value of resources to sponsors'.[31] But in the real world these conditions do not obtain. There is, therefore, a difference between resource allocation patterns optimal from the perspectives of the sponsors on the one hand and bureaucrats on the other. Sponsors will reduce resource allocation to bureaus where inefficient behaviour predominates, for by definition such behaviour reduces the organization's contribution to the achievement of the sponsors' objectives. This can be countered by bureaucrats who display 'entrepreneurial capacity' in building networks, reducing truncation, and in general taking advantages of new opportunities for reorganization. Structural changes within the organization may thus be an important means for changing the pattern of resource distribution, because such reorganization affects the capacity for entrepreneurial innovation and adaptation by the bureaucrats employed in that organization.

Different organizational structures generate different volumes and distribution patterns of trust. Trust between superiors and subordinates—vertical trust (T_v)—indicates the organization's capacity for efficient selective behaviour. Trust among bureaucrats at similar operational levels—horizontal trust (T_h)—on the other hand, measures the capacity for inefficient behaviour. Organizational efficiency can thus be conceived as being determined by the ratio T_v/T_h. The higher the level of T_v and the lower the level of T_v, the easier the accumulation of human and physical resources by the organization. This is because if T_v is high, the employee willingness to adjust to changes in work environment through, for example, the introduction of new machinery or shift procedures will also be high. The lower the T_h, the smaller is the capacity of the bureaucrats to resist such changes.

Breton and Wintrobe argue that T_v is positively associated with the frequency of promotion within an organization, since promotion usually depends upon the decisions of superiors and increased interaction between them. T_h is negatively correlated with promotion, but since the costs of promotion are significant there are likely to be 'diminishing returns' associated with the frequency of promotion. The organization must thus identify an optimal level of promotion frequency in order to maximize the effect on T_v/T_h.

T is also positively associated with discretionary perquisites—payments in cash and kind made to subordinates at the wish of superiors. It is negatively correlated with a subordinate's subjective anticipation of quitting or being fired from the organization. T_h is also negatively related to the frequency of actual and anticipated turnover. Increase in organizational turnover thus reduces the bureaucratic capacity for selective behaviour, whether efficient or inefficient. Rapid turnover among sponsors, on the other hand, increases T_h, for relations with superiors deteriorate. Thus, an increase in sponsor turnover—often associated with the growth of political instability within the environment—enhances the organizational capacity for inefficient behaviour. Conversely, the lower the turnover of superiors and the greater their number relative to subordinates, the smaller the capacity of the organization to choose inefficient behaviour patterns and work procedures.[32]

These five variables—frequency of promotions, prequisites, frequency of turnover, turnover among organizational superiors, and ratio of superiors to subordinates within an organization—are directly measurable from organizational records. They can be treated as estimators of the level of T_v and T_h and as predictors of the capacity of selective behaviour by bureaucrats. Developing an analytical framework of this sort for studying bureaucratic behaviour is, however, posited on the assumption that decision making is undertaken by utility maximizing individuals. Such a perspective has been utilized in studying international bureaucracies in works recently reviewed by Frey.[33] Needless to say, other approaches have also been adopted. In the next section I will focus upon the problems associated with an appraisal of the role and policies of the bureaucracies of IOs.

5.3 THE BEHAVIOUR OF INTERNATIONAL BUREAUCRATS

International organization theory generally recognizes the secretariats of international organizations as actors, with varying levels of independence within the international system.[34] International organizations seek to transform the international system in pursuit of organizational objectives. The secretariat seeks to define organizational objectives in a way which necessitates task expansion and creates interest coalitions within the environment and within the organization itself, which can sustain its expanded programmes. It has been suggested that growth may indeed become a goal in itself, in such a way that organizational objectives are not merely 'redefined', but abandoned and substituted by others in order to ensure growth and, particularly, survival.[35] Attempts

at explaining growth paths range widely. Some writers claim
that the processes of organizational growth are determined by
the context of the spatial situation of the organization
concerned: growth occurs in areas unoccupied by other bodies:
task expansion is limited by competition from other international organizations. The impact of the environment on the
growth path and goal structure of an IO may be far more
complex, subject to the strategy chosen by the members of the
organization and its secretariat. In particular, goal reformulation may occur as a consequence of reassessment by members
of the effectiveness of the organization concerned. In practice,
old goals are rarely abandoned altogether: they become
'restraints', which are still binding on the organization, in
pursuit of new or upgraded goals. The secretariat plays an
important role in attempting to influence the 'goal-restraints'
ordering. This reordering of organizational priorities is bound
to have an impact on the growth ability of the organization
concerned. This involves management of the processes of
alliance consolidation and disintegration between subgroups
within the environment, and within the organization itself. The
secretariat's ability to redefine goal priorities in accordance
with its own preferences depends upon the extent of consensus
concerning ultimate objectives among the membership of the
organization, and upon the extent of consensus within the
secretariat itself. In general, the wider the gap between
members' preferences, and the greater the cohesion within the
secretariat, the greater the ability of the organization's
leadership to influence the process of 'goal-restraint' reordering. Internal resistance to reformulation tends to vary in-
versely with the availability of organizational resources. Subunits of IOs generally tend to place greater emphasis upon the
attainment of subgoals which are operative, and are less
concerned about the overall goals of the organization as a
whole, as the latter are defined in general principles. The
greater the functionally specific factorization of the organization concerned, the greater is the concentration by the
subunits on the attainment of their specific subgoals. Goal
reordering is also likely to be influenced by the communication
channels linking the various parts of the organization to
various parts of its environment. These communication chan-

nels facilitate the development of interest coalitions, linking segments of the organization with groups of clients. These interest coalitions press for goal reordering, in accordance with their own interests. This is not to suggest that people support organizations only inasmuch as these organizations enable them to achieve their material or political goals. Value preferences of individuals and groups may also play an important part in determining their attitude towards the subgoals of the organization concerned. Individuals within the secretariat may develop loyalties to specific parts of the goal structure of the organization concerned. Persons loyal to specific subgoals are likely to resist a downgrading of these subgoals, and they tend to introduce an element of rigidity into the restructuring process. On the other hand, individuals may develop loyalty to the organization, or to its leader, especially to a charismatic one. This enhances flexibility in the goal structure of the organization. However, if an individual identifies himself with a subunit or its head, goal structure will tend to reflect this, and rigidity in goal structure is not likely to decrease.

In the 1960s, theorists payed a great deal of attention to the role of organizational leadership in the transformation of the environment in accordance with organizational ideology. Thus, Haas focused upon the role of the leadership in defining the organizational programme. It must build coalitions between specialists, governments and other groups interested in the pursuit of subgoals that are complementary to the overall objectives of the IO. The leadership must seek to build a consensus with like-minded environmental actors, but impose its authority on specialists within the IO who are more committed to the specific subgoals that have been choosen for strategic purpose than to the overall organizational objects: 'It is to be feared that a specialist-dominated organization would lose sight of the common purpose. In order to prevent this the leadership (must) . . . analyse the situation including the environmental constraints in which it plans to choose specific intermediate ends, devise means of action to attain them and then evaluate the consequences'.[36] Leadership must attempt to generate 'functional' controversy—that is, controversy which leads to the making of critical decisions. It must, in other words, seek 'the evolution of a programme that will solve problems only by creating new ones to be solved in turn'.[37]

In the period following the establishment of an IO, its leadership remains concerned with the problem of organizational survival. At this stage, emphasis is placed on safeguarding autonomy and distinctiveness. In the long run, the leadership's success depends upon its ability to attract new supporters and on an adroit adaptation of procedure and subgoals to fit changing environmental conditions. The attraction of new clients must not, however, be at the expense of the 'core' supporters who were responsible for the birth of the IO in the first place. Constructing and retaining the support of powerful and stable client alliances within the environment is an important criterion for the assessment of successful IO leadership. The IO leader 'must play the game of power politics to the hilt'[38] in order to arrange 'side payments' among the often antagonistic client groups which support different segments of the organization's programmes. This requires an ability to benefit from all environmental developments to enhance organizational mandate and operational capacity. The leadership must, therefore, be interested in building an effective 'feedback mechanism' which increases dependence and interaction between the IO and the most dynamic groups within its environment.

Haas sums up his recommendations for effective organizational leadership in these words: 'If the leader of an international bureaucracy has true insight, he will manipulate the subgoals in such a way as to make the organizational influence as extensive as possible: he will spread his web of clients as widely as his interpretation of organizational objectives permits. The very fact that he can rely on no homogeneous and stable body of supporters, gives him the chance to move and manoeuvre as the logic of functionalism suggests'.[39] This indicates that the leadership of IOs has significant scope for environmental manipulation and can play an important role in enhancing organizational effectiveness.[40]

The role the secretariat leadership can play depends on a number of factors. Thus, Schewebel emphasizes that the character of the executive leadership of IOs is heavily influenced by the formal constitutional powers established in the Articles of Agreement creating the IO and the interpretation of these powers by the leading powers within the IO.[41] It is also affected by the material and non-material resources the executive head has at his disposal. This includes adequate funds, a staff with an appropriate level of administrative and diplomatic skills and expertise, prestige and political salience of the office as a natural focus for the achievement of consensus among the members of the IO.[42] Much of the authority of the UN Secretary General derives from the fact that he is regarded as the primary legitimate representative of the UN.

The autonomy and authority of the secretariat leadership depends also on the character of the international environment within which the IO is situated. Non-hegemonic international systems with a relatively wide diffusion of political and economic power among nations and an expanding web of interdependent relationships, which creates an incentive for international co-operation, enhance the operational opportunities for secretariat leadership. In such circumstances IO leadership can be both active and influential. The mediating and negotiating role of the IO leadership can be most effective within systems where, despite short-run interest conflicts, countries perceive long-term mutual benefits in the avoidance of antagonistic clashes.[43] The more severe the policy and value cleavage among the IO membership, the less effective the secretariat leadership is likely to be in arranging the type of 'side payments' and 'trade offs' which ensure successful negotiation.

Finally, the personal quality of leadership incumbents also affects their performance. 'Highly important personal qualities are the incumbent's own view of the proper limits of the office and his initiative in exploiting opportunities to expand its power'.[44] The political skill of the IO leader influences the national delegates' assessment of his capability and willingness to act as a representative of the IO, safeguarding the interests of the membership as a whole rather than of some faction within it. This 'neutrality' and 'ability to be seen as impartially just' is often considered as a crucially important personal trait for successful IO leadership.

So far I have been discussing the role of the executive head in relation to the sponsors of the IO and other environmental actors. An equally important question is the attitude of the 'lower order' bureaucrats to environmental developments and to initiatives taken by the IO leadership. A study of the responsiveness of World Bank staff to such changes has recently been undertaken by Ascher.[45]

Ascher found that the World Bank's professional staff has been relatively hesitant in its response to the systemic demands for changes in operational priorities and strategies, and in the recognition of changes in the international balance of North-South interests and perceptions. It has enjoyed a high level of autonomy, being responsible for the designing and execution of the projects which the Bank finances, while the Executive Directors—the sponsors—have influence limited in the main to the general guidelines of Bank policies. As projects have grown in number and complexity, the Executive Board's ability to supervise the staff effectively has been progressively reduced. The working procedures of the Bank ensure that the policy guidelines set out by the Executive Board do not contrain the ability of the staff member dealing with recipient governments to develop 'realistic' project proposals. This has often meant that the goals of subunits have taken precedence over sponsor-defined Bank objectives. Thus, Ascher reports: 'In several prominent cases (which have to go unnamed) the country programmes division has dramatized the borrowing government's opposition to ecological and poverty alleviation concerns in ways that are consistent with their own value preferences'.[46] Indeed, the attitude of Bank staff plays an important role in determining the perceptions of its sponsors. Since the World Bank has no competitors—no international aid agency of comparable size, support or ambition—the evaluation of the performance of its staff is based on a 'theoretical' appreciation of the 'correctness' of their policies. Since the staff has included some of the leading producers of contemporary conventional wisdom in the field of economic development theory—Hollis Chenery, Paul Streeten, Anne Krueger, Mahbub ul Huq, to name a few—a 'theoretical' assessment of the Bank is inevitably value laden. The production of theory is thus an important means for safeguarding the autonomy of the Bank's staff. Those who criticize the policy of the staff can be labelled as Marxists or monetarists, and the criticism can be diverted into the safe channels of 'disputes' about 'theoretical' premises and paradigms.

Relative autonomy has meant that staff members have behaved in a manner consistent with the pursuit of objectives such as career promotion, safeguarding of positions in intra-organizational politics, and commitment to intellectual and ideological paradigms. These factors have led Bank staff to resist new development priorities, changes in techniques of project analysis, explicit politicization of bargaining procedures,[47] and incorporation of explicit political analysis in the calculations determining credit worthiness of borrower governments. Ascher argues that project personnel have been more resistant to changes in the Bank's priorities and strategies than have other professional staff members.[48]

Does the relative autonomy of the Bank staff and its resistance to changes in strategies and priorities imply that it has behaved 'inefficiently'[49] *vis-à-vis* its sponsors? The real sponsors of the World Bank are, of course, the Executive Directors of the Western countries who have a voting majority on its Executive Board and a majority of quota allocations. They are direct representatives of their governments, but they also are concerned with looking after the interests of the commercial private-sector institutions, whose loans and investments in the Third World are often negotiated through the auspices of the World Bank. Their approval for Bank policies is most clearly evident in the fact that the Bank's financial obligations carry a triple A rating from the three major US bond-rating services. Payer has pointed out that the Bank, like the IMF, plays a crucial role in reducing the threat of default by Third World governments and induces these governments to pursue 'appropriate' domestic and international policies.[50] Many Western statesmen—including members of the Reagan administration—have supported World Bank's policies and performance.[51]

It is, therefore, clearly unrealistic to regard the behaviour of World Bank staff as 'inefficient'. Despite occasional differences in terms of emphasis, priorities and procedures, they have in the main chosen to support and work towards the realization of their sponsors' objectives. This choice can be explained in a variety of ways. The traditional explanation is that common nationality is a strong binding force between the staff of an IO and their home country. In the EC, for example the 'cabinets' of individual commissioners are seen as representing the interests of the country from which the commissioner concerned comes and as being little concerned about the organizational needs and preferences of the community.[52] Other high officials nominated or seconded from the countries have less commitment to the protection of interests of their parent countries, although they are subject to a lot of pressure from national governments and also private interest groups.[53] Some officials generally tend to regard nationality as not a particularly salient factor. Michaelman found no statistically significant relationship between nationality and (social) interaction among a sample of EEC officials. However, even within this group organizational failure is often blamed on nationalistic rivalry within the community. In general, Michaelman argues that 'nationality exacerbates tensions within the organization and serves to highlight the fact that European consciousness is at times tenuous'.[54]

Like the EC the World Bank is also multinationally staffed. However, according to Ascher, national loyalties are a less important determinant of staff attitudes. More important are 'the ideological divisions of the international development community'.[55] The Bank staff seeks to influence its environment by forging links with those who share the ideological premises of important factions within the organization. Operational methods which do not originate in the theoretical orthodoxy of the Bank—such as the use of the recoupment criteria as a basis of project appraisal or the investment contracts which can provide a basis for co-financing with Islamic banks[56]—are contemptuously brushed aside as 'unscientific' and 'crude'. Pressure is applied to ensure that borrowers accept the neo-classical policy framework as technically superior, on the one hand, and value neutral on the other. This enhances co-operation between the Bank and likeminded intellectuals and policy makers within 'backward' and 'doctrinaire' governments such as Yugoslavia, Romania, Pakistan and Sudan.

Systematically developing transgovernmental and transnational links are an important means available to international bureaucracies for increasing their autonomy and influence *vis-à-vis* their sponsors. Keohane and Nye have argued that during the post Second World War era there has been a growth in both transgovernmental policy co-ordination and the building of transgovernmental alliances between segments of national and international bureaucracies. The purpose of these alliances is to oppose other such alliances—an international alliance of officials in environmental ministries may be constructed to oppose an international alliance of defence ministries within the same group of countries.[57] The emergence of transgovernmental elite networks may lead to change in attitude and to flexibility in international bargaining. Such networks provide communication channels between national bureaucracies. Transgovernmental coalition building is likely to prosper when conflict between bureaucratic subunits within the same government is high, executive power to control subordinate behaviour is low, and there is wide acceptance of the norms and procedures of international action and decision making in order to realize joint gains.

IOs can play a role in fostering both transgovernmental policy co-ordination and transgovernmental coalition building. IOs may help in defining issue area boundaries and providing a focus for national bureaucracies. IO secretariats play an important role in providing an arena and an agenda for turning potential transgovernmental alliances into 'realized' ones. IO secretariats can deliberately organize activity to assist transgovernmental coalition building and actively seek membership within them. There have been recorded cases of FAO officials 'conspiring' with African government representatives to thwart their own chief executive.[58] The World Bank staff has developed strong links with finance and planning ministries in developing countries.[59] IO secretariats have an important role in this regard when there is a need for the transfer of information to be co-ordinated through centralized international procedures. IO secretariat staff have the opportunity 'to place themselves at the centre of the crucial communications networks and acquire influence as brokers, facilitators and suggestors of new approaches . . . the relevant agencies of government (will) be dependent on them for information and for the policy co-ordination by a legitimate system-wide actor which is required to achieve their own objectives'.[60] IO secretariat officials may, of course, play a similar role *vis-à-vis* non-governmental actors. The relations of the IMF staff with the international commercial banks readily come to mind in this context. The staff of the IMF has clearly gained in authority and autonomy from the fact that the commercial banks now regard the IMF as a natural mechanism for co-ordinating borrower response to creditor needs, and usually make additional support to debtor countries conditional upon prior approval by the IMF. This shows that effective penetration of markets and interest groups by developing an understanding of the technical, economic and political characteristics of decision making in specific issue areas can pay rich dividends for the staff of an IO, and can significantly enhance its capacity for selective behaviour.

The public choice literature which has focused on the role of the international bureaucracy [61] argues that it has greater capacity for selective behaviour and a greater inclination to behave inefficiently than its domestic counterpart. This is so because there is less opportunity or incentive to control international bureaucrats. The 'output' of an IO is notoriously difficult to measure. National delegates who are the official sponsors of international bureaucracies are acutely aware that controlling IOs will be interpreted as political interference by other national delegates. National delegates prefer to become 'free riders', limiting intervention to cases where they perceive that IO activity is detrimental to their national interests or when they believe that their own nationals employed by the IO are being discriminated against. 'Due to (this) lack of effective control, none of the layers in the hierarchy has any real incentive to work towards the "official product" because there utility and the organization's official function.'[62] Hence, quotas for positions that are a feature of many international organizations drive a further wedge between the individual's utility and the organization's official function'.[62] Hence, international bureaucrats pursue 'private' goals. Growth in organizational structures and budgets become ends in themselves. A large proportion of the budget is used for the provision of benefits to incumbent bureaucrats, and a large proportion of the time is used to streamline the formalized internalized operations of these organizations. Change in the structure of these operations and in the network of relationships they create is very difficult to institutionalize. Public choice theory, therefore, predicts that rational international bureaucrats would select inefficient behaviour patterns more often than their domestic counterparts.

However, this prediction has yet to be empirically tested. There are no comparative analyses of national and international bureaucracies performing similar functions that demonstrate the relative inefficiency of the latter. The public choice approach is based on a theory of human behaviour the universal validity of which is accepted only by the neo-classical school.[63] The behaviour of international bureaucrats need not necessarily conform to neo-classical norms. They may choose to behave 'efficiently'—that is, in accordance with the objective preferences of their superiors—even if this is not in their 'interests' as perceived by public choice theorists. Moreover, the bureaucrats may play a role in defining the political and economic preferences of their formal sponsors. Thus, as I show in Chapter 9, Raul Prebisch, UNCTAD's first Secretary General, played a key role in determining the position of the developing countries at the earlier UNCTAD conferences. UNCTAD thus became the IO of the Group of 77 and a tangency was created between the interest and perception of those of its sponsors who represented the developing countries and that part of the Secretariat which identified with and was inspired by Prebisch's ideas. UNCTAD's organizational ideology could be seen as a bridge connecting the interests of dominant bureaucratic and sponsorship groups. UNCTAD bureaucrats had an incentive to behave 'efficiently' not only because sponsors would reward such behaviour, but also because sponsors identified with the organizational ideology created by the secretariat leadership.

Modelling bureaucratic behaviour in EIOs is a complex task. This chapter has discussed some of the major themes on which current researches in this area are based. In general, there is a great need for empirical studies in this field. Chapter 9 represents a small step in this direction.

NOTES

1. Weber, M. *The Theory of Social and Economic Organization*, Columbia University Press, New York (1947).
2. *See* e.g. Marx, K. *The Eighteenth Brunnaire of Louis Napoleon,* Progress Publisher, Moscow (1971) p. 33.
3. R. Michels studied the functioning of the German Social Democratic Party in the late nineteenth Century, Michels, R. *Political Parties*, Vantage, New York, 1949.
4. *See* eg. Galbraith, J.K. *The New Industrial State*, Penguin, Harmondsworth, (1957), and Marris, R. *The Economic Theory of Managerial Capitalism*, Cambridge University Press, Cambridge (1969).
5. Simon, H. *Administrative Behaviour*, Little Brown and Co., New York (1957),and March, L. and Simon, H. *Organizations*, Little Brown and Co, New York (1958).
6. Parsons, T. (ed.) *Weber: The Theory of Social and Economic Organization*, The Free Press, Glenco Ill. p. 337.
7. Rudolph, L. and Rudolph, S. 'Authority and power in bureaucratic and patrimonial administration: a revisionist interpretation of Weber on bureaucracy', *World Politics*, Vol. 38 No. 2 (1979) pp. 195–227.
8. Rudolph and Rudolph, *op. cit.*, pp. 196–9.
9. Rudolph and Rudolph, *op. cit.*, p. 209.
10. Parsons, T. 'Suggestions for a new approach to the theory of organizations', *Administrative Science Quarterly,* Vol. 1 Nos. 63–85, (1966) pp. 227–39.
11. Etzioni, A. *A Comparative Analysis of Complex Decisions*, McGraw Hill, New York (1951).
12. Friedman, M. 'Gammon's black holes', *Newsweek* (Nov. 7, 1977) p. 84.
13. Buchanin, J. *The Demand and Supply of Public Goods*, Rand McNully and Co., Chicago (1968) pp. 51–4.
14. Roberts, B. and Sullivan, J. 'Collective goods and international organization', *IO*, Vol. 26 No 4 (1971) p. 849.
15. Roberts and Sullivan, *op. cit.*, pp. 850–65.
16. That is, goods not possessing the characteristics of 'non-exclusiveness' and 'jointness'.
17. Samuelson, P. 'The pure theory of public expenditures', *Review of Economics and Statistics*, Vol. 36 No. 4 (1954) pp. 373–89.
18. Tulloch, G. *The Politics of Bureaucracy*, Public Affairs Press, Washington DC (1965).
19. Niskamen, W. 'Bureaucrats and politicians', *Journal of Law and Economics,* Vol. 18 No. 3 (1975) pp. 617–44.
20. The rest of this section summarizes the argument of their book. *An Economic Analysis of Competition, Exchange and Efficiency in Private and Public Organizations*, Cambridge University Press, Cambridge (1982).
21. Breton and Wintrobe, *op. cit.*, p. 3.
22. Breton and Wintrobe, *op. cit.*, p. 11.
23. Breton and Wintrobe, pp. 22–6.

24. Breton and Wintrobe, p. 27. This implies the assumption of certainty, Where 'uncertainty has to be assumed we postulate that bureaucrats maximize expected utility functions of the Von Neuman–Morgenstein variety', p. 27.
26. On the goals bureaucrats are thought to give priority to, *see* Niskamen, W. *Bureaucracy and Representative Government*, Aldine-Atherton, Chicago (1971), and Migue, J.-L. and Belanger, G. 'Towards a general theory of managerial discretion', *Public Choice*, Vol. 17 No. 1 (1974) pp. 27–43.
26. Breton and Wintrobe, *op. cit.*, p. 41.
27. Breton and Wintrobe, p. 80.
28. This is sometimes described as the 'cost of social cleavage'. *See* e.g. Arrow, K.L. 'Models of job discrimination' in Pascal, A.H. (ed.) *Racial Discrimination in Economic Life,* Heath, Lexington, Mass. (1972).
29. Breton and Wintrobe, *op. cit.,* pp. 94–8.
30. That is, the capacity to choose efficient or inefficient behaviour in the pursuit of the objective of maximizing utility by the bureaucrats of the organization.
31. Breton and Wintrobe, *op. cit.*, p. 119.
32. Breton and Wintrobe, *op. cit.*, pp. 133–40.
33. Frey, B.S. 'The public choice view of international political economy' *IO*, Vol. 38 No. 1 (1984) pp. 199–223.
34. *See* Haas, E. *Beyond the Nation State*, pp. 86–125, and Dufty, R. 'Organizational growth and goal structure', *IO*, Vol. 26 No. 2 (1972) pp. 479–98.
32. Etzioni, A. 'The approaches to organizational analysis', *Administrative Science Quarterly* Vol. 27 No. 3 (1960) pp. 260–9.
36. Haas, E. *Beyond the Nation State*, Vale University Press, New Haven. p. 114.
37. Haas, *op. cit.*, p. 115.
38. Haas, *op. cit.*, p. 116.
39. Haas, *op. cit.*, p. 118.
40. A well-known statement of a fundamentally different assessment of the role of secretariat leadership in IOs is to be found in Myrdal, E. *Realities and Illusions in Regard to Intergovernmental Organization*, Al George Allen and Unwin, London (1958).
41. Schewebel, S. *The Secretary General of the United Nations: His Political Powers and Practice,* Greenwood Press, New York (1952).
42. On this *see* Young, O. *The Intermediaries: Third Parties in International Crisis*, Princeton University Press, Princeton (1967).
43. Cox, R. 'The executive head: an essay on leadership in international organization', *IO*, Vol. 23 No. 1 (1969) pp. 205–30.
44. Meyers, D. 'The OAU Administrative Secretary General', *IO*, Vol. 30 No. 3 (1977) p. 516.
45. Ascher, W. 'New development approaches and the adaptability of international agencies: the case of the World Bank', *IO*, Vol. 37 No. 3 (1983) pp. 415–39.
46. Ascher, *op. cit.*, p. 424.

47. As advocated, for example, by the Reagan administration.
48. Ascher, *op. cit.*, pp. 432–3.
49. Recall the definition of 'inefficiency' in Sect. 5.2.
50. Payer, C. *The World Bank: A Critical Analysis*, Monthly Review Press, New York (1982).
51. *See* Payer, *op. cit.*, pp. 344–56.
52. Michaelman, H.J. 'Multinational staffing and organizational functioning in the commission of the European Communities', *IO*, Vol. 30 No. 2 (1977) pp. 482–3.
53. Michaelman, *op. cit.*, pp. 485–8.
54. Michaelman, *op. cit.*, p. 495.
55. W. Ascher, 'New development approaches and the World Bank' *IO*, Vol. 37 No. 3 (1983) p. 437.
56. That is, banks which use profit sharing rather than interest agreements as a basis of investment. *See* Siddiqui, N. *Banking without Interest*, Leicester, 1976.
57. Keohane, R. and Nye, J. 'Transgovernmental relations and international organizations', *IO*, Vol. 23 No. 1 (1971) pp. 44–50.
58. Keohane and Nye, *op. cit.*, p. 52.
59. *See* Ch. 4.
60. Keohane and Nye, *op. cit.*, p. 55.
61. Reviewed in Frey, B.S. 'The public choice view of international political economy', *IO*, Vol. 38 No. 1 (1984) pp. 220–1.
62. Frey, *op. cit.*, p. 221.
63. The usefulness and relevance of the neo-classical approach to international political economy has been widely questioned. *See* e.g. Barry Jones, R.J. 'International political economy: problems and issues', Part I, *Review of International Studies*, Vol. 7 No. 4 (1981) pp. 245–60, and Part II, *ibid.*, Vol. 8 No. 1 (1982) pp. 39–52. Jones writes: 'The basis of an effective analysis of the international economy must be rooted in a number of assumptions that are incompatible with neo-classical economic theory' (Part II, p. 47).

6 Are EIOs Really Necessary?

This book has mainly been concerned with selecting and integrating theoretical developments within a wide range of disciplines which are useful for assessing the performance of EIOs and for understanding their operational processes. The book has assumed that EIOs exist and will continue to remain significant forums for international decision making and implementation in the medium run. As we have seen in Chapter 2 some New Right thinkers argue for a drastic curtailment of the role of the EIOs. In their view EIOs are dispensible—and indeed ought to be dispensed with. The continuing relevance of a study of international organisation needs justification in the year when the United States has left UNESCO and Britain is preparing to do so. Moreoever similar action is planned on a wider front embracing ILO, FAO, UNCTAD, UNIDO etc. It seemed appropriate therefore to end this part of the book with a chapter that explored the alternatives to international economic organization.

6.1 INTERNATIONAL ORGANIZATION, INTERNATIONAL LAW AND THE HEGEMON

Some New Right scholars believe that international economic organization should be replaced by an elaboration and extension of international law governing commerce, investment and migration across national frontiers.

The growth of modern international law dates from the late sixteenth century when it rose in response to the need for ordering the relationships of the newly emerging nation states of Western Europe. Hugo Grotuis argued that the authority of international law was derived from 'natural law' based on reason and 'the law of nations' consisting of generally acceptable rules of 'universal validity'. As the conception of a system of natural laws fell into disrepute positivist scholars emphasised the role of explicitly and implicitly expressed consent by states (in the form of treaties and customary law) as the main foundation of international law. But it is widely recognized that an unambiguous definition of this consent is problematical and as Van Kleffens has argued 'while nobody doubts that consent can create a legal obligation, that does not mean that the ultimate basis of the validity of that obligation is consent.[1] In Van Kleffens view 'the foundations of the respect due to law belongs to the domain of sociology and morality not to the realm of law itself.'[2]

There is, however, little international consensus on moral issues. The economic obligations of states—both domestic and international—are differently defined in modern Euro-centric international law, Soviet law and islamic law, for example. This has meant that questions of foreign investment, immigration, fiscal and trade policies remain the domain of national legislatures and the provisions of international law remain strictly limited in these spheres.

The relative underdevelopment of international law as an instrument for the regulation of the world economy is partly due to the lack of effective international organization. Until the middle of the nineteenth century there was virtually no institutional machinery available for the elaboration of international law. International law could only function through the agency of separate states. The consolidation of IOs particularly after the Second World War has contributed towards the extension and elaboration of international law.

The processes of international organisation and the extension of international law are complementary, not mutually exclusive as Conneybeare and other New Right authors seem to believe.[3] IOs provide a forum for sustained deliberation and negotiations and the gradual development of mechanisms and procedures which facilitate an accumulation of knowledge and a reconciliation of national differences in perspectives and policy priorities. Both GATT and UNCLOS have played an important part in the development of international law. It may be argued that an extension of international law implies a redefinition of the role of IOs not their dismemberment. They can become channels for achieving and sustaining an international consensus on both the desired ends of international policy and on the means for achieving these ends. The New Right opponents of international organization however deny the need for the search for an international consensus on objectives. In particular the 'neo-realist'[4] school re-asserts the Hobbesian view that sovereign entities are perpetually in the state of nature and in this context 'moral discourse in mere cant';[5] state action is determined purely by self interest. Bobbes' proposed solution to this perpetual state of anarchy is the emergence of Leviathan—the all powerful state which completely depoliticizes society and by pursuing a policy of aggressive self defence, free trade and the ensuring of material abundance to all its citizens makes itself secure from external attack for all time to come.[6]

Hobbes' impact on both political realism and neo-classical economics has been profound. Realism takes from Hobbes its state centricness and ahistoricsm. In this it has been surpassed by neo-classical economics which has 'mathematicized the placeless and timeless'.[7] The New Right seeks to combine methods and insights from both these approaches and to conduct political analysis in a wholly abstract fashion claiming a discovery of superhistorical law governing social behaviour.

Neo Realist analysis regards the state as an entity with well defined objectives. The state's objectives are regarded as independent of the interests of specific groups of individuals within it. The state espouses aggregate 'national' interests and in the process provides public goods, solves the 'free rider' problem and protects citizens' welfare. In the international field the state is the sole prism through which all global interactions are refracted. The structures of the international system are produced primarily by the interaction of states. In Waltz's words 'international political systems like economic markets are formed by the co-action of self regarding units.'[8] States are prior to the international system. These states are 'individuals in origin, spontaneously generated and un-intended'.[9]

It is thus obvious that realism shares with neoclassicism the paradigm of utilitarianism. The state like 'economic man' exists prior to and independent of larger social associations. States compete against each other in a world characterised by scarcity. They seek to achieve objectives which are pre-

determined and the value of which are private to the state and
not properly the subject of theoretical discourse. Utilitarian
rationalism is strictly instrumental—the purpose being the
identification of efficient means for the realization of given
ends on which utilitarian rationality refrains from passing
judgment. The state is an efficient pursuer of the objective of
the preservation and extension of its 'national interest'—the
determination of which is beyond the scope of political
analysis—and the international order is produced by the
equilibrating 'coaction' of such independent utilitarian states
which regard each other as external objects and in the process
of exchange seek a regularisation of mutual expectations.
Institutional change within the international order is spontaneously produced as a result of changes in capabilities and
expectations of competing states. The international political
order—like the market economy—is the product of rational
behaviour reflecting a realisation of universal and objective
'truths'. It is 'unscientific' to pass normative judgment on the
allocation of economic resources by such a market economy or
the distribution of political power by such an international
system.

Neo-realism has studied the conditions for the establishment
and consolidation of such an international order. There is a
near consensus among neo-realist scholars that a heirchichal
concentration of power is advantagous for the operation of an
international order which reflects utilitarian rationality. In
Krasner's words 'the most common proposition (among neo-
realists) is that hegemonic distributions of power lead to stable
open economic regimes because the hegemon has the resources
to provide the collective goods needed to make such a system
function effectively.'[10] In this conception it is obvious that
international organization is replaced by and subordinated to a
hierarchy in which power is effectively concentrated in a
hegemon powerful enough to define the public 'good' at the
international level in terms of its own private interests and
'whose preponderant capabilities see to it that more 'good' gets
done'.[11]

It is generally believed that the need for the provision of
international public goods can be reduced by de-regulating
market structures. The unhindered operation of international

markets supported by an appropriate international legal framework would achieve a growing privatization of public goods thus ensuring an efficient allocation of resources within the global economy. EIOs—particularly governmental ones— would be demonstratably dispensible within such a system.

6.2 STATES AND MARKETS IN THE REAL WORLD

There are two principal objections to this view. First market failure—the failure to produce socially necessary quantities of most essential public goods—is sufficiently widespread to necessitate the permanent existence of non market mechanisms. The partial equilibrium models of neo-classical theory which assess behaviour on the basis of the technical Pareto criteria may be useful in cases where transaction costs are either insignificant or invariant. Usually, however transaction costs are both positive and variable. They reflect the costs of identifying trading partners and negotiating and enforcing contracts. Toumanoff has shown that many market restrictions—such as trade mark and licensing arrangements reflecting barriers to entry—exist because of the need to apportion these transaction costs.[12] The existence of the transaction costs means that the allocation of resources is influenced by the distribution of property rights reflected in different institutional arrangements.[13] Non market institutional arrangements may be effective means for dealing with externalities and concentration of monopolistic power in situations where negotiation costs of specific economic contracts are high and enforcement requires a subordination of self to group interests. Both these characteristics are particularly applicable to the international economy in a wide range of issue areas. Moreover, transaction costs of the international organisation of production, trade and finance are likely to change over time. This requires a corresponding change in the structure of market and non-market institutional arrangements for achieving the objectives of international economic policy.

The need for non market mechanism is illustrated by the existence of 'market failure' in a wide variety of circumstances.

Developing countries are for example well aware of the fact that major international market imperfections systematically reduce their gains from participation in international trade and financing arrangement. Epstein and Newfarmer, have measured the high level of concentration in the world electrical industry which is dominated by just twelve full-time producers. Major firms within the industry have formed an EIO—the International Electrical Association (IEA)—to establish and operate procedures for fixing prices and allocating markets for most export sales outside the industrialized countries. These arrangements have increased product prices to developing countries, restricted entry of domestic producers to the electrical industry and reduced domestic control of technology.[14] More general evidence on high levels of market concentration within the Western world has also not been lacking.[15] These market 'imperfections' and 'failures' have induced all modern Western governments to become direct suppliers of a wide range of public goods and also to play a regulatory role in many commodity and factor markets.

The involvement of the state in market management has not been unwelcome to the private sector. The image of the state as a parasitic body standing above society is to be found in some of the writings of Marx and Hayek.[16] Marx himself and those influenced by his views—including the so called 'neo Ricardians'—have discarded these views. The 'neo Ricardians' attempt to explain state economic intervention as a means for restoring corporate profit at the expense of wages.[17] Neo-Marxists argue that state intervention is necessary to offset the tendency of the rate of profit to fall and to sustain capital accumulation.[18] The state establishes appropriate property rights, operates an efficient monetary system, subsidises the provision of public goods and supports national capital in international markets.

These functions are not seen as unimportant by the traditional economists. Even diehard monetarists would admit the importance of the first two, Keynesians would endorse all four. But economists still fight shy of incorporating a fully articulated theory of the state within their analyses of macroeconomic behaviour. The state is sometimes regarded as a household or a firm, sometimes as a political agent, sometimes as a referee or umpire. But justification for these assumptions are rare and the nature of the state is thus one of a number of factors that economic analysis takes as given and prior to its theoretical analysis. This leaves little room for developing an understanding of the changing economic role of the State—and also of EIOs which are after all interstate bodies—within different international economic systems.

The modern international economy necessitates some state regulation not only for the provision of such public goods as economic security, a stable international monetary and trading system and physical resources which are the 'common heritage of mankind' (such as space and the oceans) but also for the growth and sustenance of the most highly developed industrial conglomerates. The need of US based TNCs for state support has been graphically illustrated by MacEvan who shows that the post war expansion of these firms is explained by the growth of foreign markets. 'Instead of being aggressive actors using their technology and capital to transform economies, (US TNCs) follow markets as they grow not creating new avenues of prosperity.'[19] The role of state policy in sustaining market expansion is documented in the case of the East Asian states by Evans and Alizadeh who note that 'the state mediated internal and external relations, planned investment and technological advance, guided industrial structure changes enabling these countries to industrialize so successfully'.[20] The state's role was particularly crucial in dealing with TNCs in highly imperfect technology markets and in the development of dynamic comparative advantage.[21] Firms in Western Europe, Japan and the United States clearly recognise the importance of state support in sustaining their corporate strategies. Today both declining (such as automobile and steel) and advanced (such as electronics) industries are dominated by business-based pressure groups which systematically seek to influence policy in Washington, Tokyo and Brussels. The number of business lobbying groups in Washington has grown from about 600 in 1974 to almost 2000 by 1980 while their contributions to members of Congress rose from $13 million to $60 million over the same period.[22] As one observer has noted: 'more than ever pricing and production decisions are arrived at not with the help of Adam Smith's invisible hand but through the interaction of corporate strategists, government planners and managers in the public sector.'[23]

6.3 A FUTURE FOR EIOs

In such a world there is a clear, indeed growing need for the state provision of public goods at the international level. This brings us to the second major objection to the neo-realists' attack on EIOs. Neo-realists argue that public goods such as international economic security can only be provided by a hegemonic power. However most observers—including perhaps a majority of neo-realists—would agree that the United States is a declining hegemonic power and there are no obvious successors.

It is generally recognised that hegemonic leaders cannot sustain their position indefinitely. The outflow of capital and technology, the growth of structural rigidities within the economy, high and rising military costs for sustaining political security within the international system—all these factors tend to erode hegemonic power and work towards a multi-polarization of international influence. An important contribution that the hegemonic power makes towards sustaining an international system is that it voluntarily assumes a disproportionate share of the operational costs of that system. It acts as a lender of last resort[24] and tolerates the imposition of protectionist measures *vis-à-vis* its exports. As the US share of world GNP has declined, it has shown an increased reluctance to bear a disproportionate share of the cost involved in the management of the international trading and monetary system. This is reflected for example in the US refusal to participate in sharing the losses which might accrue from the operation of an IMF-based substitution account which could contribute towards enhancing the stability of the international monetary system.[25] A substitution account has not yet been established within the IMF. But the failure of leading Western powers to agree on this issue cannot be interpreted as irrefutable evidence of the thesis that a hegemon is indispensible for the provision of international public goods. The substitution account represented an attractive option to

Western central banks during 1977 and 1978 because the dollar was weak in those years and currency diversification without unduly disturbing the operation of foreign exchange markets was becoming an increasingly important objective. Once the dollar strengthened, little urgency was attached to the substitution account negotiations. Gowa—who analyzed the substitution account negotiations and regards their inconclusivity as partial vindication of the position of the hegemonic school—recognizes that the substitution account did not represent a 'criticial' case.[26]

International public goods can be provided by non-hegemonic actors. Much of the literature on collective goods argues that international public goods such as economic security can be provided by relatively small country groupings with common interests and perceptions. Moreover, as Hardin points out, collective goods may be provided by 'explicit contracting' or by 'contracting by convention': the latter implies co-ordinating international action through unwritten agreements to accept certain norms of behaviour and operational procedures.[27] Collective goods, such as international monetary stability can be provided—indeed have been so provided since 1971—through 'convention contraction' among influential nation states.

It is clear that consent to provide a collective good within the international economy will depend upon a convergence of interests and perceptions of the leading economic powers. Ruggie has argued that the international economic system devised to promote 'embedded liberalism' at the end of the Second World War, continues to survive, despite the decline of American economic hegemony because new rules and institutions have been created to sustain it, and that as long as the commitment to 'embedded liberalism' endures, Western economies and Japan will continue to jointly provide support for its operation.[28] The extent to which these countries will be willing to undertake collective management for the provision of international public goods will depend crucially upon their level of support to the system.

Different views have been expressed about the possibility of the survival of the essence of the Breton woods based international economic system. Ruggie considers the main threat to the system to be emerging from 'the resurgent ethos of liberal capitalism'.[29] Buzan believes that in the absence of a hegemon 'a large scale interdependent international economy cannot develop in the essentially hostile environment of the anarchic international political system. The essence of the problem is that a liberal economy (cannot) organise itself on a scale that far outreaches the level of political organization available in the highly fragmented state system.'[30] Buzan argues that in the political environment characteristic of the 1980s a bloc mercantilist system could be a workable alternative to international economic anarchy. In his view existing economic blocs could be large enough to provide their members sufficient resources and markets. The new mercantalism would be benign, welfare-pursuing objectives would take precedence in the blocs. Within such a system the scope for international organization would be mainly limited to the co-ordination of international trade and monetary policies in Buzan's view.[31] If 'embeded liberalism' is to endure, EIOs would have to play a key role in sustaining consenus on norms and implementing rules and policies based upon these norms in a world characterized by the multipolarisation of power.

It is clear that EIOs have a role to play in international systems not dominated by hegemons. They may also be instruments of hegemonic international economic policy—as was the case with the IMF in the immediate post second World War period. That national leaders continue to expect EIOs to perform is evident from the stress laid by the Europeans on the need for international negotiation for restructuring the foreign exchange markets, and by the Americans on the need for another round of GATT talks. However attention has shifted from the EIOs as far as international theory is concerned. Integrationists, such as Haas and Lindberg, saw EIOs as of decisive importance in the structuring of international relations during the 1950s.[32] Disillusionment with the EC led to a supercession of the integrationist approach and the emergence of the interdependence paradigm which predicted a decline in the importance of 'centralized institutions' at the international level.[33] The interdependence school sees this as resulting from the down grading of market objectives in national policies and uncertainty about how different spheres of policy making relate to each other. But in denying the absence of a hierarchy of insues, interests and actors within the international system, integerationists seem to suggest that no priorities whatever can be attached to policies or the methods and instruments by means of which they are pursued. This is clearly untrue at both the domestic and international level. By blurring the distinction between the process and the subjects of international organizations (the IOs) the integerationists have come perilously close to denying the existence of any element of order in the international system. They have few explanations to offer for the continued existence of old EIOs or the emergence of new ones[34] and although they expect that the horizontal structures of international organization (increased interaction among domestic bureaucrats) will replace vertical and centralized IOs, they do not clearly identify issues in which this is likely to happen—centralized institutions continue to be particularly important for agricultural management within the EC, while this is clearly less so in the case of energy policy. Predicting that 'everything is up for grabs' as Haas does,[35] is not an adequate basis for conceptualizing the processes of economic interaction among the leading Western powers in an international environment characterized by a declining hegemon. Within such an environment Western countries will continue to make use of EIOs as a basis for negotiation, formulation and execution of international public policies. The forms and structure of international economic organization will however be influenced by the substantive context of the policies being negotiated. As long as existing market imperfections exist it is reasonable to believe that a decline in the operational efficiency of existing EIOs will lead to a decline in the provision of international public goods. Given a rise in the demand for such goods—a demand sustained by the internationalisation of capital, technological progress and increased communication—and the increasing inability of individual states to provide them,[36] the future does not look entirely bleak for the EIOs within the Western world.

What of the EIOs that are primarily concerned with the structuring of North-South economic relationships? During the 1960s and particularly during the 1970s Third World political elites made a concerted effort to use the EIOs within

the system to restructure these relationships. Many de-
pendance theorists—e.g. Peter Evans[37]—recognize and attempt to theorize the role of the state in sustaining economic
policies that restructure peripheral economies within the world
system. Yet very little attention has been paid to the formation
of alliances among Third World elites in international
economic forums. Political explanations for the survival of
these alliances have been widely available but an analysis of the
alternative policy and institutional opportunites available to
Third World rulers within the international economy are rare.
Even if it is assumed that the present stalemate in the North-
South dialogue is likely to become a permanent one does it
make sense to dismantle UNCTAD and disband the Group of
77? How many Third World national elites can hope to develop
the type of privileged bilateral relationships that characterized
US relations with Taiwan and South Korea and has been of
significance in sustaining the development strategies of these
countries.[38] One suspects that this is likely to be true for only a
handful of LDCs. Developing country elites will therefore not
easily abandon their commitment to EIOs. They will continue
to use these institutions for interest aggregation and articulation and for negotiating specific deals. They are unlikely to
accept an unrestricted opening up of their economies to
'market forces' for this will mean the disappearance of many
crucial economic sectors—such as capitals goods-producing
branches in India and China—and an erosion of national
sovereignty. Third World elites are unenthusiastic about the
rehabilitation of colonial economic policy on a global scale
because such a rehabilitation will deprive them of most of the
benefits of political independence.

The rehabilitation of colonialism cannot be restricted to the
economic sphere of the international system. The economic
'opening up' policies—symbolized by the stand by agreements
of the IMF and the structural adjustment programmes of the
World Bank must be supplemented by the deployment of
political force and in many cases the physical presence of
colonial armies. But a re-conquest of the Third World is
neither a necessary not a particularly efficient means for
ensuring Western supremacy. It is seems unlikely therefore
that the liberal economic order of the nineteenth century will

be 'born again' in the twenty-first century.

Third World ruling elites will continue to have some opportunities for re-negotiating economic deals at the international level and the majority of them will continue to find strength in unity. EIOs provide a natural home for sustaining this unity at both the global and regional level and using it as a basis for winning support for Third World elites. EIOs might however be irrelevant for Third World rulers who develop a strong political relationship with a super power, such as the Afghanistan, El Salvador and Israeli regimes and for regimes which enjoy popular support and have little need for super-power backing such as Albania, Iran and Nicaragua. The majority of Third World rulers will continue to need Western economic assistance and will therefore continue to seek an improvement in the terms on which it is made available. EIOs will remain important channels for negotiating and executing deals for regulating economic transaction between North and South.[39]

It is thus appropriate to take EIOs seriously and to attempt to study their potential, environmental impact and organizational performance. In the following chapters I have analyzed the development of the United Nations Conference on Trade and Development in the first twenty years of its existence on the basis of some of the theoretical work outlined in Part 1.

NOTES

1. Van Kleffens, E.A. 'The place of law in international relations', *United Nations Review* No. 1 (1955), p. 23.
2. Van Kleffens, *op. cit.,* p. 23.
3. Connybeare, A.C. 'International organisation and the theory of property rights', *IO*, Vol. 32 No. 3 (1980), pp. 307–34.
4. For an elaborate discussion of Neo-Realism see Ashely, R. 'The poverty of neorealism', *IO*, Vol. 38 No. 2 (1984), pp. 225–86.
5. Quoted in Walzer, M. *Just and Unjust Wars*, Basic Books, New York (1977) p. 4.
6. Hobbes, T. *Leviathan*, ed. M. Oakshott. Collier, New York, 1962. For a recent summary of Hobbes' view on this theme, see Hansaon, D. 'Thomas Hobbe' highway to peace', *IO*, Vol. 38 No. 2 (1984), pp. 329–54.

7. Hanson, *op. cit.*, p. 354.
8. Waltz, K. *Theory of International Politics*, Reading, Mass., Addison-Wesley, (1979), p. 91.
9. *Ibid*, p. 91.
10. Krasner, S. 'Regimes and the limits of realism', *IO*, Vol. 36 No. 2 (1982). p. 499. See also the discussion on regimes in this volume, Ch. 2.
11. Asheley, R. 'The poverty of neo realism' p. 246.
12. Toumanof, P. 'A positive analysis of the theory of market failure', *Kyklos* Vol. 37 No. 4 (1984), pp. 529–41.
13. Coase, R. 'The problem of social cost' *Journal of Law and Economics,* October 1960, pp. 1–44. This argument is elaborated in ch. 2.
14. Epstein, B. and Newfarmer, R. 'Imperfect international markets and monopolistic prices to developing countries: a case study' *Cambridge Journal of Economics*, Vol. 6, No. 1 pp. 33–52 (1982).
15. For the United States see, e.g. White, L. 'What has been happening to aggregate concentration in the United States?', *Journal of Industrial Economics*, Vol. 29, No. 2 (1981), pp. 223–30. For the U.K., see Haghes, A. and Kumar, S. 'Recent trends in aggregate concentration in the UK economy', *Cambridge Journal of Economics*, No. 8, (1984), pp. 238–250.
16. Discussed in Jessop, B. 'Recent theories of the capitalist state' *Cambridge Journal of Economics*, Vol. 1, (1977) pp. 353–73. Needless to say this is not the only conception of the state to be found in the work of these authors.
17. See, e.g. Gough, I. 'State expenditure in advanced capitalism', *New Left Review*, No. 92 (1975), pp. 36–64.
18. Cheprakov, V. (ed.) *State Monopoly Capitalism,* Progress Publishers, Moscow (1969).
19. MacEvan, I. 'Unstable empire: US business in the international economy', *IDS Bulletin*, Vol. 16, No. 1 (1985), pp. 40–6.
20. Evans, D. and Alizadeh, P. 'Trade, industrialisation and the visible hand', *Journal of Development Studies,* Vol. 24, No. 1 (Oct 1984), p. 27.
21. Evans and Alizadeh, *op. cit.*, p. 36.
22. *International Herald Tribune*, 5 April 1982.
23. Ballance, R., Ansari, J. and Singer, H. *The International Economy and Industrial Development,* Wheatsheaf, Brighton (1982) p. 224.
24. Kindleberger stresses this point in Kindleberger, C. *The World In Depression 1929–1939.* University of California Press (1973) pp. 291–2.
25. Negotiations for establishing the account collapsed during 1980.
26. Gowa, J. 'Hegemons, IOs and markets: the case of the substitution account', *IO*, Vol. 38 No. 4 (1984), p. 682.
27. Hardin, R. *Collective Action,* Baltimore, Johns Hopkins University Press, 1982.
28. Ruggie, J.G. 'International Regimes, Transaction and change', *IO*, Vol. 36, No. 2, pp. 379–415. The concept of embedded liberalism is discussed in Ch. 2.
29. Ruggie, *op. cit.*, p. 413.
30. Buzan, B. 'Economic structure and international security: the limits of

the liberal case', *IO*, Vol. 38 No. 4, pp. 617–18.

31. Buzan, *op. cit.*, pp. 608–16.
32. As did the classical functionalists a decade earlier.
33. Haas, E. *The Obsolescence of Regional Integration Theory,* Research Series No. 25, University of California, Berkeley (1975) p. 18.
34. This criticism is stressed in Nau, H. 'From integration to inter-dependence', *IO*, Vol. 33 No. 1 (1979), pp. 141–3.
35. Haas, *op. cit.*, p. 23.
36. For one assessment of the limits faced by individual national governments as suppliers of international public goods, see Stewart, M. *Controlling the Economic Future: Policy Dilemmas in a Shrinking World,* Wheatsheaf, Brighton and MIT Press, Cambridge, Mass.
37. Evans, P. *Dependent Development: The Alliance of Multinational, State and Local Capital in Brazil,* Princeton, University Press, Princeton, New Jersey, (1979).
38. On this see, Evans, D. and Alizadeh, P. 'Trade, industrialisation and the visible hand', *Journal of Developmental Studies*, Vol. 24 No. 1 (1984) pp. 28–31.
39. EIOs can also contribute towards structuring South-South transactions. Many regional economic groupings have been established within Asia, Africa and Latin America. Their potential is, however, as yet largely unrealised.

PART II: The United Nations Conference on Trade and Development 1964–83: an Empirical Investigation

Part II attempts to use some of the theoretical approaches discussed in Part I to study the impact and the organizational development of an EIO. I hope to demonstrate that a systemic evaluation of EIO performance and policies can be undertaken on the basis of generally available publications. The choice of analytical frameworks in the following chapters has in the main been determined by information available in these publications. Had I chosen to study another, say, the IMF or the European Community institutions, the questions asked in this part would, of course, have been different. They would have been determined by the nature of the organizational task of the EIO being studied and the information available in its official and semi-official publications. The findings of such a study would be modified by direct access to the 'inner life' of the EIO

UNCTAD has the reputation of being a relatively 'open' EIO. It has been the focus of much international attention. Over the last twenty years it has played an important role in the structuring of the dialogue between the South–UNCTAD's 'Group of 77' and the North–the Group B. It has been 'resurrected' and 'written off' in the world press at the beginning and end of each of its triannual conferences. A selective examination of the organization is thus possible and, hopefully, fruitful. This is undertaken in the following pages. Other EIOs may also be studied within the context of broadly similar analytical frameworks.

7 UNCTAD: Environment and Impact

This chapter seeks to study the influence of environmental characteristics on the development of UNCTAD's organizational ideology and to assess the organizational performance of UNCTAD over the period of 1964–1983.

The framework for analysis described in Haas's *Beyond the Nation State*[1] (and outlined at the end of Chapter 2) is utilized to address the question of the relationship between environmental characteristics and the formulation of UNCTAD's organizational ideology. I begin by asking:

(a)   What were the characteristics of the international environment at the inception of UNCTAD in 1964?
(b)   What were the shared objectives of UNCTAD constituents at Geneva in 1964, and was the secretariat's interpretation of the original mandate realistic—that is, capable of building viable interest coalitions which could sustain UNCTAD, and press for task expansion?

7.1 ENVIRONMENTAL CHARACTERISTICS:1964

UNCTAD was created with a view to restructuring the international relations of rich countries with the poor countries. Our analysis of the environment at the time of UNCTAD's inception, must enable us to understand the impulses which generated a demand for the sort of restructuring embodied in the UNCTAD ideology. In this section I attempt to isolate those environmental characteristics which bear upon the goals being pursued by rich and poor countries in their interaction with each other. What was the extent of the involvement of the Western countries in the affairs of the Third World? Why did the Western powers sustain this pattern of association? What was the extent of the dependence of the Third World and of sections within it on the West? What did the Third World expect of the West, in its quest for modernization? What was the extent of cohesion in the policies and responses of the West, and of the poor countries? In order to answer these questions I will specify the relevant characteristics of the different groups of countries.

Environmental Characteristics of the West[2]
The attitude adopted by the West, in Geneva, was influenced by a number of factors: Firstly, the Western countries in general had a strong interest in maintaining intact the economic system which had been created after the Second World War. This international economic system had made possible the unquestioned leadership of the USA, on the one hand, and the spectacular economic recovery of Europe and Japan, on the other. The Third World played little part in the management of the international economic order, and any move to redress this imbalance was likely to affect adversely the position of the West within the system.[3] Individual Western countries were, of course, concerned with these issues in varying degrees, the smaller, less influential states, such as Belgium, Denmark, Italy and New Zealand, having less at stake than the US, UK and France.

Secondly, the nature of the relationship of the Western countries to the countries of the Third World was also likely to be of significance. Some Western countries, such as the UK, France and the Netherlands, had had extensive colonial possessions in the past. This had led to the development of an intricate web of trade and investment relationships, which continued to link the former 'mother country' to her former colonies. The US, on the other hand, was the Western power which had inherited the colonial responsibilites of the European powers (and of Japan). After the Second World War, it willingly took upon itself the task of 'policing the free world'. Hence its interest in strategic and military aspects of the restructuring of North–South relationships was bound to be more pronounced than that of its Western allies.

Finally, a restructuring of the economic relationship between Western and Third World countries was also likely to affect the economic position of groups of producers and consumers within the Western countries. If major trade concessions to the poor countries were made at Geneva, for example, the consumers of primary commodities and light manufactured goods would be likely to benefit: producers of these goods would stand to lose, as would those workers who were employed in the agricultural sector, or in specific light industries. An expansion in multilateral or bilateral aid would be a victory for interest groups (such as multinational corporations, humanitarian and religious organizations, etc. which usually support aid programmes. Bearing these considerations in mind, I estimated the indicators identified in Table 7.1 to evaluate the characteristics of the Western countries in 1964.

In the year 1964, there were considerable differences in the economic characteristics of the Western countries. The GNP of some substantially exceeded that of others. Growth rates differed, though the standard deiation of indicator (ii) was small. There were large differences in the voting powers of Western countries in the international economic organizations. Trading patterns did not differ significantly, but aid and investment patterns did. In addition, the influence of groups likely to be affected by the granting of trade and aid concessions to the Third World tended to vary within the Western countries.

The US was, in terms of GNP, the richest Western country. The European countries and Japan had been growing at a faster rate than the US, and European integration had provided the impetus for the erosion of the economic power of the US. This was partially reflected in the distribution of voting power within the IMF and the IBRD. The combined voting strength of the EC (the original six member states) exceeded that of the US in both these organizations. This would indicate that a major revision in the rules of international economic management would be resisted, not only by the US, but by other major Western countries as well. Up to the middle 1960s, the economic policies of the Western countries were significantly interrelated. This is revealed by the very high proportion of intergroup trade (relative to total trade) of the Western countries. Most Western countries tended to trade mainly with other Western countries. Japan was the only exception within the group. However, there had been a rapid growth of regional trade within Europe, which tended to reduce the dependence of

Table 7.1: *Mean and standard deviation of the values of the indicators of environmental characteristics of Group B countries*

Indicator			Mean	Standard deviation
(i)	GNP	(a)	99666.6	158943.
(ii)	Rate of growth of GNP	(b)	4.5	1.42
(iii)	Voting power in international economic organizations	(c)	3.2	5.93
(iv)	Interregional trade	(d)	79.6	9.38
(v)	Arms trade with the Third World	(e)	13.9	15.49
(vi)	Exports to Third World	(f)	13.49	8.86
(vii)	Imports from Third World	(g)	14.49	8.98
(viii)	Imports from Third World of food plus raw materials	(h)	33.04	6.75
(ix)	Import from Third World of fuel	(h)	65.3	11.26
(x)	Volume of official development assistance	(i)	420.9	910.23
(xi)	Official development assistance as % of GNP		0.32	0.24
(xii)	Private investment	(j)	260.6	421.4
(xiii)	Private investment as % of GNP		0.26	0.31
(xiv)	Share of agriculture in GDP	(k)	11.07	5.21
(xv)	% of total labour force in agriculture		18.6	9.87
(xvi)	Public expenditure on agriculture as % of agricultural GDP		19.5	6.16
(xvii)	% of total labour in light manufacturing industry		41.06	10.55

Notes
(a)   In $US million for 1964.
(b)   Annual average over the period 1950–65 (percentages).
(c)   Average % of total votes in IMF and IBRD, 1964.
(d)   % of total trade of individual Western countries accounted for by trade to other Western bloc countries, 1964.
(e)   Exports of arms to the Third World as % of total exports of arms by West, 1965.
(f)   Exports to Third World as % of all exports by Western countries, 1964.
(g)   Imports from Third World as % of all imports by Western countries, 1964.
(h)   Imports from Third World as % of imports of specific commodity, 1964.
(i)   Disbursed official development assistant $US millions, 1964.
(j)   Direct foreign investment accumulated assets, 1964.
(k)   Agricultural produce as % of GDP, 1964.

Sources
Nos. (i) and (ii)   Taylor, C.L. and Mudson, M.C. *World Handbook of Political and Social Indicators,* Yale UP, New Haven (1966).
No. (iii)   *IMF Annual Report* Washington (1965).
Nos. (iv), (vi), (vii)   IMF *Directions of Trade* Washington (1964) Country tables.
No. (v)   Stockholm International Peace Research Institute *The Arms Trade with the Third World* SIPRI, Stockholm (1972).
Nos. (viii), (ix)   General Agreement on Tariffs and Trade *International Trade* (Annual) 1965, Geneva (1966).
Nos. (x), (xi), (xii), (xiii) OECD *Development Co-operation* (Annual) 1972, Paris (1972).
Nos. (xiv), (xv), (xvi)   Johnson, D.G. *World Agriculture in Discovery* Fontance (1973).
No. (xvii)   UN *The Growth of World Industry* 1953–65 New York (1966) (Country tables).

these countries on the US. Counterbalancing this, however, was the very rapid growth of US investment in Europe, and some European investment in the US.[4] Thus, the predominance of the US within the Western group stands out; although this predominance is clearly diminishing. It would have been unlikely in 1964 that other Western countries would have initiated or supported an international initiative not endorsed by the US.

Indicators (v)–(xiii) describe the nature of the relationship between the West and the Third World. The US was far and away the leading Western power in respect of military involvement in the Third World. The US had inherited the post-colonial responsibilities of these countries, and, particularly after the Indo-China confrontation of the early 1950s, the Suez crisis and the Algerian war of independence, both Britain and France seemed reconciled to the change. In analysing trade relations, we see that the United States, the United Kingdom and Japan are the major trading partners of the Third World. The EC and the EFTA countries (except for Britain and France) were generally unimportant. Not only did they account for a relatively small proportion of the total Western trade with the Third World, but their exports to the poor countries were also growing at a very slow pace. The US and Japan were most dependent on the Third World for imports of raw materials, fuels and primary goods. The dependence of the continental countries was much smaller. The US, France and Britain were the major aid donors. Aid contributions of the Western countries were insignificant. As far as private foreign investment was concerned, the US was once again the leading Western country, but the UK, France and West Germany also had significant interests. The overall picture which emerges illustrates the fact that the US alone was the key Western country as far as the Third World was concerned. No other Western country could be expected to take an interest in susbstantial changes in the economic relations between the poor countries and the rest of the world.

Indicators (xiv)–(xvii) identify further causes of the reluctance shown by Western countries towards the restructuring of international economic relationships. Though the share of agriculture within the economy of Western nations was generally small, the political leverages of the farming sector was considerable. This is indicated by the generally high level of agricultural subsidization prelevant in Western countries. Moreover, the agricultural sector still employed a significant proportion of the total labour force of most Western countries. Similarly, the proportion of labour employed in the labour-intensive light-manufactured-goods industry was also high. A liberalization of trade relations with the Third World, or a granting of trade concessions, would inevitably lead to a considerable expansion of agricultural commodity imports and light-manufactured-goods imports from the poor countries. This was bound to affect adversely a sizable proportion of Western employees and employers. It was also likely to be of considerable benefit to consumers in the Western countries, but consumers carry less political weight than producing interests do.

The general political environment of the Western bloc, in the years leading up to the creation of UNCTAD, may be briefly mentioned. Despite the Berlin Wall crisis in 1961, and the Cuban crisis in 1962, the Partial Nuclear Test Ban Treaty was signed between the US and the USSR in 1963. This signalled a relaxation in the cold war and a consequent loosening of the Western alliance system which had been formed in the late 1940s. This loosening was helped by the growing integration of the European states and a significant reduction in the power of the US. However, when UNCTAD was established in 1964, these trends were only just beginning to take shape, and major deviations from the policies of the Western group leader by the smaller (European) countries were clearly not likely.[5]

Environmental Characteristics of the Third World
The environmental characteristics of the Third World in 1964 may briefly be summarized:

(a)   the poor countries were generally ruled by elites trained in and by the West, but Western-type political institutions were not the sources of decision making;

(b)   social mobility was low and there was considerable ethnic and linguistic fractionalization;

(c) there were substantial differences in GNP levels, and the GNPs of the richer countries within the Third World had been growing more rapidly than those of the poorer countries since 1954;

(d) there were differences in production structure: the Latin American countries were much more industrialized than the rest of the Third World, where agriculture dominated the economy;

(e) trade was generally not a high proportion of GNP: most LDCs exported a few agricultural commodities, and tended to trade with a small number of developed countries;

(f) LDCs tended to encourage industrialization and discriminate against agriculture: economic policies failed to stimulate saving and investment, which were low;

(g) the poor LDCs seemed to be crucially dependent on foreign aid—which at times amounted to more than 20 per cent of their total import expenditure: the richer LDCs did not attract a great deal of aid, but they obtained most of the private investment that went to the Third World; and

(h) income disparities between various economic groups within the Third World countries were very wide, and there was no indication that these differences were being reduced.

7.2 THE IMPACT OF ENVIRONMENTAL CHARACTERISTICS ON UNCTAD'S ORGANIZATIONAL IDEOLOGY

The UNCTAD ideology, as embodied in the General and Special Principles adopted at Geneva, was accepted and endorsed unanimously by the Group of 77. Indeed the Final Act has been described as 'a program or manifesto of the developing countries'.[6] The evolution of this common attitude was a response to existing opportunities. The prospect of the conference brought about the unity of the '77', and not vice versa. The loose coalition, which became an organized group, emerged out of differing and not always complementary interests, the '77' acting together, only once the conference was assured, and the preparations virtually completed. Ever since the Bandung conference, Afro-Asian solidarity had been championed by 'progressive' regimes within the Third World. In the early 1960s, these moves received greater impetus because of the granting of independence to a large number of African states, and the adoption of the 1960s as the 'Decade of Development' by the UN General assembly. The Latin American countries also became interested in Third World solidarity as a consequence of the launching of the Alliance for Progress. Yet, up to 1961, the Latin American countries were largely uninterested in the proposed conference on trade to be held under the auspices of the United Nations. The US's own attitude towards the conference determined the Latin American response. The group of 75 (later 77) came into existence in the autumn of 1963, and, once formed, it 'accepted a measure of discipline that impressed everyone'.[7] This was despite the fact that specific short-term interests within the Third World tended to diverge, and it was clear from the outset that, in the immediate future, the relatively more advanced developing countries stood to gain more than the backward ones if trade policies were reformulated in accordance with the general and special principles adopted at Geneva.

The cornerstone of Third World unity was the organizational ideology of UNCTAD. This unity was made possible by the environmental characteristics of the poor countries. We have seen above that most poor countries were ruled by elites trained along Western lines, who had not succeeded in creating within their countries popular institutions which could be used to reorientate socio-economic relationships in accordance with their aspirations. Despite the considerable diversity in economic structure and performance, there was striking similarity in the political characteristics of Third World states. The development policies pursued by the Third World had much in common. There was a general emphasis on industrialization and urbanization (this was seen as synonymous with modernization). These policies have usually been unsuccessful in generating domestic surplus mobilization of a magnitude adequate to make possible self-sustained growth.

Hence, foreign help—in the form of trade concessions and development aid—to supplement savings efforts and stabilize fluctuating export earnings was crucial.

These factors illustrate and explain the attitude of the developing countries at Geneva. The organizational ideology won their support, because it formulated concepts—the trade gap, the need for a new international division of labour, etc.—which shifted the responsibility for underdevelopment from the poor to the rich countries, and maintained that trade concessions and increased financial assistance were essential if the Third World was to make further progress. The Third World regimes welcomed an approach which implicitly downgraded the importance of domestic policies, and argued that underdevelopment was inevitable as long as trade reforms were not enacted. Because of the inability of most Third World regimes to affect and alter domestic structual relationships directly and to institutionalize revolutionary changes of the sort which had occurred in Meiji Japan or in Bolshevik Russia, external support became vitally important. Moreover, support granted through trade concessions was much more acceptable than was increased foreign investment or aid; for the latter was seen as impinging upon the national sovereignty of the Third World countries.

This implied that UNCTAD's task expansion was sought by the '77', but the specific substantive content of the programme was allowed to be determined by the secretariat on the basis of the broad principles enshrined in the Final Act adopted at the Geneva Conference.

The programme priorities of the secretariat should have taken into account the attitude of the Western countries towards the organizational ideology, if it desired task expansion. The Western countries were not unified in the way in which the '77' were, in the years prior to the conference, or at the conference itself. The decision of the US, taken in 1962, to support the conference, was viewed with surprise and a certain degree of resentment by France and the other EC countries. The latter were especially reluctant because of the forthcoming Kennedy Round and the proposed enlargement of the EC. The Western countries, were, however, united in their determination to countenance a minimal modification of the existing institutional network regulating international trade and finance. On substantive questions, on the other hand, the Western countries differed frequently. Concessions in the field of trade and investment acceptable to some were unacceptable to other. Of the fifteen general and thirteen special principles adopted at Geneva, only three were adopted unanimously and without abstentions. Some Western countries either voted against, or abstained from voting, on all other occasions. Nearly all special recommendations adopted by roll-call votes were contested (through opposition and/or abstention) by some Group B countries. On recommendations accepted by show of hands, a number of Western countries recorded their dissent through official observations and reservations.

There was thus variation in the voting behaviour of the individual Western countries. The US voted against thirteen general and special principles and abstained on eight; on the other hand, New Zealand did not oppose any principle and abstained on only four occasions. The other developed Western countries were fairly evenly distributed between these extremes.

The same information can be viewed from another angle. The principles ranged from those unanimously adopted (e.g. those on special measures for landlocked countries and on increased technical assistance) to those vehemently opposed by the Group B countries (e.g. the principles on the granting of non-reciprocal trade concessions to the less developed countries, and on the stabilization of the prices of primary commodities). Group B countries ranged fairly evenly between these two extremes in their attitude to most other principles.

Table 7.2 summarizes the voting record of the major Group B countries on all votes recorded in the text and annexes of the Final Act document. It is clear that when the entire voting record at Geneva is taken into consideration, there is substantial variation in the voting behaviour of the Group B countries. The dispersion of votes is considerably greater in the votes on the specific recommendation of the conference. Whereas the Group B countries were more or less united in their opposition to certain general features of UNCTAD's organizational ideology, they were not so united in their opposition to the specific reforms. This conclusion is important, for it shows that, despite the avowed intention of the developed countries to countenance UNCTAD only if it maintained a forum character, they were in fact not prepared to adopt a flexible approach towards the trade and development philosophy of the Third World. On the other hand, the developed countries were not so united in their opposition to specific policies; hence, contrary to their stated position, they were enhancing the role of UNCTAD as a negotiating body. This may have served as a pointer to UNCTAD's organizational leadership. Prebisch saw UNCTAD as a pressure group, and hence placed great emphasis on the enunciation of general principles, which were the basis of UNCTAD's organizational ideology. The attitude of the developed Western countries at Geneva seems to demonstrate that these principles could only be rendered acceptable to the Western countries if a number of short-term policy changes were negotiated, which facilitated the re-ordering of international economic relationships in accordance with the UNCTAD ideology. The debate on principles was bound to be futile in the short run. The global task of UNCTAD was to affect its environment in such a way that, in the foreseeable future, its organizational ideology became meaningful and attractive to the Western countries.

What were the determinants of the voting pattern evidenced by the Group B countries at Geneva? In order to answer this question I related the voting scores of group B countries to their environmental characteristics listed above. The voting scores were computed in accordance with the method outlined by Alker and Russett in their study of voting behaviour at the UN General Assembly.[8] Scores were assigned in accordance with the ranks held by each state on a voting occasion recorded in the Final Act and Report. Support (i.e. 'yes') received the lowest rank, abstention a higher rank and opposition the highest rank. The rank assigned to a country in each group is the average rank in the group. These group average ranks are subtracted from the average rank of all countries voting. The results are then standardized so that the new voting scores have a mean of 0 and an averaged squared value of 1.[9] This method of calculating voting scores is preferable to the more straightforward one of assigning a +1 score for the 'no', a 0 for

Table 7.2:   *Voting record of major Group B countries recorded in the final act of UNCTAD I (1964)*

Country	Number of votes against and abstentions on		
	Principles	Substantive recommendation	Total
Australia	16	20	36
Austria	10	10	20
Belgium	13	22	35
Canada	18	19	37
Denmark	10	11	21
France	13	17	30
West Germany	15	13	28
Italy	13	11	24
Iceland	13	11	24
Ireland	13	17	30
Japan	14	10	24
New Zealand	4	5	9
Norway	11	11	22
Netherlands	15	16	31
Sweden	12	12	24
UK	16	17	33
USA	21	21	42
Mean	13.35	14.29	27.64
Std. deviation	3.57	4.58	7.68

Source: UNCTAD I, *Proceedings,* I, (1964) pp.18–65.

abstention, and a –1 for a 'yes', because this technique puts those abstaining against the pressure of a sizable majority, closer to those who said 'no' than to those who voted in the affirmative.[10]

Table 7.3 gives the partial correlation coefficients of the voting scores of the group B countries, with their environmental characteristics. Voting scores have been disaggregated into votes on 'principle' resolutions and 'specific recommendation' resolutions. Table 7.3 shows that a significant positive correlation exists between voting scores on the one hand and GNP, voting power in EIOs, aid given and private investment on the other. The higher the GNP, the greater the voting power, the bigger the investment and aid contribution of a group B country, the greater is the likelihood that it

Table 7.3: *Partial correlation coefficients of voting scores with environmental characteristics of group B countries at UNCTAD I*

Environmental characteristics		Voting score principle	Voting score specific recommendation	Aggregate voting score
(i)	GNP	0.6713 (0.002)	0.5327 (0.016)	0.4904 (0.023)
(ii)	Rate of growth of GNP	—0.0461 (0.431)	—0.3331 (0.092)	—0.4315 (0.047)
(iii)	Voting power in IEO	0.7207 (0.001)	0.5864 (0.007)	0.5185 (0.017)
(iv)	Inter-regional trade	0.1369 (0.301)	0.1618 (0.268)	0.2679 (0.150)
(v)	Arms trade with Third World	—0.4907 (0.023)	—0.2833 (0.136)	—0.1633 (0.268)
(vi)	Exports to Third World	0.1517 (0.281)	—0.0370 (0.452)	—0.0361 (0.446)
(vii)	Imports from Third World	0.2524 (0.165)	0.0578 (0.413)	0.0012 (0.499)
(viii)	Food and raw material imports from Third World	0.1566 (0.275)	0.0393 (0.441)	0.0368 (0.442)
(ix)	Fuel imports from Third World	0.3025 (0.119)	0.2200 (0.199)	0.0502 (0.425)
(x)	Vol. of aid	0.7315 (0.001)	0.6580 (0.003)	0.5578 (0.010)
(xi)	Aid as % of GNP	0.5925 (0.007)	0.6431 (0.003)	0.6063 (0.009)
(xii)	Vol. of private investment in Third World	0.4801 (0.026)	0.4483 (0.036)	0.3525 (0.083)
(xiii)	Private investment as % of GNP	0.2113 (0.208)	0.2950 (0.036)	0.1668 (0.267)
(xiv)	Share of agriculture in GNP	—0.3288 (0.099)	—0.2378 (0.144)	—0.2716 (0.146)
(xv)	% of labour in agriculture	—0.5060 (0.020)	—0.4917 (0.023)	—0.2825 (0.136)
(xvi)	Public expenditure on agriculture as % of agricultural GNP	0.1727 (0.259)	0.2518 (0.199)	0.0710 (0.379)
(xvii)	% of labour in light manufacturing industry	—0.4811 (0.026)	—0.4751 (0.027)	—0.3377 (0.093)

Note: Figures in parentheses are standard errors.

opposed the passage of UNCTAD resolutions. The trade indicators are variously associated with the voting scores. There is a negative relationship between the aggregate voting scores on the one hand and the Third World export indicators but a positive association on the other hand between voting score on principles and the Third World import indicators. However, association between these indicators and voting scores on substantive recommendations is weak—not significantly different from 0 in the case of both indicators (vi) and (vii). This suggests that the impact of trade relations on voting is complex and multidimensional. This would perhaps indicate that trade relations were not important determinants of voting behaviour.

Significant negative association is found between the voting scores, on the one hand, and the growth rate indicator and the indicator measuring the percentage of the total labour force employed in light manufacturing industry, on the other. Barely significant negative association was also estimated between voting scores and indicators measuring agricutlural importance within the economy. We see that on average the more rapidly growing Group B countries tended to favour trade reform along UNCTAD lines.

It is difficult to interpret the economic structure estimates, because of the existence of significant negative association (multi-colinearity) between the GNP indicator and the economic structure indicators, but it may reasonably be argued that the economic structural constraints—the desire to protect agricultural or light manufacturing industry—did not negatively influence the Group B countries at the 1964 UNCTAD conference. The structural characteristics of Group B countries did not determine their response to proposals for trade reform. What did influence this response were the economic power characteristics, and since these were negatively associated with the importance of agriculture and light manufacturing within the economy, economic structure indicators were weakly associated with voting behaviour.

Table 7.3 indicates some differences in the determinants of voting behaviour on principles, on the one hand, and on specific recommendations, on the other. The size of the correlation coefficients of the 'power' indicators (i, iii, x, xii) are higher in relation to voting scores on 'principles' than to voting scores on specific recommendations. This is also true of the economic structure indicators, but whereas the difference in the value of the power indicator coefficients on the two voting patterns is substantial, the difference on the economic structure coefficients is clearly insignificant. Finally, as noted earlier, the difference between the trade coefficients on the 'principle' and the 'recommendations' voting pattern is also considerable. The value of the partial correlation coefficient between the growth rate indicator and the voting scores on 'recommendations' is considerably greater than that for the 'principles' voting scores. This is not, however, true of the difference between the values of the partial correlation coefficients between indicator (xvi) (public expenditure on agriculture as a proportion of agricultural GDP) and the two scores. One may, therefore, conclude that power factors are less signficant, as determinants of voting behaviour on recommendations, than are trade indicators. The growth rate estimator and the estimator of agricultural subsidization are important as determinants of voting behaviour on 'substantive' resolutions.

In order to understand better the relationship between environmental characteristics and voting behaviour, use was made of factor analysis. Tables 7.4 and 7.5 show the rotated factor matrices which were obtained. Total variance in voting behaviour, explained by the environmental characteristics is about 65 per cent for votes on 'principle' resolutions, and 63 per cent for votes on specific recommendations. The two most important factors identified in the tables are factors 1 and 4. Factor 1 accounts for 36 per cent of the variation in voting scores in Table 7.4, and for 46 per cent of the variance in voting behaviour on the 'specific recommendations'. Factor 4 accounts for 12.85 per cent and 13 per cent of the variation in the two sets of votes. Factor 2 accounts for over 15 per cent of the variation in the voting on 'principle' resolutions, but for only 2.25 per cent of the variation of the 'recommendation' resolutions. Factor 3 is unimportant for either of the vote scores.

Factor 1 may best be labelled as the 'economic power' factor. Variables with high loadings on this factor are GNP, voting power in international organizations, investment and aid indicators, and the industrial structure indicators (which are

Table 7.4: *Rotated factor matrix for voting score on 'principle' resolutions*

Environmental characteristics	Factor 1	Factor 2	Factor 3	Factor 4	
(i)	0.73900	0.62981	0.15107	0.06427	
(iii)	0.65566	0.65693	0.90160	0.11662	
(iv)	0.00257	0.14985	0.23401	0.67271	
(v)	0.10310	0.83603	0.08535	0.10051	
(vi)	0.22407	0.60961	0.26037	0.72490	
(vii)	0.13421	0.62507	0.46866	0.46967	
(viii)	0.06416	0.36612	0.85310	0.06360	
(ix)	0.41673	0.03021	0.75259	0.00282	
(x)	0.83198	0.47851	0.18365	0.02830	
(xi)	0.89920	0.08913	0.13191	0.07364	
(xii)	0.74109	0.47216	0.22161	0.25492	
(xv)	0.71477	0.06951	0.05823	0.09740	
(xvi)	0.00779	0.01991	0.26694	0.71568	
(xvii)	0.89929	0.12287	0.18468	0.22998	
Voting score	0.60599	0.39700	0.02590	0.35231	0.64982

Table 7.5: *Rotated factor matrix for voting score on 'recommendations'*

Characteristics	Factor 1	Factor 2	Factor 3	Factor 4	
(i)	0.72443	0.64577	0.15350	0.06064	
(iii)	0.65415	0.64960	0.40254	0.12385	
(iv)	0.00437	0.15705	0.25023	0.69487	
(v)	0.09228	0.83646	0.08131	0.12000	
(vi)	0.20303	0.63668	0.25619	0.70471	
(vii)	0.12614	0.62809	0.46401	0.44727	
(viii)	0.04331	0.38662	0.83546	0.05376	
(ix)	0.39888	0.05752	0.74108	0.01359	
(x)	0.83015	0.48142	0.18841	0.02955	
(xi)	0.90011	0.09790	0.13895	0.08377	
(xii)	0.73283	0.50243	0.21662	0.23387	
(xv)	0.70709	0.06703	0.07397	0.06879	
(xvi)	0.01833	0.06020	0.27768	0.72859	
(xvii)	0.83793	0.14338	0.19298	0.24022	
Voting score	0.68696	0.15606	0.02779	0.36605	0.63105

correlated with GNP). The factor analysis illustrates that the economic power indicators are equally important in the determination of the voting behaviour on both 'principle' and 'recommendation' resolutions. This result is somewhat at variance with the earlier finding (derived from the partial correlation coefficients) that perhaps the 'power factors' were less important in the determination of voting behaviour on recommendation resolutions.

Factor 2, which may be labelled the 'dependency' factor, is important only for voting behaviour on 'principle' resolutions. Indicators with highloadings on this factor are 'arms trade with Third World', 'imports from Third World', 'exports to Third World', and aid and investment indicators. GNP and voting power in EIOs are also heavily loaded on this factor. However, all factors except 'arms trade with Third World' and 'imports from the Third World as a proportion of total imports', are more heavily loaded on some other factors, hence the importance of factor 2 as a determinant of voting behaviour on 'principles' resolutions is mainly a reflection of these two indicators. Strategic considerations are generally unimportant as influences on the voting behaviour of the rich countries on substantive recommendation resolutions.

Factor 3 explains less than 0.7 per cent of the variation in voting behaviour on either type of resolution. The only factors which load on it are the import component indicators.

Factor 4 may be designated as the 'economic policy' factor. It is more important as an influence on variation in 'substantive recommendation' votes than in variation on 'principle' votes. The indicators which load heavily on it, are interregional trade, trade with theThird World as a proportion of total trade, and 'public expenditure on agriculture as a proportion of agricutlural gross domestic product'. We see that the greater the amount of interregional trade in the Western world, and the greater the level of overall sub-sidization, the greater is the opposition to 'principle' and 'recommendation' resolutions at Geneva. However, the Third World export indicator loads negatively on factor 4, so that the greater the amount that a Group B country exports to the Third World, the more likely it would have been to support economic reforms proposed at UNCTAD in 1964.

The major conclusions of the factor analysis may, therefore, be summarized as follows:

(a)   Economic power variables were the main influences governing the voting behaviour of the Group B countries. Economic power is reflected in GNP, voting power in an EIO's volume of investment and aid.

(b)   the economic structure of the developed Western countries did not directly play an important part in inhibiting the granting of trade concessions in 1964, though there is some evidence of the impact of protectionism, as both intraregional trade and agricultural subsidization are important determinants of voting behaviour on both 'principle' and 'recommendation' resolutions.

(c)   Finally, export relations with the Third World were important in votes on both 'principle' and 'recommendation' resolutions. Group B countries which exported a relatively large proportion of their total exports to the poor countries were generally willing to support measures which would in the short, medium or long run contribute towards an expansion of the exports of the Group B countries to the Third World. This is once again not indicated by the partial correlation results reported in Table 7.3.

We can conclude that the original mandate which UNCTAD obtained in 1964 was affected by its environment. The poor countries expected UNCTAD to be the forum where they would win the long-term commitment of the West to the modernization of the Third World. The West, on the other hand, although conscious of the need to foster its relationship with the Third World, was unwilling to restructure, fundamentally and drastically, the international economic system which had served it so well since the Second World War. Its endorsement of the Final Act did not constitute an endorsement of UNCTAD's organizational ideology, as embodied in the general and special principles adopted at Geneva, but rather it implied the willingness of the West to explore the possibility offered by protracted negotiations, through the UNCTAD secretariat, and the Trade and Development Board

(TDB). The only substantial concession the West made at Geneva was on the institutional question. Thus, task expansion could result only from the ability of the secretariat to involve the West and the South in the pursuit of subgoals, which were seen as consistent with the general and special principles by the South, and as demonstrators of the validity and usefulness (from a Western perspective) of these principles, by the rich countries. Since the *raison d'etre* of UNCTAD was the involvement of the West as a supporter of Third World modernization, a mere reiteration of principles which the West viewed with suspicion and distaste would serve no useful purpose. UNCTAD attempted to formulate programmes and reforms which would only very gradually contribute to the vindication of the general and special principles.

In the next section I will evaluate the impact of these programs on UNCTAD's environment. I will measure the position of the Third World countries in the world economy and the nature of their relationship with the developed countries. I will also discuss the impact UNCTAD initiatives have had on the attitudes of governments and of interest groups within the West.

7.3 QUANTITATIVE CHANGES IN RELEVANT MAGNITUDES: SUBSTANTIVE CONSEQUENCES OF UNCTAD POLICIES

UNCTAD's performance could be assessed on the basis of hypothesis derived from the 'evaluation research' approach outlined in sec 3.1 UNCTAD could be regarded as effective if it could be shown to have caused movements in international trade and financial flows in accordance with its stated organizational objectives. This is clearly a rather superficial view—as we have argued above—particularly for a 'forum' type of organization. Nevertheless the evaluation research approach provides a basis for a limited and partial assessment of some aspects of UNCTAD's environmental performance. The major difficulty with this approach is that it does not allow an evaluation of the indirect environmental impact of an EIO.

Moreover such as approach permits at best an assessment of specific programme operated by an EIO. It cannot in itself be a sufficient guide for evaluating the systemic impact of an EIO.

There are also important data limitations which constrain the validity of this approach in the case of UNCTAD. The most important of these is the universal character of UNCTAD. There are no control groups against which the performance of members participating in UNCTAD sponsored programmes can be evaluated. Hypothesis tested have to be of the one group post-test design, one group pre-test design and one group interrupted time series design (tests 1,2 and 5 in sec 3.1). As noted earlier these designs do not permit a direct evaluation of the impact of the passage of time or of environmental developments, other than the initiatives of the EIO being studied, on the dependent variables. In the UNCTAD case it is possible for example to compare aid and trade levels before and after specific programatic initiatives. Changes observed in these variables may be explained by (a) the passage of time—the 'maturation trend', (b) the effectiveness of national policies, (c) developments within the international economy, such as a rise in the price of oil or depression in the West and (d) the success or failure of UNCTAD. In studying movements in variables reflecting the international economic position of Third World countries these rival explanations have been assessed in each case. The conclusions however are no more than informed judgment' and represent one plausible inter-pretation of UNCTAD's environmental performance.

In the following pages we present data to measure changes in the international development environment since the inception of UNCTAD. The following indices have been estimated:
1. Rate of growth of GNP per capita
2. Exports from Third World countries as a proportion of world exports
3. Rate of growth of Third World exports.
4. Manufacturing exports as proportion of total Third World exports
5. Trade among LDCs
6. Rate of growth of total financial flows (TFF)
7. Rate of growth of ODA
8. ODA/GNP ratios

9. Terms of aid
10. Rate of growth of private foreign investment.
Let us now turn to the presentation of the indices.

Table 7.6:   *UNCTAD development targets and their achievement: rate of growth of GNP per capita*

Target	Description	Period	Magnitude
Rate of growth of GNP	Average annual growth rate percent	1960–1982	
(a) Low income			1.1
(b) China and India			3.5
(c) Middle income			3.2
(d) High income oil exporters			5.8

Source: World Development Handbook 1984, World Bank 1984 p.218–19

Table 7.6 shows that there has been a wide variation in the growth experience of the LDCs. During the period 1950–1964 (i.e. prior to the formation of UNCTAD) the LDCs had grown in per capita terms at an annual average rate of about 2.16 per cent. The performance of the low-income countries was significantly below this level during 1960–1982; clearly UNCTAD did not succeed in raising the growth rate of this subsection of LDCs. The average per capita income growth of other LDC groups is significantly higher than in the period 1950–1964; but this difference may largely be explained with reference to environmental factors. The increase in oil prices largely accounts for the high per capita income growth of the oil-exporting countries. India's per capita income growth rate is only 1.3 per cent per annum, similar to that of may low-income countries. On the other hand, China's per capita income grew at an annual rate of over 5 per cent, but China is a relatively closed economy little affected by the international initiatives of IOs such as UNCTAD.

The middle-income countries have grown at a rate of 3.2 per cent per annum—but standard deviation of the growth rates within the group is high—2.01 per cent. The East Asian countries—South Korea, Taiwan, Singapore, Malaysia and Hong Kong—have grown at a rate of 6.5 per cent per annum (standard deviation 1.2 per cent). National policies may thus be considered important determinants of growth performance.

However, the high growth rates enjoyed by this group have been largely due to success in export expansion. If it can be shown that UNCTAD contributed significantly to the export growth of the LDCs, it would be possible to accept the hypothesis that it had a positive impact on the growth of at least the middle-income group of developing countries.

Table 7.7 presents various measures for assessing the export performance of the LDCs.

Over the period 1965–82 the share of developing countries in world exports has increased from 21 per cent to 29 per cent. In

Table 7.7: *UNCTAD development targets and their achievements: trade indicators*

Measure	Period	Non OPEC LDCs	OPEC
1. Share of Third World exports in total world exports (%)	1965–71	18.25 (0.73)	2.92 (0.20)
	1972–6	18.46 (3.62)	5.45 (1.72)
	1977–82	21.62 (1.07)	7.47 (0.77)
2. Rate of annual growth (%)	1965–71	8.73 (2.90)	6.99 (4.93)
	1972–6	26.45 (23.12)	96.00 (29.41)
	1977–82	10.50 (16.62)	9.78 (16.56)
3. Export of manufacturers as % of total Third World exports: annual averages %	1964–71	21.42 (3.12)	—
	1972–6	32.34 (2.30)	—
	1977–82	37.55 (2.16)	1.3 (0.2)

Note: Figures in parentheses are standard deviations.
Source: IMF *Directions of Trade* (Annual) Washington, various.

the period 1960–72 the share of LDC exports in world exports had stagnated. This share was 21.4 per cent in 1960, by 1965 it had reached 19.5 per cent and by the end of this period, (i.e. 1972) LDC exports accounted for about 22 per cent of total world exports. UNCTAD clearly did not succeed in stimulating exports during this period. LDCs' share in world exports reached 23 per cent by 1976, but this was largely due to the very high export earnings of the OPEC countries—their export receipts increased by more than 400 per cent over these four years.

During 1965–71 LDC exports grew more rapidly than during 1960–65 (by an annual average of over 8 per cent as against 6.4 per cent). However, UNCTAD had no particular trade expansion programme in operation during this period. The Generalized Preference Scheme (GSP) became functional from 1971 onwards. During 1972–76 OPEC exports grew substantially faster than non-OPEC LDC exports, but the trend was reversed during 1977–82, when non OPEC LDC exports grew at the rate of 8.7 per cent. During this period the exports of developed market economy countries grew at 9.2 per cent per annum. Total world exports grew at the rate of 9.7 per cent per annum.

The relatively rapid growth of non OPEC LDC exports during this period cannot be explained with reference to the GSP. The idea of a generalized system of preferences was first mooted by Prebisch, who in 1964 called for 'preferential treatment to be granted in principle to all imports from developing countries, subject only to certain specified exclusions as well as certain safeguards'. This was interpreted by the LDCs to mean a scheme which: (a) guaranteed preferential access to the markets of the DCs for all manufacturers and semi-manufacturers of the LDCs without any volume limitations for a specified period of time, (b) allowed importing countries under specified conditions to exclude certain products and apply safeguards, (c) compensated LDCs which in 1964 enjoyed special preferential treatment and took into account the special needs of the least developed LDCs, and (d) provided for international supervision of the scheme.[11]

Agreement on the GSP was finally reached in October 1970,

and rules of origin were adopted in December of that year. Individual DCs submitted separate lists for the granting of preferences to LDC exports. These lists specified products from BTN categories 25–99, which would be excluded from preferential treatment, and products from BTN categories 1–24, which would be granted preferential treatment. DCs also specified specific safeguards, and although they agreed that consultations could be held, they all reserved the right of unilaterally suspending GSP in a specific area. Preferences were to last for ten years. GSP could not prevent inter-DC tariff reductions negotiated bilaterally or through GATT. Self-election criteria for claiming beneficiary status were retained. No special concessions for the least of the less developed countries (LDDCs) were included. In general, the final agreements were close to the initial submission of the developed countries; and the LDCs had to concede almost all the specific demands they had made on the preferences issue, once the principle of establishing the GSP had been accepted. For the African and other LDDCs this represented an important setback. They were unlikely to gain substantially from the operation of the GSP scheme, their special requirements were not taken into account, and product coverage of most national schemes excluded semi-processed products. They accepted the final agreement because of the retention of a transitory period for special preferences, and in order to preserve Group of 77 unity. All in all, the GSP which was formally initiated in 1971 looked quite different from the initial proposal.

The rich countries were not able to agree on one single scheme . . . [They differed] with regard to produce coverage and the method of preferential treatment. The rich countries argued that processed agricultural goods and other semi-manufactures should be excluded from the scheme, and different rich countries gave different product classifications . . . Japan and the EEC members set quantitative ceilings . . . Other rich countries specified that they would withdraw the preferences if domestic problems necessitated such action. On top of all [this] . . . there was no legal guarantee that the rich countries will in fact . . . continue the schemes that they have formulated.[12]

The overall ineffectiveness of the GSP has been documented in a series of reports by the UNCTAD Secretariat. Murray has estimated that products covered by the scheme accounted for only about 2 per cent of the total imports of the preference-granting countries, whereas if all the restrictions with which national schemes were hedged in were removed at least 20 per cent of the imports of the 'donor' countries would have been covered by these schemes.[13]

An important concern of those pressing for the adoption of the GSP was an increase in the Third World's share of global manufactured exports. Table 7.7 shows that the share of manufactured exports in total exports by developing countries has increased during 1977–82. In 1957 the share of manufacturing exports in total Third World exports was only 13 per cent. The ratio rose from about 17 per cent in 1964 to about 23 per cent in 1971, but the period 1972–6 saw a rapid increase in export revenues generated by oil and other primary commodities. A similar phenomenon although on a somewhat reduced scale was repeated in 1979 and 1980—nevertheless the share of manufactured exports in total exports of non OPEC LDCs had reached 36 per cent by 1982.

The share of developing countries in world manufacturing exports increased from 4.4 per cent in 1965 to 9.2 per cent in 1982. Four East Asian countries—South Korea, Taiwan, Hong Kong and Singapore—currently account for almost 40 per cent of the total exports of manufactures from the Third World. Twelve developing countries accounts for 60% of manufactured exports from the Third World.[14]

This high concentration of exports illustrates that it was the national policies of individual countries that were mainly responsible for the growth of manufactured exports. The effectiveness of the GSP in this regard has been noted by a study sponsored by the World Bank.

Trade creation consequent on the implementation of the GSP by the developed countries amounted to 0.9 per cent of the total imports of the Western countries in the first year of operation of the scheme. This is less than 5 per cent of financial assistance provided by DCs in the same year. The GSP schemes currently in operation generated very limited incentives for encouraging manufactured exports from [LDCs]. Products covered by the schemes cover only 2 per cent of the total imports of the preference-granting countries. Quantitative restrictions (further) . . . negate the positive effects which might otherwise occur.[15]

UNCTAD has also stressed the importance of the growth of

intra Third World trade. Table 7.8 presents intra Third World trade flows.

Table 7.8:   *UNCTAD development targets and their achievements: intra Third World trade flows*

Period	Intra Third World exports as a percentage of total Third World exports	Intra Third World imports as a percentage of total Third World imports
1965–71	20.24 (0.35)	18.62 (0.82)
1972–6	27.00 [5.7] (1.19)	28.00 [12.51] (3.61)
1977–82		
OPEC	25.97 [1.45] (3.45) [(0.35)]	18.39 [2.24] (2.26) [(0.61)]
Non-OPEC	30.23 [6.58]	32.43 [14.65]
Third World	(1.64) [(0.86)]	(1.07) [(1.64)]

Note: Figures in parentheses are standard deviations; figures in square brackets are exports to and imports from OPEC countries by OPEC and non-OPEC Third World countries.
Source: IMF *Directories of Trade* Washington (annual), various.

Once again it is evident that there is an inherent upward trend. The share of intra Third World exports has increased from 20 per cent in 1960 to over 30 per cent in 1982. Imports have also expanded and currently account for about one-third of total LDC imports. However nearly half of these are oil imports from OPEC. In terms of non-oil imports, intra Third World trade has remained relatively constant: 16 per cent during 1972–76 and about 17 per cent currently. This is one aspect of the growing balance-of-payment deficits of many Third World countries. Over the period 1977–82, for example, exports of non-oil-exporting Third World countries grew by 117 per cent but imports grew by 215 per cent.[16] Developing countries remain dependent on the West as suppliers of crucial capital, technology and food imports, but are gradually developing new export markets, particularly for their manu-factuured products.

It is difficult to assess UNCTAD's impact on these

developments, as the organization adopted no specific programme initiative in this area and technical assistance remained very limited.

Another area in which UNCTAD showed involvement was that of development assistance. The New Delhi Conference (UNCTAD II) adopted resolutions committing the donor states to provide 1 per cent of GNP in the form of total financial flows to LDCs and 0.7 per cent in the form of Official Development Assistance (ODA). There have also been a large number of recommendations regarding the softening of the terms on which aid is provided. Table 7.9 assesses changes in the structure and terms of public and private capital flows to the developing world.

Total financial flows from developed to developing countries have grown at a rate of 3.4 per cent per annum over the period 1970–82 in real terms. This has been higher than the GNP growth rate of the DCs during this period, with the result that the ratio of total resource flows to GNP has increased from 0.76 per cent in 1970 to 1.15 per cent in 1982. Thus the OECD countries had as a group achieved the 1 per cent target established in 1960 and formally accepted by them at UNCTAD II in 1968.[17]

The share of ODA in total resource flows declined from 40.6 per cent in 1970 to 34.7 per cent in 1982. The ODA/GNP ratio, however, rose from 0.40 over the period 1971-3 to 0.45 during 1980-2. In 1964 the ODA/GNP ratio was 0.48. The most important component of total financial flows to the LDCs have been non concessional funds. They grew at an average rate of about 40 per cent over the period 1971–82 and increased their share in total financial flows from 31 per cent during 1971-3 to 69 per cent over the period 1977–82. Much of this lending was by commercial banks for relatively short periods at variable interest rates, and the burden of servicing these loans has continued to rise for many developing countries. As against this, the burden of servicing official debt has remained fairly invariable. An improvement in terms occurred during 1967–75, but over 1975–82 the average interest rates on ODA loans has increased and the grant element within these loans has declined. The rising debt burden of the developing world has not led to an institutionalization of general debt relief

Table 7.9:   *UNCTAD development targets and their achievements: aid indicators*

Indicator	Period	Value
1. Total net receipts of LDCs at constant 1981 prices: US$billion	1970–4 1975–9 1980–2	57.98 (7.46) 92.82 (8.28) 98.75 (8.00)
2. Official Development Assistance (ODA) at constant 1981 prices: US$billion	1970–4 1975–9 1980–2	23.75 (3.28) 31.67 (2.14) 35.90 (0.84)
3. Non-concessional flows at constant 1981 prices: US$billion	1970–4 1975–9 1980–2	31.92 (4.67) 59.12 (7.12) 60.66 (7.63)
4. ODA as a proportion of total net receipts per cent	1970 1975 1982	40.6 36.0 34.7
5. Concessional flows as a proportion of total: net receipts per cent	1970 1975 1982	55.1 61.6 63.3
6. Net flow of resources from DAC countries to LDCs as percentage of GNP	1971–3 1977–9 1980–2	0.76 1.16 1.14
7. Net flow of official resources from DAC as percentage of GNP	1971–3 1977–9 1980–2	0.40 0.41 0.46
8. Net flow of official resources from OPEC to LDCs as percentage of GNP	1970 1975 1982	1.18 2.92 1.22
9. Grants as percentage of ODC commitments	1967 1975	63 69
10. ODA Loan structures (a) Average interest rate percentage	1967 1975 1982	3.5 2.6 2.8
(b) Maturity (years)	1967 1975 1982	28.6 28.9 29.8

Indicator	Period	Value
(c) Grace period (years)	1967	6.7
	1975	7.7
	1982	8.5
(d) Grant element	1967	57
	1975	62.3
	1982	58.3

Note: figures in parenthesis are standard deviations
Source: Development Assistance Committee *Development Co-operation* OECD
  Paris (Annual)

schemes envisaged by UNCTAD, but to the periodic rescheduling of the debt of particularly severely affected countries—Mexico, Brazil, Sudan—under IMF surveillance. The improvement in the terms of official aid is at least partly due to the work of the Development Assistance Committee of the OECD. UNCTAD's contribution in the development finance field remains confined to its role in mobilizing international public opinion for the meeting of the 'one per cent' target formally endorsed by both developed and developing countries at UNCTAD II.

In general we may conclude that UNCTAD played a relatively modest part in the restructuring of international economic relations. During 1964–72, the position of the developing countries within the world economy continued to worsen. The share in global trade continued to decline and aid levels stagnated. The improvement during 1973–76 was largely due to the rapid increase in the price of oil and a small group of other primary commodities. In the period 1977–82, the international performance of the East Asian 'gang of four'—Taiwan, South Korea, Hong Kong and Singapore—accounts for much of the export success of the Third World in the markets for manufactures. The oil price boom of 1979–80 also helped the oil-exporting countries. These two factors largely caused a rapid expansion in intra Third World trade. The period, however, saw no breakthroughs in the economic relations of the developed and developing countries.

The period of 1977–82 has seen a gradual disintegration and abandonment of the North–South dialogue. After the watering down of the Common Fund proposals[18] and the seemingly never-ending negotiations for its formal establishment, UNCTAD has not launched any other major substantive initiatives. International developments during this period are less directly related to its work than in the previous period. Even during those periods UNCTAD's substantive contributions were rather limited.

This is, however, not altogether surprising. At its inception, UNCTAD was conceived of as a forum organization, not a negotiating one. Naturally, the concrete decisions of the TDB were limited in effect. The broader resolutions and recommendations of the conference, on the other hand, lacked legal sanction, and dissenting states felt no obligation to abide by such decisions. It may, therefore, be argued that formal decisions taken are an unsatisfactory estimator of UNCTAD's influence. Those who hold this view may contend that the targets set by the TDB and the conferences were not crucial in themselves, but rather in their impact on the attitudes of member states and other international organizations. Thus, to dub UNCTAD as an ineffective organization on the grounds that 'an organization is effective [to the extent that] what is formalized verbally by that organization, or done by its agents, has a causal effect on the settlement of issues',[19] is to take a narrow and short-run view. For what was formalized at UNCTAD conference and TDB sessions was of little more than symbolic value. The extent to which UNCTAD has succeeded in creating an evolving consensus on the problems of development is the change in attitudes and policies of governments and international organizations occasioned by UNCTAD. The next section attempts to evaluate changes in attitudes of Western governments and international organizations on major issues raised by UNCTAD.

7.4 CHANGE IN ATTITUDES OF WESTERN GOVERNMENTS AND INTERNATIONAL ECONOMIC ORGANIZATIONS

Prebisch saw UNCTAD as a forum organization. One of its main aims, as noted in the UN resolution calling for its establishment, was 'to formulate principles and policies on international trade and related problems of economic development'. The establishment of UNCTAD was in itself an act of endorsement of the Prebisch–Singer structuralist trade 'heresy'. Since the late 1940s, orthodox neo-classical teaching on trade theory and policy had come under attack by UN-based economists, who maintained that the coventional framework for international trade policies discriminated heavily against the LDCs. They argued that a new and more realistic world view, of the processes of international economic interaction, was necessary in order to appreciate the nature and causes of the major structural deformities within the world economy. Prebisch set out to formulate such a world view in his report to UNCTAD I.[20]

Western governmental and mainstream academic reaction to this initiative was initially fairly hostile. The 'UNCTAD doctrine' was attacked from many sides, and it was argued that UNCTAD's substantive policies ought not to be linked to Prebisch's all-encompassing theory of trade and development. However, Prebisch's conceptual framework has proved enduring. The issues he highlighted and the approaches he suggested have been the focus of UNCTAD's voluminous research activity, on the one hand, and of the 'North–South' encounter, within many international forums, on the other. Since Prebisch's departure, the UNCTAD secretariat leadership has attempted to seek a negotiating role within the UN family, but they have been unwilling (or unable) to depart from Prebisch's conceptual framework, and their 'agenda for negotiation' identifies issue areas which would undoubtedly be regarded as of great priority within the Prebisch framework. Furthermore, Prebisch's concern for seeking a generalized solution to Third World problems is also maintained: hence the approach to the establishment of the common fund in 1974 is little different from the approach to the inception of the GSP at UNCTAD II. In both cases, UNCTAD sought a unified Third World platform, seeking the establishment of international transfer mechanisms which would be based on generalized preferences and concessions given by the rich Western countries. In both cases, the Western bloc was prepared to endorse in a limited and guarded style, the underlying principles on which the proposed policies were based, but was unwilling to set up international bodies charged with the legal responsibility of ensuring that the proposed policies were implemented. Western governments have demonstrated a preference for bilateral commitments and for a piecemeal approach as far as specific concessions are concerned.

The unwillingness to implement UNCTAD proposals does not originate in ideological opposition to 'UNCTAD doctrine'. but in opposition to the generalized character of many of the proposed reforms. Western academics and policy makers are willing 'in principle' to concede many, if not most, of the theoretical scenarios which provide the background to UNCTAD recommendations; hence the unanimous adoption of all resolutions finally considered by the conference in 1976.

The most common attitude on the part of the Western countries has been to make a positive or a near-neutral response to UNCTAD proposals and policies. A hard core of rejectionists including the US, Britain and sometimes West Germany usually adopt negative attitudes and vote against majority-sponsored resolutions. During 1964–76 this hard core was often overruled by the moderates, and the adoption of UNCTAD resolutions committed the member governments to detailed negotiations in specific issue areas. The negotiations themselves have rarely been fruitful in achieving substantive changes in the economic relationship between rich and poor countries. Thus, the acceptance of the general principles put forward by UNCTAD did not have a significant political or economic cost as far as the moderate Western countries were concerned. Since 1979, however, the rejectionists have prevailed over the moderates in UNCTAD as in most other international economic forums. The result is that UNCTAD V and UNCTAD VI did not lead to new negotiations, and UNCTAD remains largely confined to the performance of the tasks endorsed by the conferences up to 1976.

It is clear, therefore, that the attitudes of the major Western governments have significantly deteriorated since 1979. They are less willing to countenance task expansion by this organization today than they were ten years ago. It may be argued that this is because UNCTAD has refused to concern itself with the task of identifying groups, particularly within the developed countries (DCs), whose long-run economic interest can be shown to be in line with UNCTAD's organizational ideology. If such groups can be identified, only then can UNCTAD move on to the deriving of policies which might transform the environment in accordance with its ideology, and. hope that there will be political support within the system to sustain this transformation. But are non-governmental economic and political interest groups interested in participating in the North–South dialogue directly?

7.5 UNCTAD AND ECONOMIC AND POLITICAL INTEREST GROUPS IN GROUP B COUNTRIES: A PILOT QUESTIONNAIRE STUDY

In order to answer this question, the author of the present study sent a questionnaire in December 1976 a few months after the Nairobi Conference (UNCTAD IV)—to:

(a) 10 consumer associations in the UK;
(b) 29 NGOs involved in aid support programmes in the UK;
(c) 100 trade union associations in the textile, chemical, leather, food, drink and tobacco industries in the UK;
(d) 100 leading industrial companies in the UK with subsidiaries in Third World countries.

The main results are summarized in Table 7.10. The response rate is 20.08 per cent, not entirely unrespectable. However, the response rate for the trade unions (TUs) is extremely low, and there are no grounds for taking opinions expressed by respondent trade unions as representative of the opinion of the population of trade unions in the industries specified. The response rate for consumer associations (CAs) is surprisingly high, but that for the NGOs is disappointingly low, given their active involvement in UNCTAD work. The response rate from industrial companies (ICs) is, in the writer's view, satisfactory.

A surprisingly large number of the respondent ICs monitored UNCTAD in 1976, although they did so mainly

Table 7.10:   *Western interest groups and UNCTAD: main results of questionnaire study*

	No.	as % of Total
1. No. of organizations to which questionnaire was sent	239	100.00
2. No. of replies[a]	48	20.08
of which were industrial companies (ICs)	26	26.00
of which were NGOs	11	37.93
of which were trade unions (TUs)	6	6.00
of which were consumer associations (CAs)	5	50.00
3. Delegation of responsibility to a person or department to monitor UNCTAD during part (or whole) of 1976:		
ICs	13	50.00
NGOs	8	72.72
TUs	0	0.00
CAs	0	0.00
4. The UK's negotiating position at UNCTAD IV satisfactory:		
ICs	22	84.61
NGOs	4	36.36
TUs	3	50.00
CAs	4	75.00
5. Group B's negotiating position at UNCTAD IV satisfactory:		
ICs	21	80.76
NGOs	4	25.00
TUs	—	—
CAs	4	75.00
6. Major weaknesses in UK/Group B position:		
(a) Attitude too rigid:		
ICs	2	7.69
NGOs	5	45.45
TUs	3	50.00
CAs	1	20.00
(b) Ignored commercial possibilities:		
ICs	2	7.69
(c) Ignored possibilities of co-operation:		
NGOs	2	18.18

	No.	As % of total
7. Negotiating position of group of 77:		
(a) Unsatisfactory:		
ICs	24	92.3
NGOs	2	18.2
TUs	3	50.0
CUs	4	75.0
(b) Weakness in group of 77's position. Attitude too rigid:		
ICs	18	69.2
CAs	4	75.0
(c) Ignored economic considerations.		
ICs	6	23.0
8. Major obstacles to implementation of UNCTAD policies:		
(a) Technically unsound:		
ICs	22	84.6
TUs	2	33.0
(b) Economically unrealistic:		
ICs	24	92.3
TUs	3	50.0
CAs	5	100.0
(c) Politically controversial:		
ICs	2	7.6
NGOs	10	90.9
TUs	1	16.6
9(a). Representation at UNCTAD: desirable:		
ICs	2	7.6
TUs	1	16.6
NGOs	10	90.9
CAs	2	40.0
9(b). Consultative role to national governments of UNCTAD: desirable:		
ICs	26	100.0
TUs	6	100.0
NGOs	11	100.0
CAs	5	100.0
9(c). Multilateral bargaining with Third World governments preferred:		
ICs	10	38.4
TUs	4	66.6
NGOs	11	100.0
CAs	4	75.0

	No.	As % of total
9(d). Multilateral bargaining with Third World NGOs preferred:		
ICs	10	38.4
TUs	5	83.3
NGOs	10	90.9
CAs	0	
9(e). A new international organization needed:		
ICs	4	66.6
NGOs	11	9.0
CAs	3	60.0

Note: a = as % of total questionnaires sent in item 1. In all other cases, figures are given as % of respondents.

from their London headquarters. A large number of NGOs also kept in touch with UNCTAD, but none of the TUs or the CAs did so. The vast majority of ICs regarded the UK and group B's negotiating position at Nairobi as satisfactory, as did 75 per cent of the responding CAs; against this, 7 out of 11 responding NGOs did not consider these positions as satisfactory: 5 of them felt that it was too rigid, and 2 NGOs and 2 ICs felt that the UK had ignored possibilities for economic co-operation with the LDCs. Twenty-four out of 26 responding ICs felt that the negotiating position of the '77' had been unsatisfactory; 18 regarded this position as too rigid, and 6 as ignoring economic considerations. All responding CAs felt that UNCTAD policies could not be implemented as they were economically unrealistic. Forty six ICs felt that UNCTAD policies could not be implemented, because they were technically unsound and economically unrealistic and hence incapable of implentation, against 10 out of 11 respondent NGOs who said they UNCTAD policies could not be implemented because they were politically controversial.

This survey was undertaken after the conclusion of perhaps the most successful UNCTAD conference, which committed the developed countries to intensive negotiations. The outcome of these negotiations has, however, fallen short of the initial expectation of the secretariat, with the consequence that private interest group concern about the activities of UNCTAD has probably declined. If the survey undertaken in 1976 had been repeated in 1983 after the Belgrade conference, we would probably have found a decline in the proportion of the sample of respondents who monitored UNCTAD during that year. Similarly the proportion of respondents interested in participating in multilateral negotiations with the Third World is also likely to have fallen. The results of the 1976 survey, however, indicate that at the time of UNCTAD's greatest international salience important non-governmental interest groups—in particular transnational corporations—were interested in its work, and an opportunity existed for initiating a dialogue and establishing a network of expanded contacts. This opportunity was in the main missed by the UNCTAD secretariat.

7.6 THE INFLUENCE OF UNCTAD: A SUMMING UP

We have seen that the substantive impact of UNCTAD on its environment has not been particularly strong. Modification in the level and form of transactions between DCs and LDCs have been modest. Acceptance by IGOs and Western governments of UNCTAD principles has not led to a radical change in their policies *vis-à-vis* the poor countries. This limited impact in substantive terms was also sustained by the international political environment. Both within UNCTAD and outside it, East–West rivalry did not seriously affect the development issue. From the middle of the 1960s there was no particular reason why the US or the USSR should look to the Third World. The Socialist bloc had tended to opt out of the North–South dialogue; and the UNCTAD secretariat did not mount any initiatives for playing the East against the West in the interests of the Third World. The political impact of UNCTAD was mainly confined to a systematic pressurizing of the DCs—particularly within the conferences, but also at the TDB sessions—in order to induce them to give concessions to the LDCs. This political embarrassment did have some effect in modifying the attitudes of the West, but they soon learnt to cope with it.

The limited impact which UNCTAD has had does not, of course, mean that it has been 'ineffective'. That depends on how we perceive the 'effect' that it wants to create. If its primary concern is with interest articulation, then clearly its contribution to world politics has not been insubstantial. As against this, its ability to restructure international economic relationships has been modest over the period 1964–83, as this chapter has tried to show. The political salience and the economic effectiveness of UNCTAD reflect its scope and level, its structure of decision making and the distribution of organizational influence. It is to an analysis of these questions that I turn in the following chapter.

NOTES

1. Haas, E. *Beyond the Nation State,* Stanford (1964), p. 77.
2. The following countries are included in this category: Australia, Austria, Belgium, Canada, Denmark, France, Iceland, Ireland, Italy, Japan, Netherlands, New Zealand, Norway, Sweden, UK, USA, West Germany. These countries are included in Group B within UNCTAD, which also includes certain other European states, i.e. Greece, Portugal, Spain and Turkey. These latter may more properly be regarded as less developed states in 1964.
3. The socialist countries had no part in the running of the international economic order either. This has been a cause of increasing concern to them, as economic isolationism has been abandoned. The USSR has repeatedly called for the creation of an International Trade Organization, and other East European states have shown great interest in the expansion of East–West trade.
4. On this see Rolfe, S. and Damm, W. (eds.) *The Multinational Enterprise in the World Economy,* Praeger, New York (1970).
5. No mention has been made of the internal political structure of the Western countries. All these countries may be described as possessing 'competitive' policies. Such policies are reputed to be 'open', i.e. more receptive to the implementation of the decisions of IOs.
6. Gosovic, B. *UNCTAD: Conflict and Compromise* Sijthoff, Leiden (1972), p. 28.
7. Cox, R. *International Organisation: World Politics*, Macmillan, London (1969) p. 261.
8. Alker, H. and Russett, B. *World Politics in the General Assembly,* New Haven, Yale (1965).

9. If x_i is country i's voting rank, $\bar{x}$ is the average voting rank, and s_x is the standard deviation of the x_i's $(s_x^2 = \dfrac{1}{N} \sum_{i=1}^{N} (x_i - \bar{x})^2$, then a standardized voting rank $(z_x(i))$ is given by the formula $z_x(i) = \dfrac{\bar{x}_i - \bar{x}}{S_x}$, *ibid.*, p. 31.

10. However, there is also a strong case for lumping the no's together, for the practical consequences of opposition to and of abstention on UNCTAD resolutions were similar. Countries which did not support a specific recommendation did not feel obliged to abide by it.

11. See Gosovic, B. *UNCTAD Conflict and Compromise* Part II.

12. Singer, H. and Ansari, J. *Rich and Poor Countries*, George Allen and Unwin, London (1982) p. 130.

13. Murray, T. 'How helpful is the GSP *'Economic Journal'*, Vol. 79. No. 3, (1973) p. 449–55.

14. These estimates are taken from UNIDO, *Industry in a Changing World: Survey for UNIDO IV*, New York (1983) Ch. VII pp. 188–93. The estimates do not include exports from China. Estimates for Taiwan have been separately obtained.

15. Igbal, Z. 'The GSP Schemes', *Finance and Development*, Washington (Sept. 1975) pp. 38–9.

16. These figures have been calculated from IMF *Directions of Trade 1984*, Washington (1984).

17. However, in 1982 nine of the seventeen DAC members had not reached this target—this was a higher proportion than for any year since 1975. *See* DAC *Development Corporation 1983*, OECD, Paris (1983). Appendix Table A4.

18. The impact of UNCTAD's work in the commodity field has not been detailed because analysis and conclusions are broadly similar to those in the case of trade and aid.

19. Ogley, R. 'Towards a general theory of international organisation' *International Relations*, No. 4 (1970) p. 60.

20. Prebisch, R. *Towards a New Trade Policy for Development* UN, New York (1964).

8 UNCTAD's Organizational Development

In this Chapter we will assess UNCTAD's scope and level, estimate its organizational autonomy and durability and evaluate its decision-making processes. The study will be based on an eclectic application of some of the theoretical approaches outlined in Chapter 4.

We begin out study of UNCTAD's organizational performance by estimating its scope and level over the period 1968–83. This is done by:

(a) Enumerating the groups involved in the making, implementation, and follow-up of UNCTAD's decisions. Composition of the Trade and Development Board (which is UNCTAD's main governing body responsible for the implementation of Conference decisions) and of the delegations at the UNCTAD Conferences will be analysed, with a view to assessing the national groups represented in UNCTAD's decision-making forums.

(b) Enumerating the national interest groups which could be affected by the implementation of UNCTAD policies in Western countries, and assessing the political and economic significance of these groups.

(c) Assessing the level of delegations sent to UNCTAD, by comparing the rank size of delegation sent by country A to UNCTAD I with the rank size of delegation sent by country A to UNCTAD VI, to see if there has been a decline in interest in UNCTAD by some key Western and Third World countries over the years.

(d) Studying decision-making processes within UNCTAD, with a view to ascertaining the extent of willingness to devolve decision-making in a specific area to an UNCTAD forum or subunit. This will be done with reference to the major substantive decisions taken by UNCTAD: the 1 per cent aid target, the GSP, and the Common Fund.

8.1 UNCTAD's SCOPE

8.1.1 Decision makers within UNCTAD

Table 8.1 gives a breakdown of national delegations to Trade and Development Boards meetings.

From Table 8.1 we can see that, for the period for which data are available, delegations to the TDB from the Group B countries were usually dominated by representatives from foreign ministries. Moreover, the proportion of foreign ministry representatives in Group B delegations has been increasing over time. They constituted 47.71 per cent of Group B delegates over the period 1965–7, but 68.60 per cent over the period 1981–3. The second-largest group in Group B delegations represents the ministries of trade, commerce, and industry; but their representatives have been a declining group: they constituted almost 25 per cent of the Group B delegates to the TDB over the first period, but during the years 1981–3 their share had dwindled to only 13.52 per cent. The third main element within the Group B delegations represents the finance ministries, and their proportionate share has also moderately declined, from 8.97 per cent in 1965–7 to 5.8 per cent during 1981–3.

Group of 77 delegates to the TDB were also predominantly composed of foreign ministry officials. The share of foreign ministry officials in Group of 77 delegations increased from 52.8 per cent in 1965–7 to 80.2 per cent in 1981–3. The proportion of representatives from the trade and industry ministries (which constituted the second largest group in their delegations) declined from 23.24 per cent in the first period to only 12 per cent (approximately) during the second. Thus the change in the composition of the delegations to the TDB was broadly similar for the Group B and the Group of 77 countries. The Socialist countries also displayed a similar trend.

In the national delegates at the UNCTAD conferences, also the largest group within the Group B delegations were representatives from foreign ministries over the period 1964–83. Their share in the Group B delegations has risen from about 37 per cent during 1964–76 to about 43 per cent over 1976–83. The second main constituent of the Group B delegations to the conferences came from the trade, commerce

228 UN Conference on Trade and Development

Table 8.1: Composition of delegations to Trade and Development Board 1965-83

	1965-7			1971-7			1981-3		
	B	77	D	B	77	D	B	77	D
Foreign affairs	47.71	52.30	38.52	63.03	69.43	48.05	68.60	80.18	48.25
Planning and economic	7.92	10.42	2.16	10.15	5.91	3.57	9.83	5.04	2.36
Central bank	1.76	3.76	0.00	0.31	1.15	0.00	0.00	0.25	0.00
Agriculture	4.40	0.51	0.00	2.09	0.30	0.08	1.12	0.12	0.00
Trade, commerce industry	24.47	23.24	41.99	12.56	16.28	36.68	13.52	11.88	37.22
Treasury and finance	8.97	3.58	3.46	6.17	2.30	4.87	5.81	0.83	3.37
Legislative and executive	0.70	1.02	4.32	1.46	0.07	0.32	0.78	0.32	2.44
Transport	2.28	0.61	0.86	0.73	0.61	1.02	0.00	0.19	0.83
Other	3.34	3.41	8.65	3.41	3.91	4.37	0.33	1.21	5.52

Overall Unaccounted=4.27%

Note: Ministerial breakdown for delegations to the Trade and Development Board over the years 1968-70 not available.
Source: Trade and Development Board Records, Geneva (various).

and industry ministries, whose share fell from on average about 21 per cent during 1964–76 to 17 per cent during 1976–83. The third major group were the representatives from the finance ministries. Finally, representatives from Western parliaments and cabinet offices constituted about 5 per cent of the delegates at UNCTAD.

Delegations from the Group of 77 to the conferences were increasingly dominated by representatives from the foreign ministries. These constituted 20 per cent of total delegates in 1964, but this proportion had increased to 45.6 per cent by 1983. Representatives from the trade, industry and commerce ministries accounted for approximately 25 per cent of total LDC delegates, and the share was relatively stable. Representatives from 'other' groups, including unspecified delegates, were the third major group, and they showed a moderately declining tendency. Finance ministry representatives constituted about 5 per cent of LDC delegates.

Group D delegations were dominated by representation from the trade, commerce and industry ministries, on the one hand, and from the foreign ministries, on the other. Representatives from the former group of ministries constituted an increasing proportion of total delegates over this period. As against this, representatives from foreign ministries declined consistently, as a proportion of total Group D delegates, from 1968.

The relatively high percentage of delegates in the 'other' categories is accounted for by the fact that 83.6 per cent of Group of 77 delegates, and 61 per cent of Group B delegates, in this category, either are secretarial/translation staff, or else are unaccounted for in the UNCTAD documents. Roughly speaking, about 6 per cent of Group B delegates came from ministries and government departments not listed. About half of these (i.e. 3 per cent of the total Group B delegates) came from non-governmental organizations, mainly chambers of commerce, commodity councils, and trade unions. Less than 1 per cent of Group B delegates represented aid support non-governmental and semi-governmental organizations. The Nordic countries, Switzerland and Canada tended to send a relatively large contingent of non-governmental and semi-governmental representatives as parts of their delegations.

The ministerial classification has been formulated on the basis of the following assumptions:

(a)   Representatives from foreign ministries are likely to be concerned with the 'strategic' and general political impact of UNCTAD decisions.

(b)   Representatives from the trade, industry and commerce ministries are likely to adopt a 'forward-looking' approach, and support suitable initiatives for task expansion likely to increase the level of trade and investment.

(c)   Representatives from central banks and finance ministries of Group B countries are likely to exercise a 'conservative' influence. They are likely to be mainly concerned with spelling out the cost to the West of concessions given. Representatives from planning or economic affairs ministries of the West are also likely to be concerned with the evaluation of economic costs, but they are likely to take a longer-run view than the finance ministry officials.

(d)   Representatives from the planning and finance ministries, and from the central banks of the Group of 77 countries, are most likely to evaluate the short- and long-run implications of specific proposals at UNCTAD, as far as the economic strategy of the LDCs is . concerned. They are thus likely to be important in formulating negotiating positions for the Third World.

(e)   Representatives from research organizations and from parliaments are likely to be influential in reformulating attitudes and approaches.

(f)   Representatives from the agriculture and transport (particularly marine transport) ministries of the Western countries are likely to be adversely affected to a significant degree, if concessions are given to the Third World.

Table 8.1 has shown that foreign ministry representatives from DCs and LDCs have been an increasing and dominant delegation constituent in TDB meetings. They constituted the largest group within the national delegations at the conferences, and their proportion in both Group B and Group of 77 country delegates at the conference increased substantially.

As against this, delegates from the commerce, industry and trade ministries declined as a proportion of both Group B and Group of 77 delegations to the TDB. They also declined as a proportion of Group B delegations in the conferences. Representatives of finance ministries declined as a proportion of both Group B and Group of 77 delegations to the TDB. Finance ministry representatives increased as a proportion of Group of 77 delegations, as did the representatives from the planning ministries. There was no consistent trend in the representation from agriculture and transport ministries of the Group B countries. Parliamentary representatives from Group B countries increased, but they came largely from the smaller countries, such as Switzerland and Norway.

It is evident, therefore, that decision makers at UNCTAD are primarily concerned with strategic and diplomatic questions. Group of 77 delegates are primarily interested in mounting political pressure to win concessions from the West. Group B delegates are also basically concerned with minimizing the political cost of the UNCTAD deliberation processes. The transformation of UNCTAD from a forum to a negotiating organization concerned with technical economic deliberation must involve a change in the composition of national delegations, a significant increase in trade, commerce and industry representatives from Group B and Group of 77 countries, an increase in the planning and economic affairs representatives from the Group of 77 countries, a decline in representatives of foreign ministries from the Group B countries, etc. The existing trends are largely contrary to this form of restructuring. The 'conservative' interests have increased their representation in Group B delegations to the conference, and the decrease in the proportion of trade, commerce and industry ministries in Group B delegations to the conference has been evident. Similarly, the representation from planning ministries in Group of 77 delegations to the conferences has also declined. Thus, those who can formulate realistic negotiating positions on specific economic issues are overshadowed by foreign ministry representatives, preoccupied with political and strategic questions, at conferences and TDB meetings.

The economic salience of the UNCTAD negotiating process

has been limited, partly because those who participated in this process were not primarily concerned with increasing this salience through formulation and implementation of specific policy proposals. This, of course, does not mean that the political salience of UNCTAD has also declined. If the level of representation is a measure of political importance, then the political importance of UNCTAD has been undisputed. In the 1983 conference, for example, most Group B delegations were led by cabinet ministers. Similarly, UNCTAD IV adopted resolutions to ensure that the TDB should meet at ministerial level before every conference. Moreover, even though ministers do not stay long at the conferences and TDB meetings, Nye has pointed out that 'representatives at board meetings generally held high bureaucratic posts, which handled political aspects of apparently technical subjects'[1] These representatives from the Group B countries are mainly based in their respective national capitals and are closely briefed by their governments. Thus, over the period 1965–83 delegates from permanent missions constituted a far smaller proportion of Group B delegations to the TDB and the conferences than was the case with Group of 77 delegations. The relatively high level of the Group B delegations, according to Nye, is accounted for by: (a) a desire to participate in the making of principles on which international economic policy may eventually be based, (b) a desire to present a favourable political image, and (c) a realization of the long-run political importance of the development problem.[2]

Thus, if UNCTAD does not achieve substantive shifts in policy, it is not because its members do not take it seriously; it is rather due to the fact that those who make decisions within UNCTAD forums are not primarily concerned with short-run changes in economic policy: they are interested in enunciating, interpreting and opposing general policy guidelines, and in evaluating political costs and benefits of the acceptance or rejection of these policies. In the economic field, changes in national policy generally involve not so much a debate on diverse economic perspectives, as an appreciation of tangible potential gains, realizable through a feasible co-ordination of the initiatives of relevant interest groups. Thus, Western governments generally operate in the economic field through manipulating private economic interests by gradual and marginal shifts in policy. Radical shifts in economic perspective—such as the endorsement of Keynesianism in the US and the UK—require the prior generation of high levels of political tension, and pressure for the abandonment of the old economic policies and the acceptance of the new ones. Thus, if decision makers within UNCTAD had proved capable of mounting and sustaining a level of political pressure which could significantly affect the lives of ordinary men and women in the West,[3] then the articulation of a new economic orthodoxy might have resulted in a radical shift in economic policy. Delegations from the Third World were, however, never in a position to mount any significant external threat to the West. They concentrated on making use of UNCTAD machinery as an instrument for interest articulation, and delegates from the West found that most of their time was spent in explaining why the general principles enunciated in UNCTAD could not be translated into international economic policy. Diplomatic skill is thus a much-needed asset at UNCTAD sessions. The Third World needs it to achieve and maintain group solidarity, and to present a unified and coherent programme for the sort of international economic restructuring which they desire. The West needs it to parry the diplomatic thrusts of the Third World, and to avoid 'loss of face' and of some political influence, consequent upon its refusal to enact policies on the basis of principles of international trade and investment, which it is powerless to prevent UNCTAD from endorsing.

Delegates interested in negotiating feasible changes in international economic policy at UNCTAD play a subdued role. Ostensibly, the whole organizational process is justified in terms of its impact on the actual economic magnitudes which reflect the position of Third World countries within the world economy, but decision-making and bargaining procedures within UNCTAD are geared to interest articulation, and the enunciation of general principle, not task expansion by concluding feasible agreements in an expanding range of issue areas. If UNCTAD is to be transformed from a 'forum' to a 'negotiating' organization, the composition of delegations to UNCTAD will have to undergo a change. These delegations will have to consist of people interested primarily in issues, such as export promotion, greater investment, and an increase in international liquidity. Delegations representing strategic interests, and diplomatic personnel, will have to be reduced. That not even the Group of 77 countries' delegations reflect this trends points to the fact that, contrary to their official statements, the LDCs are not willing to turn UNCTAD into a negotiating organization. They value its role as a forum for interest articulation. However it must be stressed that dependence of LDCs on local diplomatic staff reflects a shortage of trained negotiators and lack of travel funds. This is less true of Third World leaders such as India, Mexico, Brazil and South Korea but even their delegations to UNCTAD have been dominated by career (political) diplomats.

If UNCTAD has remained a forum organization, concerned mainly with interest articulation on behalf of the Third World, this is because there are no significant political pressures for turning it into something else. In order to understand UNCTAD's organizational processes, one must identify the national groups likely to be affected by UNCTAD's policies. The next section attempts to do this and to raise the question: why have these groups not pressed for rapid task expansion in specific issue areas? Since Group B countries have been mainly responsible for mounting active resistance to the implementation of UNCTAD's policy recommendations, the analysis will focus upon national interest groups within the developed countries.

8.1.2 National Interest Groups Affected by UNCTAD

The major substantive decisions taken by UNCTAD to date are likely to have had an impact on a number of interest groups within the developed countries. In this section I intend to identify these groups, and to evaluate their realized and potential political significance.

8.1.2 (a) Interest groups and aid studies of national policies generally hold that there is little grass-roots enthusiasm for foreign aid in most Western countries.[4] Both multilateral and bilateral agencies have frequently argued that loans to developing countries have to be placed within the conventional commercial framework, otherwise the international capital markets or the national finance ministries will not approve. In the Nordic countries, concern with the education of public opinion is a permanent feature of their aid policies. However, it is rather unlikely that unfavourable public opinion has been a major restraint upon the expansion of development assistance. Political parties have rarely won or lost significant proportions of votes on the basis of their development policies and performance.

Aid programmes within the developed countries are strongly influenced by the existence of pressure groups. These groups may broadly be categorized as follows:

(a) *Economic interest groups.* This category may be further subdivided into (i) investment-based interest groups, and (ii) trade-based interest groups. The former group consists mainly of those multinational corporations which have invested in the developing world. They seek foreign aid for the LDCs, primarily because such aid facilitates the development of a socio-economic infrastructure for successful investment. Both in the UK and in the US investment-based interest groups have constituted a very important segment of the aid lobby. For the UK, the influence of this group is described by White: 'New Overseas Investors[5] assessment of aid was conditioned by assessment of the developmental impact of aid programmes. This group was outstanding among non-governmental groups in that the nature and function of its channels of communication with the Government were clear'.[6] This group did not place an emphasis on expansion in aid programmes as a major priority item in their dealings with home governments, because most multinationals invest in a large number of countries, and investment in developing countries constitutes a relatively small portion of their total capital. These multinationals thus, typically, are much more concerned with the negotiation of arrangements on tax, employment, interest rates and on changes in domestic economic policies of the Western countries, as well as on their inter-group trade policies, than with Western attitudes and policies *vis-à-vis* the Third World. Their influence on the composition of the aid effort is evident from the fact that during the 1960s and 1970s Western countries tended to increase aid flows related to the development of new relatively high technology industries, or of the socio-economic infrastructure necessary to sustain them.

As far as the trade-based groups are concerned, their major interest in aid is mainly related to the question of aid tying. Both in the US and in the UK, major exporters to Third World countries take an active interest in negotiations leading to specific agreements on aid use. There is little evidence to suggest that bilateral aid is less 'tied' today than it was in the early 1960s.[7] The exporters have not, however, generally attempted to influence the volume of aid. This may again be explained by the fact that well over two-thirds of total exports of Western developed countries is accounted for by trade with each other. Hence the major exporting groups within the Western countries were mainly concerned with intra-group Western trade, and were not primarily concerned with stimulation of demand for their goods in the poor countries.

(b) *Religious and humanitarian interest groups.* The political effectiveness of these groups is constrained by the nature and content of their pro-aid programme. They stress the importance of assistance to the underprivileged on moral grounds. And, in an increasingly materialistic culture, arguments of this nature are not capable of generating much political momentum. Moreoever, the general endorsement of an expanded aid programme does not create pressure within Western-type polities, unless this is accompanied by support for specific policies. Traditionally, on questions of aid, pressure mobilized by voluntary agencies has tended to remain general and diffuse. Since the early 1970s, there are indications that this is being realized, and religious and humanitarian bodies have published analyses of and responses to specific proposals. Generally these studies represent a ready acceptance of the position taken by the developing countries.[8] The religious and humanitarian organizations face the problem that, to increase their political impact on the aid question, they have to appeal to specific material interests, but this may lead to a toning down of the moral content of their appeal.

(c) *Government departments.* Aid administrations generally do not occupy a position at the highest levels of political decision-making processes. They are usually subsumed by the ministry of trade, the foreign ministry, or both. Finance and defence ministries may also evidence considerable interest in the aid programme. The finance ministry is concerned with the impact of the foreign aid programme on the domestic economy. Aid represents an immediate balance of payments cost, but this may be offset by export earnings occasioned by that aid or by increased profit remittances of multinationals benefiting from the deployment of aid funds on infrastructure developments. Defence and foreign ministries are concerned with aid, to the extent to which it can be used as an instrument of foreign policy.]

It is easy to see why these ministries did not push for aid expansion along the lines of UNCTAD's policy. Intra-group trade of the West was more important than North–South trade, in terms of both volume and growth rate, hence the trade establishment had little incentive for supporting the aid programme. The major aid donors—the US and the UK in particular—found themselves facing a series of balance of payments crisis during the 1960s especially, hence the finance ministries envisaged little enthusiasm for aid expansion. (Countries which had a balance of payments surplus, and in which the finance ministries did not veto new aid proposals, performed much better than the established donors, and their aid volumes went up considerably.) The cold war cooled off significantly during the 1960s, and Third World non-alignment was no longer considered to be a threat to Western security, hence the defence and foreign ministries saw no strategic case for the expansion of foreign assistance. They were in particular opposed to the generalized increases in aid volume which the UNCTAD proposals seemed to envisage.

Thus, aid volumes remained fairly stagnant during the past two decades. This was so because there were no politically significant interest groups willing to exert enough pressure on the aid policy makers to implement the UNCTAD resolutions. The major drive for aid expansion during the 1950s had come from newly perceived military and strategic needs by the West. In the 1960s and 1970s the situation had stabilized, and aid levels stabilized with it.

(d) *Interest groups and trade.* UNCTAD proposals for trade expansion envisage the expansion of output by LCDs in those industrial branches in which they have an international comparative advantage. These are 'problem industries' for the

West, and enjoy high levels of protection and subsidization. They include the food-processing industry, which benefits from generally high levels of protection accorded to agriculture by Western countries. Other protected industries include chemicals, textiles and leather, which are typically employment intensive and face stiff competition from the Third World. Pressure to protect these industries is accentuated by a desire to protect employment. These industries pose significant employment problems for the developed countries. As technological development takes place, there is a natural impetus, generated within the developed economies, to concentrate heavily on the production of technology-intensive products, and firms attempt to shift resources in the less sophisticated industries to low-wage countries. However, this is a painful process; for the shifting of resources from the low to the high technology industries, or the changeover from labour- to capital-intensive methods of production within these industries, releases a large volume of unemployed labour, which is very difficult to absorb within other parts of the economy. Both the US and the UK have experimented with 'adjustment assistance' programmes— particularly to counteract labour displacement in the textile industry—but the results have not been very encouraging.[9] Governments of developed countries thus resist the dismantling of tariff barriers in this area, since they apprehend that such a policy would entail the commitment of sizable proportions of public money to 'adjustment assistance' schemes, which have not proved very fruitful in the past.

Furthermore, the levels of industrial concentration in the 'protected' industries are generally high. High rates of concentration imply increased co-ordination in business strategy. Such industries can bring about more pressure to bear upon their governments. Thus, the 'protected' industries are in an advantageous position to ensure that governments of developed countries do not endorse policies which would increase competition, and which would, therefore, lower prices in their markets. Moreover, groups interested in reducing the prices of these products are weak, disorganized, and generally without significant bargaining power within the Western countries. Thus, of the thirty-six product markets studied by Walsh, in his analysis of monopoly in the UK—including fourteen products manufactured by British 'protected' industries—only four product markets of those in which developing countries had an interest had significant consumer interest coordination and pressure, and all the markets were characterized by high levels of concentration.[10] Moreover, this consumer pressure was exercised, in the main, by retailing chains, which were primarily interested not in low prices, but in maintaining profit margins. If the consumers were willing to pay a higher price, the retailers saw no point in attempting to depress it. Consumer associations themselves had little and insignificant impact on the policies of either firms or governments within the Western countries.

We see, therefore, that the structure of the 'protected' industries was an important factor in inducing the governments of the developed world to adopt a rigid postuɪe *vis-à-vis* the proposed GSP product coverage lists of the UNCTAD Secretariat. These industries account for a large proportion of total manufacturing production, and employment. They have high levels of concentration. Redeployment of the labour force is a difficult and expensive operation. Pressure to reduce prices of the products of these industries was negligible. These factors, coupled with the inbuilt restrictiveness of agricultural trade policy, determined the attitude of the Western countries.

(e) *Interest groups and commodities.* In this section we will try to identify the main Western groups involved in dealings on world commodity markets, and explain their response to UNCTAD initiatives in this field. Nearly all primary products produced in the developing countries are traded (either by the LDCs or by other producers) in international markets. Theoretically, a 'manufactured' product differs from a 'primary' commodity by the relatively low level of processing of the latter. However, in practice it is almost impossible (in most cases) to identify unambiguously the stage at which a commodity ceases to be 'primary' and becomes 'manufactured' or 'semi-manufactured'. This is because many existing processes of production and marketing technically link primary commodities to manufactured products. Vertically integrated transnational corporations (TNCs), operating globally, aim at a continuous centralization of control over these production and marketing processes. Owing to their monopoly in the field of technological innovation, their organizational skill and their financial power, a relatively small number of TNCs have succeeded in obtaining a vantage position in many primary commodity markets.

Leading TNCs in the market of ten 'core' commodities included in UNCTAD's Integrated Commodity Plan controlled almost 60 per cent of the total volume of transactions in the mid 1970s. Moreover, marketing at the international level remains largely under the dominance of the TNCs. This is true, for example, of copper, bauxite, aluminium and crude oil,[11] in all of which nationalization of foreign enterprises has been a growing tendency in recent years. Market structures of many primary commodities are no longer characterized by the predominance of inter-firm transactions, but by bilateral bargaining between governments and TNCs and by 'open' transactions between TNCs, speculators, state trading corporations, etc. In most cases the TNC plays a vital role in establishing prices and output levels of primary commodities traded in most international markets. The influence of the TNCs in these markets reflects their size—annual average sales of the twenty-seven leading TNCs in primary commodity markets was equivalent to 36.5 per cent of the GNP of the 'average' primary producing LDC, and the combined annual sales of these TNCs was equal to 37.8 per cent of the combined GNP of the primary producing LDCs in the late 1970s.[12]

The TNCs thus are an important source of decision making in world commodity markets. The TNCs seek internationalization, in order to benefit from worldwide sourcing, they aim at vertical integration of production and management processes, and they seek to develop and consolidate their control by constructing conglomerates.[13] TNCs thus have a natural tendency to seek expansion of production complexes—TNCs in primary producing industries generally have larger production complexes than do TNCs in manufactured industries[14]—and a natural tendency to centralize authority in the hands of relatively small groups of key top executives, based at central headquarters and at regional head office. These characteristics of TNC strategy are often at variance with the economic policies and objectives of LDCs.[15]

Such interest divergence in the primary goods industries is

not uncommon, and has been an important factor behind the spate of nationalizations and partial take-overs of these industries by some LDCs during the 1960s and 1970s. According to one study, almost 350 cases of nationalization in primary goods industries were recorded during the period 1960–74.[16] Attempts at establishing national control through appropriation were particularly marked in the crude oil, bauxite and copper industries.[17]

Variance of interests between TNCs and primary producing LDCs may find expression in price policy. Generally speaking, LDCs desire stable prices for primary exports and favourable terms of trade between primary and manufactured goods in world markets. After the commodity price boom of the early 1970s the LDCs sought to achieve these aims in UNCTAD through the creation of international mechanisms, which would regulate fluctuations in the prices of ten 'core' and eight other primary commodities. We have seen that the level of concentration in the world markets of the ten core commodities is high. There was little discernible support from these TNCs for the international initiatives of the LDCs in these markets. Price formation in most primary commodity markets reflects the bargaining power of participants. Prices may be fixed on the basis of one- or two-year contracts between suppliers and purchasers, or they may be determined directly or indirectly (i.e. by being linked) by transactions on international spot or future markets. Prices may also be determined by the TNCs internally, if the company acquires possession of a raw material at an early stage of processing, and its production process centre on its continued processing and fabrication. The more monopolized a market, the greater is the influence of the TNC's 'internal' price structures on the process of market price formations. In the minerals markets in particular, the influence of the commodity exchanges on price determination is unlikely to be more important than that of the TNCs' internal price policies, as only a very small proportion of the physical movement of a commodity takes place at the international commodity exchanges.

The TNCs' attitude on price levels in specific commodity markets reflects the structure of demand in these markets. Generally speaking, the lower the price elasticity of demand of a given commodity, the greater is the likelihood that an increase in its price will contribute towards a growth in profits. Most of the core commodities have high price elasticities. An increase in the price of most of these commodities would have a large negative impact on quantity demanded, and TNCs would find it difficult to pass on price increases to consumers, owing to the existence of a large number of substitutes. Moreover, the income elasticity of demand is low. Thus, their demand does not grow as rapidly as GNP in the developed countries. TNCs thus seek to incorporate prices of these commodities in the prices of products with favourable price and income elasticities, and there are few significant group interests in maintaining high price levels for the core primary commodities identified by UNCTAD. This is less true, of course, of Western agricultural producers of commodities included in the IPC, (Integrated Programme for Commodities), but their interests are taken care of by the national and regional agricultural policies of the Western countries, and, in any case, they produce a relatively minor proportion of world output in the agricultural primary commodity markets covered by the IPC. TNCs, however, had little cause to support the IPC.

8.2 UNCTAD's LEVEL

8.2.1 Changes in representational level

The preceding sections have looked at the scope of UNCTAD. This section will study changes in the level of represenation, by asking the question: has there been a significant change in the level of interest and participation in UNCTAD's decision-making process by countries which exercise influence within the international system? We assumed that the greater the relative level of participation of the 'key' developed and developing countries, the greater is their commitment to UNCTAD, in terms both of continuity and of technique. The 'key' developed countries have been identified as the US, France, Japan, the UK and West Germany, and the 'key' LDCs have been identified as India, Brazil, Yugoslavia, Argentina, Pakistan, Indonesia, Egypt, and Nigeria. This list is based on Cox and Jacobson's study of the distribution of power within the international system in the year 1967. They calculated national power as a component of five indicators—GNP, population, per capita GNP, offensive nuclear capability and international prestige. The pattern of power distribution remained fairly stable over the period 1950–67, according to Cox and Jacobson's calculations. Thus the list of the most powerful developed countries from 1950 and 1958 contains four of the five countries in the 1967 list. The LDC list is slightly more subject to change. A tentative attempt at drawing a picture of the pattern of national power distribution in 1983 showed that there was no significant difference from Cox and Jacobson's list of 1967. We, therefore, used this list to identify the most powerful nations.

In order to assess changes in the level of participation by the different countries in UNCTAD I have used the method developed by Keohane.[18] This method involves a comparison between states' ranking on basis of size of delegation to different meetings. Keohane compared sizes of national delegations to UN General Assembly Nos. 16–20 with the size of national diplomatic emissaries sent during 1963–4, Keohane writes 'this procedure will provide us with a measure of *relative*[19] attention paid by states to the General Assembly . . . The method creates a distribution of mean approximately zero (distorted slightly by tied scores)'.[20]

We will compare state rankings by size of delegations to UNCTAD I and UNCTAD VI. This will indicate changes in level of relative participation within UNCTAD by the 'key' states.

Table 8.2 indicates that there is little correlation between the sizes of state delegations to UNCTAD I and UNCTAD IV. The value of Spearman's rank correlation coefficient is very low. Theoretically, as Keohane has pointed out, the distribution of states should have a mean of 0, but due to the abundance of tied scores we get a mean of 1.12 (which, however, does not differ significantly from 0). We also obtain a standard deviation of 12.86 from a mean of 0. It must be emphasized that the table is a very rough estimator of levels of participation. It predicts that the nth state of the 1964 list will have a delegation size equal to the nth state on the 1983 list. Thus Sweden was no. 3 on the 1964 list. The table predicts that it would have had a

Table 8.2:   *Level of participation in UNCTAD: UNCTAD I v. UNCTAD VI*

Rank order by delegation to UNCTAD I	Predicted delegation size to UNCTAD VI	Actual delegation size to UNCTAD VI	Rank diff.	Rank by UNCTAD VI	
1 USSR	127	36	-91	Yugoslavia	1
2 Mexico	73	15	-58	Japan	2
3 Sweden	45	19	-26	West Germany	3
4.5 West Germany	42	45	+3	France	4
4.5 Argentina	36	25	-11	USSR	5
4.5 Netherlands	33	33	0	Netherlands	6
7.5 USA	32	23	-9	Belgium	7
7.5 Italy	30	20	-10	India	8
9.5 Yugoslavia	29	127	98	UK	9
9.5 Austria	28	28	0	Austria	10
11 UK	26	29	3	Brazil	11
12 Brazil	25	26	1	Argentina	12
13 France	23	42	19	USA	13.5
14 Japan	23	73	50	South Korea	
15 Spain	22	15	-7	Venezuela	
16 Czechoslovakia	22	12	-10	Greece	15.5
17 India	22	30	8	Australia	
18 Israel	20	8	-12	Italy	
19 Switzerland	20	16	-4	Indonesia	18.5
20 Ghana	20	8	-12	Egypt (UAR)	
21 Egypt (UAR)	19	20	1	Sweden	
22.5 Romania	19	15	-4	Tunisia	21.5

22.5	Morocco	18	16	Finland	-2	
24	Senegal	18	6	Cuba	-12	23.5
25.5	Nigeria	18	14	Denmark	-4	
25.5	Poland	18	17	Canada	-1	
26.5	Belgium	17	32	Poland	15	27.5
27.5	Venezuela	17	22	Algeria	5	
29.5	Bulgaria	17	14	Iran	-3	
29.5	Turkey	16	14	Switzerland	-2	30.5
31	Chile	16	9	Morocco	-7	
32.5	Portugal	15	10	Mexico	-5	
32.5	Indonesia	15	20	Spain	5	
34.5	Finland	15	18	Romania	3	32.5
34.5	Algeria	15	17	Philippines	2	
34.5	El Salvador	15	3	Colombia	-12	
34.5	Ivory Coast	14	11	Nigeria	-3	
34.5	Greece	14	22	Bulgaria	8	
34.5	Cuba	14	18	Turkey	4	
40.5	Australia	14	22	Hungary	8	37.5
40.5	Peru	14	7	Norway	-7	
40.5	Hungary	14	14	Saudi Arabia	0	
43.5	Denmark	12	18	Czechoslovakia	6	
43.5	Thailand	11	6	Ivory Coast	-5	
43.5	Norway	11	14	New Zealand	3	
43.5	Uruguay	11	5	Uganda	-6	
43.5	Guatemala	11	3	Liberia	-8	43
47.5	Trinidad + Tobago	11	5	Iraq	-6	
48.5	Iran	11	17	Sri Lanka	6	44.5
48.5	Niger	11	3	Tanzania	-8	
50.5	Costa Rica	10	9	Portugal	-1	
50.5	Pakistan	10	9	Malaysia	-1	51.5
50.5	Ecuador	10	6	Panama	-4	

continued

Rank order by delegation to UNCTAD I	Predicted delegation size to UNCTAD VI	Actual delegation size to UNCTAD VI	Rank diff.	Rank by UNCTAD VI	
50.5 Malaysia	9	10	1	Chile	
55.5 Burma	9	3	−6	Costa Rica	
55.5 Madagascar	9	3	−6	Pakistan	
55.5 New Zealand	9	11	2	Jamaica	54.5
55.5 Uganda	9	11	2	Kenya	
55.5 Philippines	9	15	6	Nicaragua	
55.5 Cameroon	9	7	−2	Haiti	
55.6 Tunisia	8	19	11	Israel	
55.5 Liberia	8	11	3	Ghana	
55.5 RSS Byelorussia	8	5	−3	Ethiopia	61.5
64.5 Colombia	8	15	7	Central Africa	
64.5 Dominican Rep.	7	7	0	Peru	
64.5 RSS Ukraine	7	5	−2	Cameroon	
64.5 Canada	7	18	11	Dominican Rep.	
64.5 Iraq	7	11	4	Upper Volta	
69.5 South Korea	7	23	16	South Vietnam	65.5
69.5 Libya	7	6	−1	Rwanda	
71.5 Ethiopia	7	8	1	Zaire	
71.5 Saudi Arabia	7	14	7	North Yemen	
71.5 Guinea (Conakry)	6	6	0	Senegal	
71.5 Mongolia	6	6	0	Thailand	
75.5 Sri Lanka	6	11	5	Ecuador	
75.5 Jamaica	6	9	3	Libya	
75.5 Gabon	6	6	0	Guinea	
75.5 Sudan	6	1	−5	Mongolia	
75.5 Panama	6	10	5	Gabon	73.5

Rank	Country	Score		Score	Country	Change	Rank
81.5	Kuwait	6		5	Honduras	−1	
81.5	Ireland	6		5	Syria	−1	
81.5	Afghanistan	6		3	Nepal	−3	
81.5	Kenya	5		9	Uruguay	4	
81.5	Togo	5		2	Trinidad + Tobago	−3	
81.5	Honduras	5		6	RSS Byelorussia	1	
81.5	Mali	5		3	RSS Ukraine	−2	
81.5	Upper Volta	5		7	Kuwait	2	83.5
89.5	South Vietnam	5		7	Ireland	2	
89.5	Luxembourg	5		3	Holy See	−2	
91.5	Cyprus	5		4	Chad	−1	
91.5	Nicaragua	5		9	Burundi	4	
91.5	Syria	4		6	Cyprus	2	
91.5	Nepal	4		6	Bolivia	2	92.5
91.5	Tanzania	4		11	Jordan	7	
91.5	Mauritania	3		1	El Salvador	−2	
91.5	Bolivia	3		4	Guatemala	1	
91.5	Holy See	3		5	Niger	2	
99.5	Rwanda	3		7	Burma	4	95.5
99.5	Congo (Zaire)	3		7	Madagascar	4	
99.5	Haiti	3		9	Afghanistan	6	
102	Chad	3		5	Mali	2	
103	Central Africa	3		8	Luxembourg	5	
104.5	Jordan	2		4	Togo	2	103
104.5	Burundi	1		5	Mauritania	4	104.5
104.5	Yemen	1		7	Sudan	6	
	GDR	19					

Note: Only states which participated in both UNCTAD I and UNCTAD VI (*n*=106) included.
Source: UNCTAD I *Proceedings*, Vol. 1; UNCTAD VI *Proceedings*, Vol. 1.

delegation size equal to the state which was no. 3 on the 1983 list—which was West Germany with a delegation size of 45. Sweden, however, sent only 19 delegates to UNCTAD VI. Its score was calculated as (19–45=–26), and its relative level of participation has declined since 1964. In the table, however, there are relatively few states about which we can make such 'predictions' accurately. Thus, Italy, for example, ranks 7.5 in the 1964 list, but no state has this rank in the 1983 list. Thus the 'score prediction' is only approximate, and, since this is true of most states, the effect on the rank correlation and standard deviation estimates is likely to be considerable. Thus, Table 8.2 is indicative only of broad trends.

The evidence in Table 8.2 shows that it is not possible to establish a lowering of the level of participation in UNCTAD conferences, as far as the key developed countries are concerned. Japan, Britain, France and West Germany had positive scores. The US alone had a negative score of –9. The ranks of the former four countries rose in 1983 compared with 1964. The evidence with regard to the eight key LDCs, on the other hand, is clearly mixed. Four of the key states had positive scores, and three, Argentina, Pakistan and Nigeria, had negative ones. Argentina alone had a high negative score (–11), and the average score of the key LDC states (excluding Yugoslavia, which hosted UNCTAD VI and sent the largest delegation) was –1. Thus, there is no clear evidence to indicate a substantial decline in the level of participation of key LDC's. As against this, there is some reason to believe that the relative level of participation of key DCs had increased—the major exception being the US.

Thus, there is no clear evidence for the generally held view that the relation level of participation of the Group B countries within UNCTAD has declined. However, there is some justification for the view that the absolute level of representation of the different groups has fallen since the early years of UNCTAD's inception (Table 8.3). The average size of the delegations of all groups declined substantially from 1964 to 1968. The average Group of 77 delegation at UNCTAD II was 35 per cent smaller in size than the average Group of 77 delegation at UNCTAD I. The average Group B delegation at Delhi was 30 per cent smaller than the average Group B

Table 8.3: *Level of representation of groups at UNCTAD conferences*

	1964	1978	1972	1976	1979	1983	X
Group of 77	12.84	8.31	8.90	8.91	9.71	9.17	9.64
Group B	25.85	17.89	20.64	20.32	23.48	21.68	21.64
Group D	21.90	15.60	13.40	14.10	15.54	14.68	15.86

Source: UNCTAD Conference *Proceedings* I, II, III, IV, V, VI, Vol. 1.

delegation at Geneva. There was an increase in the average delegation size of both B and '77' groups at UNCTAD III, relative to UNCTAD II, and no significant change in the average size of Group B and Group of 77 delegations subsequently. There have been no substantial changes in delegation size since 1976.

Given the fact that the level of participation at the earlier sessions was—to quote Nye—'surprisingly high', we cannot explain UNCTAD's apparent inability to transform North–South relations solely by pointing to low levels of participation of the 'key' states. This inability is also related to the process of decision making within UNCTAD. It has been argued that the commitment of a state to an international organization can be measured by the extent to which it is willing to devolve decision making in a specific issue area to a subunit of the organization concerned. Thus, an organization is likely to achieve environmental transformation in accordance with its ideology if its members agree to institutionalize decision making processes which subordinate national autonomy in specific issue areas to the international organization concerned. Let us look at the major substantive decisions taken by UNCTAD, and see to what extent there was a willingness on the part of the 'key' states in invest UNCTAD with the authority to make decisions as and when they become necessary.

8.2.2 Commitment to UNCTAD and delegation of authority in specific issue areas

(a) The Generalized Scheme of Preferences Prebisch, in his report to the 1964 UNCTAD, had formulated some ideas about preferences.[21] The US objected to the GSP on

principle. France and Belgium advocated selective preferences. This specifically allowed the DCs themselves to determine the terms of the GSP. The UK and West Germany favoured a single preferential scheme. In their proposal the developing countries insisted that there should be international supervision of the scheme. In the aftermath of UNCTAD I, a Group on Preferences was established, which launched a study of the technical aspects of a scheme fairly similar to the proposal made by the Group of 77. Following the US conversion to the GSP, Group B countries co-ordinated their policies in this issue area with the OECD Group of Four, but continued to insist that they had the right to determined product coverage individually, and to work out safeguards and escape clauses within Group B. On the other hand, the Group of 77 insisted strongly on the establishment of an international scheme with clearly defined objectives and methods of operation. This necessarily implied an extension of UNCTAD's role, although in reconciling their own intra-group differences the Group of 77 felt compelled to shelve international supervision. However, the LDCs seemed more concerned with getting Group B to commit itself to operating a liberal and wide-ranging GSP, and less concerned with establishing an international supervisory mechanism. Thus the crucial issue on which the GSP debate was deadlocked in the last days of the New Delhi conference was product coverage. The New Delhi conference adopted a resolution which endorsed the principle of preferential treatment of LDC's exports. It recommended that a Special Committee on Preferences be established within UNCTAD. This committee was to continue negotiations on this issue. Negotiations within the developed countries generally by-passed the Special Committee, which remained inactive in the first half of 1969. The developed countries forwarded their GSP proposals individually to the OECD.

The developed country submissions differed significantly in terms of product coverage, safeguards, exemptions and extent of tariff cuts. The GSP, as adopted, meant that each DC was itself ultimately responsible for the operation of its own scheme. Safeguards would be reviewed and applied unilaterally by individual DCs, who could withdraw from the whole GSP if they so wished, though UNCTAD was allowed to review that operation of the GSP schemes. It was to consider the effects of GSP on exports, economic growth and industrialization, and the interaction of the GSP with the specialized preference system. Group B established a parallel review mechanism within the OECD, to assess the impact of GSP on burden sharing, and the use of safeguards by the Group B countries. Thus the GSP schemes do not represent an attempt at subordinating national autonomy to the authority of UNCTAD. UNCTAD may review and comment upon the schemes; but LDCs have not placed any great emphasis on establishing UNCTAD's role as a supervisor of the implementation of the GSP, and UNCTAD's annual GSP reviews have not had a noticeable impact on the performance of the DCs in this area.

(b) The Integrated Commodity Programme After the third session of UNCTAD in 1972, intensive intergovernmental consultations were initiated for thirteen commodities on a case-by-case basis, but though these served to elucidate problems, they failed to lead to the adoption of measures to alleviate them.

In 1974, a committee open to membership by all states was established to consider a new approach to commodity policy.

UNCTAD made some headway in organizing negotiation sessions for a number of commodities, and agreement on the establishment of a Common Fund was reached in 1979. The establishment within UNCTAD of institutional mechanisms on this issue has, however, not meant a subordination to international co-ordination and negotiation of national decision making processes. If a realistically sized Common Fund could be established, it would imply acceptance by Western developed countries of international regulatory and management mechanisms, which would circumscribe the ability of national decision makers to act independently in commodity markets. That the Common Fund has been envisaged as a relatively minor financial operation indicates that, despite agreeing to the establishment of a subunit within UNCTAD specifically responsible for conducting negotiations, the DCs do not subscribe to the view that permanent international machinery should be established for effective intervention in commodity markets. As against this, the LDCs insist on the need for a substantial Common Fund, capable of significant intervention in commodity markets. This seems to indicate that LDCs have become conscious of the need for international regulatory mechanisms, which can override government and private-sector policies in this field. This is in contrast with the earlier position of the LDCs on the GSP and the Aid Target issues where, as we have seen, they were more concerned with the granting of concessions and with the acceptance of general principles than with the establishment of institutional machinery. The eventual establishment of the Fund, and its operational performance, will determine the extent to which UNCTAD has acquired an interventionist and supervisory role in this field. Writing in late 1984, one cannot afford to be optimistic on this score.

There are no a priori reasons for expecting the scope of UNCTAD to have widened, or its level to have risen over time. UNCTAD is a good example of what Roderick Ogley has called a 'blunt' organization. Its membership is not selective. Its specialized committees are open to very wide membership. States are allowed to be represented as they wish. Consensus is required for any concrete action to the initiated—although, at least in the earlier days, the enunciation of general principles did not seem to require the emergence of consensus. UNCTAD's recommendations are not legally binding. There have been few successful attempts to 'sharpen' UNCTAD. This is explained by the all too obvious fact that by 'sharpening' UNCTAD the Group of 77 would not increase the commitment of key states to UNCTAD policy. Thus, although there is general endorsement of the desire to raise the level of some UNCTAD organs such as the TDB, which is periodically convened at the ministerial level after 1976, there has been no attempt to sharpen them.

The fact that the scope of UNCTAD has not widened, and its level has not significantly risen over time, should not be allowed to obscure another equally significant aspect of the development of this organization: that is, the relatively high level of state participation in its processes. This high level of participation is coupled with a low level of commitment on the part of the key states to the policies which these processes generate. Thus the 'acceptability' of UNCTAD is not in question. Since decisions are not binding, can easily be ignored and are potentially 'reversible', there are no great political or economic costs attached to participation within it. Moreover, UNCTAD's role as a forum for interest articulation in the development issue are is unique.

If UNCTAD is to be transformed into a negotiating body, this must mean an increase in the level of commitment to its policies. This implies a sharpening of its constituent bodies and of its decision-making processes. This may mean a lowering of the level of state representation, but it will also mean a widening of UNCTAD's scope. In other words, it must mean increasing participation in UNCTAD processes of groups likely to be affected by the formulation or implementation of its policies. It is not clear whether such a 'sharpening' of UNCTAD is likely to be considered important by either the Group of 77 or Group B. To answer such questions we must assess the organizational autonomy of UNCTAD and the pattern of influence distribution which characterizes its decision-making processes.

8.3 ORGANIZATIONAL AUTONOMY

One approach to the measurement of the level of autonomy of an organization may be the ascertaining of the length of service of its secretariat officials and its delegates. The author was not permitted to compile internal staff lists, stretching from 1965 to 1983, of Secretariat officials, hence a correct estimate of the average length of service of Secretariat officials, and the extent to which personnel from within the organization are promoted to higher posts, could not be computed. However, from the record of the TDB it was possible to compile a list of 'experienced' delegates (i.e. delegates who had attended more than one meeting of a committee or of the TDB) for the TDB and a number of its committees.

Experienced delegates at the TDB and its committees constitute a small minority of those attending. Like other UN bodies, UNCTAD also has a highly variable 'delegate clientele', which consists of individuals who have had the burden of representing their countries in a number of forums, as well as performing domestic duties. This is perhaps inevitable for the LDCs, who have at their disposal a fairly limited number of diplomats and negotiators. The proportion of experienced delegates in Group of 77 delegations was lower than that in Group B and Group D delegations at the meeting of the board and its committees during 1964–83. Given the fact that Group D delegates considered themselves to be largely outside the negotiating processes, and unaffected by UNCTAD decisions, the higher proportion of experienced Group B and Group D delegates does not indicate that these delegations identified themselves significantly with the organizational ideology. UNCTAD's organizational autonomy was thus not augmented by the presence of a significant number of delegates with long experience of UNCTAD functioning and a sense of identity with UNCTAD's objectives. The group with the lowest proportion of experienced delegates, the Group of 77, tended to support task expansion by UNCTAD, more than either Group B or Group D. Delegates' identification with organizational ideology was thus not an important factor, as far as the institutionalization of UNCTAD was concerned.

Another indicator of the level of autonomy attained by an organization is the pattern of office distribution prevailing within it. Following Volgy and Quistguard,[22] we have attempted to relate office-holding patterns in UNCTAD to 'environmental', 'interaction', and 'legislative' variables. Table 8.4 describes the estimated variables. A significant positive association between the office-holding scores and the 'legislative' indicators would suggest that UNCTAD is a quasi-parliamentary body, which has the capacity to reward states which participate actively and fruitfully in its decision making processes. A negative and/or an insignificant relationship between these variables would indicate that UNCTAD has been unable to reward those states which took an interest in its affairs. A strong positive association between the office-holding scores, on the one hand, and the 'environmental' and 'interaction' variables, on the other hand, would suggest that office-holding patterns within UNCTAD were determined on the basis of extraorganizational considerations. An organization whose own decision-making processes did not have a significant bearing on the distribution of executive responsibilities within it could not be regarded as being significantly autonomous.

Table 8.5 reports the results of relating the office-holding scores to the 'environmental', interaction, and 'legislative' variables. We see that the average values of the 'legislative' coefficients is significantly greater than that of the 'environment' or 'interaction' coefficients. Also, five of the six 'leigslative' coefficients are statistically significant.

The two zeros which occur are explained by the fact that variable 13 is calculated only for Group B countries. Variable 12 is calculated only for the Group of 77, as almost all Group B countries joined UNCTAD in 1964. One 'legislative' variable has the wrong sign. It is variable 13, that is, 'Votes against cast by Group B countries'. (A high tendency to vote against would be expected to correlate negatively with office-holding scores.) Only five out of the twelve 'environmental' coefficients, and three of the six 'interaction' coefficients, are statistically significant. Two of the eight 'environmental' coefficients, and two of the six 'interaction' coefficients have the wrong sign.

These results are largely similar to those of Volgy and Quistguard, who found that 'legislative' characteristics best explained office holding within the UN General Assembly,[23] but our results are at variance with the studies of Weigart and Riggs,[24] and Singer and Sensening,[25] who found 'environmental' variables to be important determinants of office holding within the UN. We have found that UNCTAD is a 'quasi-legislative' body, which gives office to those who are involved in its processes. As far as the LDCs are concerned, none of the 'environmental' or 'interaction' characteristics seem to be an important determinant of office holding—except perhaps the number of missions sent abroad (Var. 8). For the Group B countries, on the other hand, some 'environmental' characteristics were found to be somewhat more important, but even here the 'legislative' variables were far more significant.

The study of office-holding patterns thus shows that UNCTAD enjoyed a significant degree of autonomy. Another indicator of the level of organizational autonomy enjoyed by an international organization is the distinctiveness of its ideology. UNCTAD, at its inception, was identified with an

Table 8.4:   *Measures for determining patterns of office-holding in UNCTAD,*
1963-76

Variable	Method of calculation
Dependent variable	Countries were ranked separately in Group 77 and Group B according to number of offices held at: (1) UNCTAD conferences, (2) TDB sessions, (3) TDB committee meetings.
UNCTAD office-holding score	Different weights were attached to different offices—a score of 3 was assigned to the office of vice president and rapporteur, and a score of 5 to the chairmanship of a committee.
Independent variables	
I Environmental characteristics:	
1. GNP	Group rank according to GNP average in US$ 1964-83.
2. GNP per capita	Group rank according to GNP p.c. in US$ 1964-83.
3. Rate of growth	Group rank according to GNP p.c. growth in US$ 1960-83.
4. No. of radios	Population average 1966-1983.
5. Military expenditure	Group rank according to military expenditure/ GNP ratios 1982.
6. Education index	Group rank according to persons in higher education per million inhabitants 1982.
II Interaction characteristics:	
7. Memberships	Group rank according to membership in international organizations 1982.
8. Missions abroad	Group rank according to number of missions sent abroad 1982.
9. Trade	Group rank according to mean trade/GNP ratio, average 1964-86 (US$).
III Legislative characteristics	
10. Participation in committees	Group rank according to membership of committees of the conference and of the TDB.
11. Delegation size	Group rank according to size of delegation to UNCTAD conferences.
12. Membership	Group rank according to length of membership of UNCTAD.
13. Voting	Group rank of Group B countries according to number of *votes against* and abstentions on all resolutions at UNCTAD conferences.

Source: 1. World Bank, *World Atlas*, Washington (various).
2. GATT, *International Trade*, Geneva (various).
3. UNESCO *Statistical Yearbook*, New York (various).
4. UN *Statistical Yearbook*, (various).
5. Taylor, *World Handbook*, Yale (1972).
6. UNCTAD *Conference Proceedings* (various).
7. UNCTAD *Trade and Development Board Records* (various).

Table 8.5: *Office-holding patterns in UNCTAD: environmental, interaction and legislative correlates of office-holding scores*

		Office-holding	
		B	77
V.1	GNP	0.6933	0.0805
V.2	GNP p.c.	0.3872	0.3102
V.3	Growth rate	0.4648	0.3071
V.4	Radios	0.2129	0.3281
V.5	Military expenditure	0.1789	0.0200
V.6	Higher education	0.1581	0.2575
V.7	Membership in international organizations	0.3568	0.3226
V.8	Missions abroad	0.5299	0.4631
V.9	Trade/GNP	0.2142	0.4358
V.10	Membership of committee	0.4888	0.4672
V.11	Size of delegation to UNCTAD	0.6573	0.3458
V.12	Duration of membership	0.0	0.8170
V.13	Votes against (Group B)	0.3184	0.0

organizational ideology which was not explicitly shared by any other existing international organization. The IMF, the GATT and the IBRD had been born as part of the Bretton Woods system of 1944, and were firmly wedded to the philosphy of economic liberalism and *laissez-faire*. The purpose of the creation of the IBRD was to 'guarantee loans for productive reconstruction and development projects both with its own capital funds and through the mobilization of private capital ... the records of the Bretton Woods deliberations indicate that the emphasis from the beginning was not so much on what the Bank could lend directly out of its paid-in capital, as on the concept of the Bank providing a safe bridge over which private capital could move in the international field'.[26] Commercial viability was thus the most important criterion for the guaranteeing of development assistance by the IBRD. Despite the recent concern of the IBRD with taking a longer-term view of the development process, and its endeavour to move into areas such as agriculture, infrastructure creation and population control, the overriding concern with commercial feasibility has tended to persist.

Like the IBRD, GATT also sees itself as a custodian of a

liberal international trading system. Competition between UNCTAD and GATT has been stiff: each has tried to appropriate the others' functional mandate. Some observers believed that this competition would transform the nature of GATT. In particular, the adoption of Part IV of the General Agreement, incorporating a recognition that LDCs were justified recipients of non-reciprocal trade concessions, raised these hopes, but time has shown that 'Part IV provisions do not change the content of the first three parts in any decisive way'.[27] The concrete commitments of Part IV were disappointingly few, and Article IV, entitled 'Principles and Objectives', 'contains the most abstract verbiage . . . it follows the elegant but indefinite style which has tended to characterize the work of those international organizations where the appearance of action has too often been substituted for action itself'.[28] There is no mention of preferences, or of any specific commitment with regard to agricultural goods, and a large number of escape clauses, enabling DCs to postpone Part IV recommendations, are included. Thus, the adoption of Part IV has not affected the character of the GATT, which remains wedded to its ideal of a liberal world trading system.

UNCTAD's organizational ideology, on the other hand, has profoundly affected the thinking of the core UN system. Although institutional links between UNCTAD and the organs of the General Assembly are no greater than UNCTAD's institutional links with the specialized agencies, UNCTAD thinking has tended to prevail whenever the developing countries have had a voting majority. The UNCTAD Secretariat has played a crucial role in the formulation of Third World demands for the building up of the NIEO, and, in the process of negotiations launched since the UN General Assembly Seventh Special Session for the implementation of the various NIEO proposals, the UNCTAD Secretariat prepared the main background paper which provided the basis for the NIEO resolutions. There is little wonder that the NIEO proposals on commodities, on trade in manufactures, on financing and on multinational corporations are permeated with UNCTAD ideology. These proposals recognize 'the imperative need for redressing the economic imbalance between developed and developing countries'. They advocate that 'concerted efforts should be made in favour of the developing countries' in the field of trade, international monetary reform, international investment, science and technology, etc.

The identification of the General Assembly with UNCTAD's ideology has not, however, meant that UNCTAD's organizational autonomy has been curtailed. In the 1970s, there were some signs that this might indeed be so. The UN General Assembly, at its Seventh Special Session, had set up an *ad hoc* committee on restructuring economic and social programme of the UN system. In 1975, a resolution was passed by UNIDO II at Lima, recommending that the United Nations Industrial Development Organization (UNIDO) should become a UN specialized agency; the North–South dialogue, based at Paris, gained new momentum following the success of the Seventh Session. However, nothing much has come of these developments. Most important, the North–South dialogue has collapsed without setting up any new institutional machinery. We may, therefore, argue that UNCTAD may, in the foreseeable future, reasonably expect to be the focus for the articulation and implementation of programmes based on its organizational ideology. This indicates that UNCTAD has significant organizational autonomy.

Organizational autonomy may also be assessed by looking at an organization's ability to control its own budgetary resources. UN General Assembly resolution 1995—UNCTAD's Constitution—lays down that 'the expenses of the Conference, its subsidiary bodies and Secretariat shall be borne by the regular budget of the United Nations which shall include a separate budgetary provision for such expenses'. Estimates of total financial requirements, and of the distribution of the funds, are worked out by the UNCTAD Secretariat, and submitted for adoption by the General Assembly. Proposals with financial implications may be forwarded by the board or any of its subsidiary organs within the framework of estimates supplied by the Secretary General of the UN. Gosovic has remarked that 'the relationship between UNCTAD and its parent body the UN General Assembly has essentially been a trouble-free and complementary one'.[29] At its inception, LDCs argued that UNCTAD ought to be given complete autonomy in the use of its budgetary resources, and in the early years neither the UN General Assembly nor the Headquarters Secretariat tended to exercise much direct control over the budget's administration and the allocation of expenditure by UNCTAD. Since 1971, the UN Advisory Committee on Administrative and Budgetary Questions (ACABQ) has tended to look a little more closely at the UNCTAD budget and its use. The UNCTAD Secretary General however has considerable freedom, though he cannot make appropriations at his discretion, and though he is formally supervised by the UN Controller, the UNCTAD allocation of the UN budget is directly allocated to the UNCTAD Secretary General, which ensures that he has considerable autonomy. As UNCTAD has grown, so has its budgetary resources. It may thus be concluded that UNCTAD enjoys considerable autonomy as far as the use of resources allocated to it is concerned: its autonomy is nowhere near as great as that of some specialized agencies such as the IBRD and the IMF, which can mobilize resources on their own, but imminent threats to control its purse strings are not emerging. The Western countries are not likely to be enthusiastic about an expansion in its budget, but as long as it remains essentially a 'forum' organization there are no great gains to be made by attempting to control rigorously the funds allocated to UNCTAD.

High levels of organizational autonomy are not necessarily associated with high levels of organizational effectiveness. Organizational effectiveness depends upon a number of other factors, among the most important of which is the distribution of influence within the organization. It is to an analysis of this question that we now turn.

8.4 UNCTAD: THE ANATOMY OF INFLUENCE

The distribution of organizational influence depends upon the internal structure of the organization. Similarly, the internal organizational structure also affects organizational autonomy and organizational effectiveness. Generally speaking, the greater the importance of organizational subunits dominated by environmentally influential actors, the greater the effectiveness of the organization concerned. In attempting to evaluate the structuring of influence within UNCTAD we must ask:

(a) What is the relationship of UNCTAD's major internal units to each other, and what is their respective role in the process of decision making?

(b) What is the level of influence possessed by different groups in each of these subunits?

Internal organizational structure

Turning to the first question, we see that UNCTAD's constituent instrument—UN General Assembly Resolution 1995 (XIX)—established the triennial conference as the supreme plenary body of UNCTAD, responsible for carrying out the principal functions determined by the general assembly. The conference is largely free to adopt its own rules of procedure and programme of work. The conference supervises the work of all the other organs of UNCTAD. It elects its own officers, appoints sessional bodies and adopts the agenda (on the basis of the recommendations of the TDB) for a session. The number of sessional committees, and the number of items on a conference agenda, shrank over the period 1964–76, but have expanded somewhat subsequently.

The TDB is 'a permanent organ of the Conference . . . (which) adopt(s) its own rules of procedures . . . (and) meet(s) as required in accordance with its rules'.[30] Members of the TDB are elected at regular sessions of the conference. When the conference is not in session, the TDB performs its functions. It is responsible for follow-up action on decisions taken by the conference, and for conference preparatory work. It prepares the provisional agenda for the conference. On several occasions it has organized intergovernmental meetings at ministerial level, to discuss matters which may not be included in the conference agenda. LDCs have generally argued that the TDB should also be made responsible for seeing that UNCTAD resolutions are implemented. But to date the TDB has not had a significant role in ensuring policy implementation. The TDB is responsible for maintaining relations and co-ordinating action with international organizations within and without the UN system. The TDB is also empowered to 'establish such subsidiary organs as may be necessary to the effective discharge of its functions'.

The terms of reference of the committee established by the TDB have been determined after taking into account the desirability of avoiding duplication and overlapping of responsibility within the UN system. The committees usually meet twice, in regular sessions, between sessions of the conference. The TDB may convene a regular session of the committees when necessary. The committees may establish their own permanent or *ad hoc* subsidiary organs. Many such bodies have been established by the board and the committees.

Resolution 1995 (XIX) laid down the voting and conciliation procedure, which was to provide the basis of the decision-making process. Within the conference, and its committees, 'decisions of the Conference on matters of substance shall be taken by a two-thirds majority of the representatives present and voting on procedure (all decisions) shall be taken by a majority of the representatives present and voting . . . In the Board and its organs a majority of the representatives present and voting . . . shall determine (a decision)'.[31] The conciliation procedures laid down in General Assembly Resolution 1995 have never been made use of. UNCTAD has tended to make increasing use of the consensus method in reaching decisions in all its deliberations. Even at the conference, where the LDCs face the temptation of articulating their voting strength, most significant decisions were taken by consensus. In the TDB and the committees the consensus method is far more common. The articles of establishment do not include consensus as a method of decision making within UNCTAD. It is regulated by rule-of-thumb criteria. It involves intensive negotiation under the guidance of the chairman of the group, until consensus is reached on a specific issue. This consensus is submitted in the form of a draft resolution by the chairman who announces that if there is no opposition to this proposal it will be considered as adopted.

As time has gone on, there has been a recognition that a wider level of state participation is desirable, hence the emphasis on decisions via consensus, and hence also the increase in the membership of UNCTAD's main organs.

All members of UNCTAD are members of the conference. Originally, TDB members were elected at UNCTAD conferences; but after UNCTAD IV, General Assembly Resolution 1995 (XIX) was amended, enabling all countries to be members of the TDB if they so wished, simply by notifying the Secretary General of UNCTAD of their intention. Membership of the board now lasts indefinitely. UNCTAD IV also adopted a resolution requesting that 'the TDB (should) hold sessions periodically at the ministerial level . . . (ensuring) . . . that important policy issues will receive high level attention at UNCTAD more frequently than in the past'.[32] Conference also requested the board 'to reform and rationalize the continuing machinery of UNCTAD'. This has meant a considerable expansion in the membership of the TDB committees.

Officers of the TDB and the committees are elected on the basis of the group system, whereby UNCTAD members have been divided into three groups. The TDB president and rapporteur posts are subject to rotation among the groups, on a ten-year cycle and a five-year-cycle respectively. The chief officers of the main committees are also elected on the basis of the same rules of procedure, which are amended from time to time. Membership of committees is determined by the board, taking into account group representatives and states concerned with the issues which the committee is likely to consider. Members of committees are elected at the beginning of a board session, but 'it is becoming increasingly common for all member states to take part if they wish, in some UNCTAD subsidiary organ'.[33] Thus, from the point of view of the different groups, what is important is not whether any particular member state participates in a particular body or holds office within it: rather, what is of significance is the relative strength of the group within a particular UNCTAD forum.

There is remarkable degree of stability in the proportion in which offices are distributed within UNCTAD. The distribution of offices at TDB meetings and at meetings of its main committees have remained virtually unchanged since 1964. The typical TDB session elects seven officers, four from the Group of 77 and two from Group B. There has been a decline in the relative strength of the Group B delegations, as the committees and the TDB have become large; but Group B countries have not objected to this, as most issues are determined through consensus, and voting majorities do not pose the sort of threat that they did in 1964.

To get on an UNCTAD committee and to hold office is a relatively effortless matter. Countries with special interests, and large countries, find that there are no major hurdles confronting them when they seek membership of a committee or the board: offices are distributed by the different groups. Chairmanship of groups rotate in alphabetical order. Legislative performance plays an important part in determining a claim to office. Nomination to office depends also upon the size of the country, its geographical representativeness, its contribution to the group's and to UNCTAD's resources, its level of participation in world trade, and investment, and flexibility in negotiating position. This last is singled out for emphasis by Nye, who writes 'the forum role of UNCTAD makes it difficult for a moderate to prevail over a more legitimate extremist in the early stages of discussion (but) . . . flexibility and diplomatic skill are useful resources in the final stages of discussion when it becomes clear that something must be done to salvage a meeting'.[34]

Distribution of influence

We used Nye's methodology[35] to estimate the influence of different state members of UNCTAD. On the basis of an analysis of TDB and conference documents it becomes possible to identify eight decisions over the period 1964–83 where:

(a)   states which proposed a certain decision;
(b)   states which opposed a certain decision; and
(c)   states which acted as brokers and successful negotiators

could be ranked along the Nye scale, which is presented in Table 8.6, and Table 8.7 summarizes the results of the exercise.

These results ought to be viewed with extreme caution. The only basis on which particular decisions were selected was availability of sufficient discussion in the UNCTAD documents. This ensured that the decisions studied were the more important ones, but scores assigned to different states were based entirely on subjective evaluation. This was particularly tricky when assessing the role of brokers. Moreover, we did not have the opportunity to supplement the document study with

Table 8.6: *The Nye scale for measuring influence in UNCTAD*

Direction of influence	Action	Score
Negative	Prevents easily and independently	3
	Prevents by alliance with group members	2
	Prevents by alliance with members inside and outside the group	1
	Wants to but cannot prevent	0
Positive	Initiates successfully, individually	3
	Initiaties successfully, with support of the group	2
	Plays the role of broker between groups	1
	Wants to but cannot initiate successfully	0

Ranking states along this scale we get the following results (Table 8.7).

Table 8.7: *Ranks of influential states within UNCTAD (maximum score=24)*

		Score	+	−
1.	USA	20	6	14
2.5	France	17	4	13
3.	India	16	12	4
4.	UK	16	7	9
5.5	Japan	13	6	7
5.5	Australia	13	5	8
7.	Yugoslavia	12	12	10
7.5	West Germany	12	6	6
7.5	Saudi Arabia	12	8	4
7.5	Philippines	12	11	1
11.5	Nigeria	10	10	1
11.5	Pakistan	10	8	2
13.5	Netherlands	9	6	3
13.5	Chile	9	4	5
13.5	Denmark	9	6	3
13.5	USSR	9	5	4
17.	Iran	8	6	2
18.5	Sweden	7	6	1
18.5	Romania	7	3	4
20.	Egypt	6	5	1

interviews and observation of meetings. Nye did make use of these methods. His results, therefore, are more firmly based.

Bearing this in mind, it is reassuring to note that these results are not significantly different from Nye's. Although some countries included in our list are not included in Nye's, they have low rankings. Spearman's correlation coefficient between our list and that of Nye is 0.38. Moreover, the pattern of the influence identified by this work is similar to that of Nye. The Western countries have higher negative scores—the USA has the highest negative score—and India the highest positive score. There are nine developing countries and nine Western countries in our list, and in Nye's list eight developing countries and twelve Western countries.

In general, countries which rank highly in terms of their share in world trade have little positive influence in UNCTAD. Influence patterns in UNCTAD do not accurately reflect the distribution of influence within UNCTAD's specific environment. Though the major world traders are influential in UNCTAD, they find that they can exercise this influence mainly negatively. They are unwilling to initiate policies and have little interest in expanding UNCTAD's global task. This is the most important determinant of the relative ineffectiveness of UNCTAD, in its quest for system transformation, in accordance with its ideology. Furthermore, increasing UNCTAD's bluntness may not necessarily lead to an increase in the West's role within this organization. Such a policy can, at best, persuade the West that UNCTAD does not pose a threat to its economic interest, and can induce the Group B countries to tolerate its existence and countenance moderate expansion in its level of activity.

The internal organizational structure of UNCTAD has tended to become blunt over time. This has contributed to the growth of conciliation and compromise within the organization; however, as we saw in the last section, environmentally powerful states are not sufficiently influential within the organization to initiate or sustain task expansion in accordance with their own view of UNCTAD's role in co-ordinating international trade and investment. These states, however, do have significant blocking power, and can frustrate attempts at task expansion which are at variance with their own perceived international economic interests. The states which do have organizational influence, and can foster and sustain organizational initiates, are environmentally weak. The Secretariat thus faces the dual task of persuading LDCs to support organizational initiatives, and inducing the developed Western countries to tolerate UNCTAD's environmental initiatives. I will evaluate the strategy of the Secretariat in the next chapter, with a view to assessing the extent to which it has succeeded in pursuing these goals.

NOTES

1. Nye, J. 'UNCTAD: poor nations' pressure group', in Cox, R. and Jacobson, H. (ed.) *The Anatomy of Influence,* Yale, New Haven (1973) p. 346.
2. *Ibid.,* p. 347.
3. Something which occurred prior to the adoption of Keynesianism via the post-1929 Great Depression and the Second World War.
4. Major studies on British aid policies include Hart, Judith *Aid and liberation; a socialist study of aid policies.* Gollancz, London (1973); Seers, D. and Streeten, P., 'Overseas development policies', in Becherman, W. (ed.) *The Labour Government's Economic Record 1964–1970,* Macmillan, London (1972); White, John *The Politics of Foreign Aid,* The Bodley Head, London (1974). On US aid policies, *see* Mason, E.S. *Foreign Aid and Foreign Policy,* Harper, New York (1964); Milikan, R. and Rostow, I. *A Proposal: Key to Effective Foreign Policy,* Free Press, New York (1957); Walters, R.S. *American and Soviet Aid: a Comparative Analysis,* Pittsburgh University Press, Pittsburgh (1970); Westwood, A.F. *Foreign Aid in a Foreign Policy Framework,* Brookings Institution, Washington (1966); Wall, D. *The Charity of Nations: the Political Economy of Foreign Aid,* Macmillan, London (1973); For other countries and comparative studies, *see* Edgren, R. 'Growth and Equality—the Dual Aim of Swedish Development Assistance', *Development Dialogue,* Part I, (1972) p. 17–23; Hayter, T. *French Aid,* (ODI, London (1966); Rabin, J. *The Conscience of the Rich Nations DAC and the Common Aid Effect,* Free Press, New York (1966); White, J. *Japanese Aid,* ODI, London (1964); White, J. *German Aid: a Survey of the Sources, Policy and Structure of German Aid,* ODI, London (1965).
5. That is, multinational corporations. The traditional overseas investors with interest in plantations and in the commercial sector were not so concerned with aid policy, as the infrastructure necessary for the operation of such enterprises already existed. They were more concerned with trade policy, as we shall see later.
6. White, J. *The Politics of Foreign Aid,* p. 281. For the US, *see* the evidence in Wall, *op. cit.* pp. 64–81.
7. Singer, H.W. and Ansari, J.A. *Rich and Poor Countries,* George Allen and Unwin, London (1982) pp. 170–173.
8. *See* e.g. Tanner, J. *The Tide Has Turned: a First-hand Report on the Outcome of UNCTAD 4,* (World Development Movement (1976)).

9. On this *see* Singer and Ansari, *op. cit.,* Ch. 5. *See also* Miles, Caroline *Lancashire Textiles: A Case Study of Industrial Change,* NIESR Occ. Paper 23, Cambridge University Press, Cambridge (1971).
10. Walsh, D. *Recent Trends in Monopoly in Great Britain,* NIESR Occ. Paper 27, Cambridge University Press, Cambridge CUP (1974) pp. 102–10.
11. Hveem, H. *The Political Economy of Third World Producer Associations,* Universitetsporiaget, Oslo (1977) p. 21.
12. Hveem, *op. cit.* pp. 32–3.
13. UN, *Multinational Corporations in World Development,* UN, New York (1973) p. 7.
14. Chandler, A. *Strategy and Structure,* MIT Press, Cambridge Mass (1962). *See also* Hymer, S. 'The multinational corporation and the law of uneven development' in Bhagwati, J.N. (ed.) *Economics and World Order from the 1970s to the 1990s,* Macmillan, London (1972).
15. Streeten P. 'Costs and benefits of multinational enterprises in LDC's' in Dunning, J.H. (ed.) *The Multinational Enterprise,* George Allen and Unwin, London (1971) pp. 240–59.
16. UN, A/ 9716, Sept. 1974 and E/C 7/53 Jan. 1975.
17. Hveem, *op. cit.,* p. 23.
18. Keohane, Robert 'Who cares about the General Assembly?', *IO*, Vol. 19 No. 1, pp. 141–9.
19. Keohane's emphasis.
20. Keohane, *op. cit.,* p. 142.
21. Prebisch, R. *Towards a New Trade Policy,* UN, New York (1963) pp. 35–40.
22. Volgy, I. and Quistgard, R. 'Correlatives of organizational rewards', *IO* Vol. 28, No. 2., (1974) pp. 207–33.
23. Volgy and Quistgard, *op. cit.,* pp. 189–92.
24. Weigart, K.M. and Riggs, R.E. 'Africa and the United Nations elections', *IO*, Vol. 19, No. 1, (Winter 1969), pp. 1–19.
25. Singer, M. and Sensening, B. IV 'Elections within the United Nations', *IO*, Vol. 13, No. 4 (Autumn 1963) pp. 901–25.
26. The World Bank, *The World Bank, the IFC and the IDA,* Washington (1962) p. 3.
27. Dam, K.W. *GATT, Law and International Organization,* Chicago University Press, Chicago (1970) p. 22.
28. *Ibid.,* p. 238.
29. Gosovic, B. *UNCTAD: Conflict and Compromise,* Sijthoff Leiden, p. 177.
30. UN General Assembly Resolution 1995 (XIX) December 1964.
31. UN General Assembly Resolution 1995 (XIX) December 1964.
32. Resolution 90 (IV) of 1976, TD/216 September 1975, p. 27.
33. Haquani, Z. *UNCTAD: Towards a New Economic Order,* UNCTAD, New York, (1978).
34. Nye, J. 'UNCTAD: poor nations' pressure group' in Cox, R. and Jacobson, H. (ed.) *The Anatomy of Influence,* Yale University Press, New Haven (1975) p. 353.
35. Nye, *op. cit.,* p. 353–62.

9 The Strategy of the UNCTAD Secretariat

There exists a strong prima-facie case for examining the UNCTAD Secretariat's strategy. The failure of the Belgrade Conference has opened up the debate about the future of the NorthSouth dialogue. The consensus of opinion within the Third World seems to be that the niggardliness of the West is the sole or at least the main factor responsible for the stalemate. The attitude of the West was, however, quite different in the early 1960s and after 1974 when many Third World countries had demonstrated considerable 'producers power'. Were there really no opportunities to be seized during the 1960s and 1970s, and why was so little achieved during this period? A scientific and dispassionate examination of the Secretariat's strategy may take us some way towards answering these questions.

The Secretariat of the UNCTAD played an important part in determining the attitude and negotiating stance of developing countries. It may be argued that the organizational strategy of UNCTAD has had an important impact on the evolution of international economic relations since 1964. In this chapter I have attempted to evaluate this strategy on the basis of hypotheses derived from an (admittedly eclectic) reading of international organization theory. This theory has been discussed in Chapter 5. The period covered extends from 1964 to 1983—that is, from the time of the convening of UNCTAD at Geneva to the conclusion of UNCTAD VI at Belgrade.

The following hypotheses have been derived from international organization theory and used as a basis for studying the strategy of the UNCTAD Secretariat.

9.1 THE STRATEGY

Hypothesis 1: Growth is a specific organizational goal that takes precedence over stable client-related tasks.

Organizational growth implies an increase both in the material resources possessed by the organization and in the power and influence of the organization within the international system. A concern with increasing the international influence of UNCTAD can be read into the 1964 report of UNCTAD's first Secretary General, who formulated a cogent criticism of the role of the GATT within the world economy. GATT, he argued, had only 64 members and could by no means be described as a universal organization. It was not primarily concerned with the problems of development. Its impact upon intro-LDC trade as well as on trade between DCs and LDCs had been minimal. All this underlined the necessity for the creation of a universal trading organization with extensive powers to deal with the special requirements and needs of the LDCs.

Prebisch played a crucially important role in bringing about reconciliation between the developed and developing countries on the institutional question at Geneva,[1] and the final resolution adopted gave UNCTAD a mandate that could be fairly widely interpreted, although it does not invest UNCTAD with the authority to oversee or subjugate any other UN body. The DCs had wanted UNCTAD to be basically a forum organization, but the UN General Assembly resolution 1995 (XIX) recognized its role both as initiator of negotiations for the adoption of multilateral legal instruments, and a body 'that shall take . . . appropriate action for the implementation of the resolutions . . . of the Conference'. As is well known, the Secretariat has been pressing for the enhancement of UNCTAD's negotiating role. Thus, though the greatest success in this field has been in connection with the conclusion and ratification of international commodity agreements, the Secretariat has also attempted to play a negotiating role in the field of preferences, supplementary financing, shipping legislations, etc. Prebisch had also been strongly concerned about improving UNCTAD's ability to supervise the implementation of decisions taken within it. Corea had also insisted that the Common Fund proposals can be meaningfully implemented only if UNCTAD is permitted a supervisory role.[2]

Corea had also concerned himself with seeking an expansion in the material resources available to UNCTAD. Budget appropriations for UNCTAD had represented roughly about 5 per cent of the total UN budget over the period 1964–75. After the Nairobi Conference 1976, agreement was reached between the UN Secretary General and Corea on the need for a substantial rise in the budget resources. Total appropriations amounted to $33.5 million for the 1976–9 period.[3] The budget has continued to expand and has reached $55.2 million over the period 1984–5.[4] The concern of the Secretariat with organization growth has meant a continuous search for issues on which task expansion seems most feasible. The feasibility of task expansion in specific issue areas is determined primarily by the environment within which such task expansion is sought. UNDTAD has been acutely conscious of the need to focus attention on problems that have become salient because of developments within the international environment. Thus UNCTAD I concerned itself primarily with a consolidation of the newly emerging unity of the developing countries. Without an effective instrument for interest aggregation, synthesis and articulation, it was improbable that Third World unity could have been long-lasting. Prebisch provided a basis for the consolidation of Third World unity within international economic forums.

The international environment provided an opportunity for working for the consolidation of Third World unity. A large number of African countries had gained independence in the early 1960s. Aggressive non-alignment was being gradually mellowed as the cold war was losing its intensity. The economic problems of LDCs were appearing formidable. At the same time, foreign aid levels were falling, as the West stopped competing with the Soviet bloc for Third World allies. All factors highlighted the need for a new international economic strategy by the Third World. Prebisch tailored UNCTAD's organizational ideology to meeting this need. UNCTAD I concentrated attention on winning Third World support for

UNCTAD's organizational ideology, and on winning First World tolerance for the creation of a permanent UN forum where the Third World could articulate its interests and voice its aspirations. At New Delhi the Secretariat concentrated attention, not on the acceptance of general principles, but on the 1 per cent Aid Target and on the Generalized Preference Schemes. The emphasis on preferences was once again determined very largely by developments within the world economy. In 1967 the Kennedy Round of GATT negotiations had concluded without any substantial gains to the LDCs. In 1967 the USA also announced its willingness to support preferences in principle as a major concession to Latin American heads of states.[5] Similarly the debate on the aid target resolutions at New Delhi reflected the previous consensus within the UN system on the desirability of meeting these targets 'in principle'—a fact which was also highlighted in the report of the Pearson Commission submitted less than a year after the New Delhi Conference.

The major resolutions at Santiago also reflected developments within the international environment. An important event from UNCTAD's point of view during the period 1968–72 had been UNCTAD's acceptance as a participating agency within the United Nations Development Programme. In 1969 a Technical Co-ordination Unit was established within the UNCTAD Secretariat. This development provided a natural background for the adoption of the Transfer of Technology resolutions unanimously adopted at UNCTAD III. These resolutions requested the UNCTAD Secretariat to provide technical assistance for technology transfer to LDCs within the context of the UNDP.[6]

UNCTAD III also saw a major attempt to achieve a breakthrough on the 'aid SDR link' question. By the early 1970s it had become quite clear that the decline in official development assistance was of a secular character. The collapse of the Bretton Woods system in 1971 had created a need for the replacement of the United States dollar by a new international currency. The Special Drawing Rights of the IMF created in 1968 could potentially play this role, provided there was a substantial increase in the volume of SDRs in circulation. Such an expansion was desired by the major industrial trading countries, which had endorsed the need for an expansion in SDRs within the IMF Group of Ten. Perez-Guerero—UNCTAD's second Secretary General—sought to establish a 'link' between expansion in aid and in international liquidity, hoping to benefit from the need of the DCs for an expansion in SDRs.

UNCTAD IV was dominated by the discussion of Mr Corea's 'Integrated Programme for Commodities'. This concern with commodities could once again be traced to developments within the international system. Commodity prices—not just the price of oil, but the price of a number of other industrial raw materials—had risen sharply in the period 1971-4. The LDCs were deeply concerned to consolidate the gain that had been made in the commodity markets during the early 1970s, and there was a general realization that the commodity boom was not likely to last very long. The Sixth and Seventh Special Sessions of the UN General Assembly, held in April 1974 and September 1975 respectively, addressed themselves specifically to the task of mobilizing the 'commodity power' of the Third World to build a New International Economic Order. UNCTAD's Secretary General played an important part in preparation for the Seventh Session of the UN General Assembly, and many of the resolutions of this session entailed specific proposals for consideration at UNCTAD IV.[7] The most important of these proposals related to the Integrated Commodity Plan, which had been put forward by Corea soon after coming into office in 1974, and the proposals on the granting of permission for the rescheduling of debt and institutionalization of other forms of debt relief for the LDCs. The oil price boom following the Ramadhan War, and the emerging food deficits of 1974 had created a need for granting of debt relief to countries most seriously affected by these crises. This need had been recognized within the UN system—the MSA (most seriously affected countries) category had been formally established—and by the IMF, which had established its 'oil facility' in 1975. UNCTAD sought to win concession on this question.

The main issues considered at Nairobi thus were determined by developments within the international environment. However, by 1979 it was clear that the establishment of the

Fund would not lead to a restructuring of the world economy. It was also evident that the international economy was in the grip of a recession that would significantly weaken the position of the developing countries. There would be an increase in protectionist measures used against LDC exports and a hardening of terms on which private-sector loans were extended to the Third World. These concerns of the Group of 77 were reflected in the now famous 'Item 8'—a discussion of the possibility of moving towards a negotiated restructuring of the international economy, on the agenda of UNCTAD V. Group B countries were unwilling to commit themselves on this issue. The pressure on commodity prices had been significantly reduced, and the prolonged recession made the rich countries cautious and somewhat inflexible. The Secretariat preferred to press ahead with the 'restructuring resolution' in the hope that this would ensure the support of its main client group and facilitate organizational growth.

By 1983 LDCs had lost the initiative, and international economic restructuring seemed to be both an unrealistic and an undesirable objective to the monetarist New Right regimes of the United States, Britain and West Germany. In the early 1980s the West was in the grip of a serious economic recession. Corea, therefore, emphasized that UNCTAD VI could play a role in initiating and sustaining world economic recovery. No specific new proposals were put on the Belgrade agenda. UNCTAD VI was based on the new theme 'recovery and development'. Corea stated 'what we are seeking today is not so much to negotiate major new innovations in policy but rather to give effect to approaches and goals which have for long been the subject of consensus in the international community'.[8] Proposals for accelerating the development of the LDCs—such as the resolution recommending a special allocation of SDRs equivalent to $30 billion to them—were invariably justified by the positive impact such measures could have on the state of the world economy.

We may conclude therefore that organizational growth is a specific organizational goal. It takes precedence over the performance of stable client-related tasks, if client-related tasks are defined in terms of specific proposals put forward at UNCTAD conferences. If the Secretariat had insisted on seeking the implementation of these proposals, the resources and influence of UNCTAD would in all probability not have increased significantly, for it soon became apparent that Group B countries were not likely to countenance a major role of UNCTAD as a supervisor, and resistance on such a role would almost inevitably have meant organizational stalemate. As the systemic resistance to the actual implementation of these resolutions became apparent in negotiations, UNCTAD did not seek to stick to the letter of these resolutions. Thus the New Delhi and Santiago Conferences did not stress the need of UNCTAD to assume a specific 'supervisory' role in the field of aid administration and the operation of the GSP schemes. It sought instead to circumvent this impasse by redefining the issues in terms of resolutions that had greater chance of systemic appreciation. Thus in 1972, instead of just asking for meeting the 1 per cent Aid Target, the Secretariat tried to link the provision of aid to expansion of international liquidity. In 1976, instead of limiting itself to proposals about increasing the efficiency of specific GSP schemes in operation, the Secretariat sought to link trade concessions with a stabilization of commodity markets. A similar modification of the Manila 'restructuring' resolution was evident at Belgrade. UNCTAD has also considered an expansion of its role as a provider of technical assistance, to be best sustained within the context of a redefinition of its global task. Thus it seeks an expansion in those areas of technical assistance that are related to its major policy initiatives. The need for organizational growth is thus an important factor in determining the form and content of UNCTAD's task expansion. Organizational growth has necessitated the development of considerable flexibility on the part of the Secretariat.

Hypothesis 2: Threat from rival international organizations is countered by political opposition if client support remains, otherwise new goals will be sought.

The UNCTAD Secretariat has never been seriously threatened either by goal fulfillment or by changing client preferences. The Secretariat played an important part in shaping the global aspirations of the developing countries. The

Secretariat's wish to transform UNCTAD from a 'forum' to a negotiating body is undoubtedly related to the realization that a large number of LDCs desire marginal modifications within the system of international trade and investment relationships to occur concurrently with the articulation of a bold initiative for the grand overhauling of the system as a whole. These two tasks are not seen as mutually incompatible either by the Secretariat or by the Group of 77. Thus a negotiating role for UNCTAD was recognized clearly at the time of its inception. The nature of negotiations conducted under the auspices of UNCTAD has reflected the aspirations of the Group of 77. Thus Prebisch frequently spoke of the need to adhere to his concept of 'international reciprocity' (as against the traditional views of reciprocity advocated within GATT) whereby a combination of political and economic commitments would be jointly undertaken and mutually respected by both rich and poor countries.[9]

At the time of its inception UNCTAD was confronted with what many conceive of as a direct political threat from GATT. GATT sought to retain the support of the LDCs by adoption of Part IV to the GATT Agreement under the title 'Trade and Development'. Prebisch saw the incorporation of Part IV within GATT as a deliberate move to secure for GATT an image like UNCTAD's, although there was a fundamental difference in orientation and ideology between these two organizations. GATT was challenging UNCTAD's right to assume a negotiating and implementing role in the area of international trade. UNCTAD, however, did not respond by initiating a duplication feud. This was so despite the fact that at the Geneva Conference and in 1965 Prebisch had explicitly taken exception to GATT's task expansion in the development field.[10] Competition between the GATT and the UNCTAD Secretariat during the period 1964–8 was intense. During the Kennedy Round, the GATT Secretariat assisted many LDCs in drafting request lists and advised about advantageous negotiating positions. GATT scheduled many meetings to clash with similar meetings held under UNCTAD auspices. According to Gosovic 'this appears to have been the favourite tactic of the GATT Secretariat.'[11] This tended to intensify hostility between the two Secretariats, which had a basis in the personal animosity that existed between Prebisch and Wyndham White—an animosity born of Prebisch's unsuccessful attempt to win GATT support for the establishment of the Latin American Free Trade Association.

Such attitudes ensured that considerable duplication between the activities of GATT and UNCTAD was unavoidable. The possibility of such duplication existed in the area of commodity agreements, the operation of the GSP schemes, trade expansion among LDCs and technical assistance in the field of export expansion. Prebisch argued that collaboration between the two Secretariats should be based upon a clear functional differentiation between GATT and UNCTAD. During 1966 he gradually recognized that LDCs could not be wooed away from GATT—that many LDC delegations resented being dragged into what they regarded as jurisdictional disputes between two sets of international civil servants: the Algiers Charter, the common platform adopted by the LDCs prior to UNCTAD II, noted the wish of the LDCs to see co-operation and harmonization appear in the policies of GATT and UNCTAD.[12] From 1967 co-operation between these two organizations started to replace overt confrontation. Arrangements were made for informal consultations at the secretariat level. In 1967 Prebisch proposed the establishment of a GATT–UNCTAD Centre of International Trade for the co-ordination of their export promotion activities. LDCs endorsed this proposal enthusiastically at the Fifth Board, and the Centre came into existence in 1968. By that year the UNCTAD Secretariat seems to have accepted that GATT's task expansion in the development area could not be contained. Since the departure of Prebisch and Wyndham White, the animosity between GATT and UNCTAD has diminished, but co-operation has not flourished.

UNCTAD's inability to contain GATT by launching a political initiative has taught it caution in its dealings with other EIOs. Its Secretariat was careful not to appear in a negative role when the United Nations Industrial Development Organization and the United Nations Commission on International Trade Law were established in 1966. Co-operation between UNCTAD and both these bodies has proceeded fairly harmoniously. A joint shipping legislation section has been established by UNCTAD and UNICTRAL, and co-operation with UNIDO for the implementation of the 'Lima Target' has also been developed. At the time of its inception UNIDO had represented a potential threat to UNCTAD, particularly when the issue of the creation of a 'Department of Foreign Trade' was raised within UNIDO. In 1967 Prebisch succeeded in getting support in New York for naming the department as 'The Department for Export Orientated Industries' thus obtaining vague assurances that the new department would concern itself with production rather than trade and, although duplication has not been entirely avoided, co-ordination of UNCTAD and UNIDO policies has been frequent and fruitful.

Similarly UNCTAD has not seen the emergence of a new forum for conducting the debate between rich and the poor countries the Conference on International Economic Co-operation, CIEC, established in Paris in 1975 and abandoned in 1978 as a threat. The CIEC was initiated as a consequence of the Seventh Special Session of the UN General Assembly. UNCTAD had played an important role in preparing for this as well as for the Sixth Special Session on Raw Materials and Development. Resolutions adopted at these sessions had created new avenues for task expansion by UNCTAD. The Group of 77 recognized that their endeavours to build a New International Economic Order implied an enhanced role for UNCTAD within the UN system. The relationship between the NIEO resolutions, the progress of the Paris Dialogue and the success of the Nairobi Conference was recognized by all sides. In its preparatory statement for the EEC delegation to the Sixteenth Session of the TDB, the Commission of the European Communities wrote 'The links between UNCTAD IV and the Dialogue (CIEC) are, and will be close'.[13] Corea saw 'the Fourth Session of UNCTAD following closely after (the VIIth Special Session) as providing the first opportunity for decisions to be taken by the international community in an international forum on specific issues so as to create some of the essential elements of a new order for the development of the Third World'.[14] The establishment of the NIEO initiatives within the UN and of the CIEC were thus not seen as a threat by UNCTAD but as an opportunity for task expansion.

Institutional initiatives since 1978 have been few and far between. Resources available to the World Bank have shrunk. But the role of the IMF has grown and though this may be interpreted as representing an indirect threat to UNCTAD; the Secretariat has done little to forestall or counter it.

Having learnt that the Third World is in general in favour of a proliferation of agencies dealing with development, the UNCTAD Secretariat seeks compromise and conciliation, and avoids political confrontation with EIOs that enter the development field. The second part of the hypothesis is not testable, as UNCTAD has not lost client support during any period of its existence.

Hypothesis 3: UNCTAD moves into areas where other EIOs are weak or non-existent.

UNCTAD's main function—and the one it paid its greatest attention to at the time of its inception, was the aggregation and articulation of the interests of the Third World within the world economy. This was a function that was then not being performed by any other organization within or without the UN system. The substantive resolutions adopted at the Conferences—resolutions the implementation of which requires a negotiating or supervisory role—did tend to create the possibility of UNCTAD moving into areas that were being worked by other organizations. Thus the various proposals on aid reform implicitly referred to an expanded supervisory role within this field. Co-ordination and scrutiny of Western aid policies had been the function of the Development Assistance Committee (DAC) of the OECD since the middle 1950s. Both UNCTAD and DAC prepare annual reports on aid performance, but most agreements on aid softening have been negotiated within DAC. Similarly, most UNCTAD resolutions on compensatory and supplementary financing have been implemented by initiatives within the IMF and the IBRD, and UNCTAD has not sought for itself a role as a financing agency. In the area of preferences, UNCTAD resolutions implied some initiative in an area traditionally under the control of GATT and national government agencies responsible for the administration of special preferential schemes.

UNCTAD was the forum in which the new GSP schemes were negotiated, and thus it did pre-empt GATT's role to some extent. But the operation of the national schemes remained the responsibility of individual governments, and UNCTAD was denied a supervisory role. In the area of commodities agreement negotiation, UNCTAD impinges least upon the jurisdictional authority of other international organizations. At its inception the two UN bodies dealing with commodity agreements—the Commission on International Commodity Trade (CICT) and the Interim Co-ordinating Committee for International Commodity Agreements (ICCICA)—were disbanded, and UNCTAD was given the responsibility of international co-ordination on commodity problems.

The functions of ICCICA and CICT were taken over by UNCTAD and its Committee on Commodities was given responsibility of co-ordinating all international agencies working in this field, but developed countries have argued that UNCTAD does not have the exclusive right to convene commodity conferences. The role of UNCTAD as a manager of international commodity agreements has expanded, particularly since 1974. UNCTAD's Committee on Commodities duplicates FAO's Committee on Commodity Problems (set up in the 1950s). UNCTAD has a tendency to enter into pre-negotiations on individual commodities (e.g. oil seeds, bananas, tea) which technical discussions in FAO's commodity study groups have demonstrated as futile or counterproductive. In the field of technical assistance, under the UNDP programme UNCTAD was in competitition with both GATT and UNIDO as far as the provision of expertise for export promotion by LDCs was concerned. In the area of technical assistance for shipping some competition with the International Marine Organization (IMO) was likely, but technical assistance for insurance, tourism and economic integration among LDCs did not involve competition and duplication with any intergovernmental body. In the field of shipping legislation UNCTAD task expansion has meant competition with UNICTRAL, which created an *ad hoc* working group on international shipping legislation and included shipping legislation as a priority item on its agenda in 1966,[15] specifically to counter the threat from UNCTAD. In the area of economic integration among LDCs, UNCTAD is not really in competition with the regional organizations. To secure DC support for LDC integration schemes was an important factor in the consistent support given by the Group of 77 to the Secretariat's original proposal for establishing the Committee on Economic Co-operation among LDCs.

In the area of transfer of technology there was evident duplication within the work of ECOSOC's Advisory Committee on Application of Science and Technology to Development. The Secretariat urged that ACAST was largely occupied with technical and scientific questions, and a discussion of the economic and political aspects of technology transfer to LDCs would create no duplication in the work of UNCTAD or any other intergovernmental body.[16] DC hostility to UNCTAD involvement in this field reflected their tendency to avoid UNCTAD's concern with questions that affected big business and transnational corporations. The Committee on Transfer of Technology and the various Intergovernmental Groups to look at transfer of technology within UNCTAD have dealt with issues that are related to the operation of multinationals as transmitters of technology to the LDCs. This refers in part to the role of the UNCTAD Intergovernmental Group of Experts on a Code of Conduct for Transfer of Technology and to the role of the UNCTAD Secretariat in the revision of the Paris Convention for the Protection of Industrial Property. The tasks involve competition with the International Union for the Protection of Industrial Property and the World Intellectual Property Organization, and the difference in the codes proposed by Group B and the Group of 77 reflect the reluctance of the former to countenance international surveillance of restrictive business practices in this field.

Finally UNCTAD has also sought to expand its role *vis-à-vis* ECOSOC. At the Geneva Conference the developed countries had failed to subordinate it to ECOSOC's authority. In August 1975, encouraged by the growing militancy of the Group of 77, Gamani Corea called for 'serious consideration of the option of ... extending the present competence of UNCTAD—the Conference, the TDB and the Secretariat—so that it could become the central body of the United Nations in the field of international economic relations.'[17] Such a move, if successful—and of now there are no signs of success—would entirely pre-empt ECOSOC's role.

Since UNCTAD IV the Group B countries have constantly sought to pre-empt moves which they apprehend might lead UNCTAD to enter areas worked by other EIOs. Thus, in 1978, UNCTAD proposals for an international programme covering all aspects of trade in the meat and livestock industry were countered by the establishment of the International Meat Council under the auspices of GATT.[18] DC representatives have continued to raise objections to the enhancement of ECDC programmes on the grounds of duplicity with existing EIOs.

We see, therefore, that the UNCTAD Secretariat has not limited task expansion to areas where other EIOs are absent. Rather it has challenged their legitimacy to operate in these areas and has maintained that they have not concerned themselves with issues relating to development.

Hypothesis 4: Old goals are rarely abandoned, but are given lower priority and are incorporated in other more comprehensive programmes.

UNCTAD has shifted emphasis significantly from interest articulation to substantive negotiations over the period 1964–79. During 1979–83 there was a clear reversion to interest articulation once again. Moreover, issues highlighted have also altered from institutionalization at Geneva, to preferences at New Delhi, to the SDR-and XR link at Santiago, to the Common Fund and the Integrated Commodity Programme at Nairobi, to restructuring at Manila and to world economic recovery at Belgrade. However, although there was emphasis on UNCTAD's negotiating role in 1976, the Nairobi Conference noted that 'the evolution of UNCTAD as a negotiating arm of the United Nations in the trade and development field must take place while maintaining its traditional role as a forum for the development of new ideas and new policies',[19] and a formulation of principles and policies have never been abandoned by UNCTAD. Most of the resolutions adopted at UNCTAD IV—by common consensus the most successful and path-breaking conference held so far—have precursors in UNCTAD I. Thus the Integrated Commodity Programme can be described as a 'descendant' of Resolutions 16 (II), 17 (II), 18

(II) and 20 (II) of the 1968 Conference. The generalized preference scheme is referred to in the resolution on a comprehensive strategy for industry. The resolution called for an improvement of the existing GSPs and extension of duration. Similarly, UNCTAD IV resolutions on the debt problem were 'descendants' of UNCTAD I Resolution 29 (I), 30 (I) and 31 (I). UNCTAD IV also considered the 1 per cent Aid Target, and LDCs had put forward proposals for the method of achieving it. No consensus could be reached on this issue because DCs rejected these proposals. Finally it may be noted that UNCTAD IV resolutions on the institutional strengthening of the organization had predecessors in UNCTAD I Resolutions on Institutionalization of UNCTAD.

Similarly UNCTAD VI also reflected the commitment to earlier goals. Corea described UNCTAD VI as 'unlike UNCTAD II or UNCTAD IV where a particular proposal had matured and was ready for decision ... UNCTAD VI will deal with issues over a wider range ... issues that are central to the crises of today'. Nevertheless much of the unfinished business of UNCTAD IV and UNCTAD V was placed on the agenda of UNCTAD VI. Shifting emphasis in goals and subgoals is evident over the years, but the old goals seldom entirely disappear. They are reformulated in new proposals and provide a basis for task expansion. Most old proposals are thus 'collapsed' into new ones. We may, therefore, conclude that old goals have an influence upon the development of new proposals put forward for task expansion by UNCTAD, and it is rare for them to be entirely abandoned

Hypothesis 5: The environment has determined UNCTAD's priorities.

Table 9.1 summarizes a distribution of UNCTAD's budget resources to different sectors over the period 1971–84/5.

The table illustrates that sectorial allocations have largely been influenced by the environmental developments. Thus in 1971 the allocations to both 'commodities' and 'money and finance' were roughly similar. Money allocated to commodities increased by 10.3 per cent over 1970–1. As against this, money allocated to money and finance increased by 11.2 per cent over the same period. This reflected the fact that the main

Table 9.1:   *Allocation of UNCTAD Secretariat expenditure 1971–84/5 (as percentage of total)*

	1971	1973	1978/9	1982/3	1984/5
Money, finance and development	19.8	17.6	16.9	15.9	15.7
Commodities	19.6	20.1	15.9	17.9	14.7
Manufacture	14.9	15.1	9.7	8.7	8.8
Shipping	14.2	10.4	8.0	6.7	7.0
Transfer of technology	2.1	5.9	6.8	6.8	6.7
Trade with socialist countries	4.6	4.1	3.7	3.3	3.4
Economic integration in LDCs and least developed country aid	8.3	7.5	8.2	10.8	11.4
Insurance and trade facilitation	3.1	2.6	2.0	2.4	2.5

Sources: TDB XII Session *Records* Annex p. 24.
Haqani, Z. *UNCTAD: for a New Economic Order* p. 52.
UNCTAD: personal communication Ref TDO/221/1/71.

concern at Santiago was with the SDR–aid link. By 1973 money allocated to Commodities had increased to over 20 per cent of the total allocation, reflecting UNCTAD's perception of the importance of the commodity issue. However, by 1978/9 the commodity share had fallen to about 15 per cent—UNCTAD IV had shown that substantial breakthroughs were unlikely in this area. The pattern of budget distribution remained relatively stable over the subsequent years, with an approximately equal allocation to commodities and finance. Allocations to finance were directed to exploring ways for dealing with the debt crisis of the LDCS.

Thus, although the environment plays a role in determining goal priorities, the relationship between environmental changes and goal reordering is a complex one. The old goals are rarely drastically downgraded or abandoned, and financial allocation patterns remain fairly stable over time.

Hypothesis 6: The Secretary General plays a significant role in goal reformulation.

Martin Hill ('the doyen of the UN corps' according to Kurt Waldheim[20]) has noted 'the immense influence exercised by most heads of agencies (within the UN system). The basis of this influence is not only personal but constitutional since in most agencies the executive head is responsible for preparing, submitting, and executing the programme, as well as submitting the budget and administering the fund'.[21] Moreover, the growing diffusion and dispersion of authority within the UN system has made the agency head more powerful and autonomous, *vis-à-vis* the office of Inter-Agency Affairs and other co-ordinating agencies within the UN system. In constitutional terms the Secretary General of UNCTAD finds himself in a strong leadership role within the organization. His principal functions include ensuring that the Secretariat properly services the Conference and TDB, drawing up the agenda of the deliberative bodies, arranging for the meeting of the Conference, the Board and its Committees, supervising the implementation of UNCTAD decisions, preparing UNCTAD's budget estimates and annual programme of work, convening UN commodity conferences (on behalf of the UN Secretary General) and participating in the work of the UN Administrative Committee on Co-ordination.

The strong constitutional position was fairly taken advantage of by Prebisch—UNCTAD's first charismatic, prophetic, innovative Secretary General. Few would dispute that UNCTAD's organizational ideology has been indelibly stamped by the intellectual vigour and distinctiveness of Prebisch's theories about the nature, causes and cures of underdevelopment. The recurring themes in all UNCTAD debates over the period 1964–83 can be traced to the conceptual formulations in Prebisch's two small pamphlets: *Towards a New Trade Policy for Development* and *Towards a Global Strategy for Development.* In the early days in particular, 'the UNCTAD Secretariat was almost totally identified with the person of its first Secretary General, Dr Raoul Prebisch'.[22] His influence extended beyond the intellectual sphere and his style of work—as well as the ideology he espoused—was an important determinant of UNCTAD's programmatic orientation. Prebisch's relations with government representatives, and they were many and varied, were focused on attempts to sell them new ideas and win their support for new concepts and perspectives. This style of work made substantial involvement in negotiations difficult. Prebisch was at ease and could trust only that small group of UN men who had come with him to UNCTAD and who shared his ideology. His reluctance to delegate authority within the Secretariat reflected his unwillingess to make negotiations dictate UNCTAD's posture on international economic issues. He was willing to negotiate on specific issues, and himself played the role of a broker repeatedly at UNCTAD I and II, but the organizational ideology itself could never with him be a bargaining counter. This made it inevitable that Prebisch and the UNCTAD Secretariat were accused of partiality for the Group of 77. After Prebisch the Secretariat made studies and reports its basic policy weapon, and made little attempt to cultivate relations with national delegations. Prebisch's insistence on the primacy of ideas meant that he did not care over-much about the financial resources at UNCTAD's disposal. His good relations with the UN Advisory Committee on Administrative and Budgetary Questions (ACABQ) reflected his willingness to accept only moderate increases in UNCTAD's budget. His amicable relations with the Department of Economic and Social Affairs shows that he was willing to adapt a conciliatory approach on the questions of UNCTAD's role as a service organization—recall in particular Prebisch's position on UNCTAD's place as an agency of UNDP, a position that was vehemently rejected by a majority of the Group of 77. As against this moderate stand on policy questions, Prebisch jealously guarded his theories. He did his own thinking. 'The role of the Secretariat was not so much to generate ideas as to work out supporting documentation'.[23]

In sharp contrast to Prebisch, Perez-Guerero was a mediator and a broker. He believed that UNCTAD should no longer be a focus of controversy, but should attempt to bridge the gap between DCs and LDCs on specific issues. He brought to Geneva a long experience of dealing with situations of conflict and compromise in international negotiations within the OPEC. He had played a constructive role in the negotiations on preferences during 1966–7, which won him the confidence of both sides. He believed that organizational performance could be substantially improved by concentrating on details and specifics. He spent a large proportion of his time at Geneva, instituted regular directors' meetings, delegated authority to subordinates and succeeded in getting Rossen of Norway appointed as his second in command. During Perez-Guerero's term of office, the Secretariat emphasized its role as a mediator and negotiator, and ostensibly avoided public statements.

This emphasis on negotiations, and on the role of the Secretariat as a mediator for the achievement of *rapprochement* between the DCs and LDCs has been continued by Gamani Corea, who became UNCTAD's Secretary General in 1974. Perez-Guerero and Corea sought to achieve task expansion for UNCTAD within the context of the Prebisch ideology. The 'link' proposals and the 'Corea Plan' on commodities do not represent conceptual innovations. Both Corea and Perez-Guerero continued to press for a restriction of Conference agenda and a raising of the delegation level at TDB Sessions and at Conferences, and Corea succeeded in reorientating activity within the Secretariat towards partici-pation in promotion of conferences. During 1977–9 the Secretariat's main concern was the organizing of commodity negotiating sessions for the establishment of the Common Fund and other elements of the Integrated Commodity Plan. Thus the main policy tool of the Secretariat became the negotiating session and not the policy and research docu-ment—at least in the field of commodity agreements.

The UNCTAD-sponsored negotiations have, however, failed to achieve the type of institutional and substantive breakthrough that Corea envisaged. Corea saw the Common Fund as a step towards 'the restructuring of the whole gamut of North–South relations', but subsequent negotiations so watered down the original conception that it cannot be anything but a very marginal operation in view of the size of the commodity markets and the huge price swings to which they are subject.

Corea is a British-trained Sri Lankan civil servant who, until one year prior to his assuming UNCTAD's Secretary Generalship, had held senior national posts such as Permanent Secretary Ministry of Planning and Deputy Governor Central Bank of Sri Lanka. His international experience prior to 1974 was somewhat limited. Unlike Prebisch and Perez-Guerero, Corea lacked international contacts, and his intense concern with the commodity issue at a time when the West was apprehensive of 'rising commodity power' has stamped him as a 'third world spokesman'. He has not been a successful international negotiator. On the other hand, he has not fostered the development of new theoretical perspectives. At the Belgrade meeting, Prebisch commented 'the problem is not a decadence of the system but a decadence of ideas'.[24] UNCTAD's decreasing salience in the international system is at least partly due to the diplomatic ineffectiveness of its Secretary General.

We may conclude therefore that the Secretary General has played an important role in goal reformulation within the UNCTAD Secretariat. This reformulation of goals—and hence the Secretariat's strategy—has not been endorsed in part by the main client of UNCTAD, the Group of 77. Thus, despite Prebisch's opinion and Perez-Guerero's insistence, UNCTAD III debated a very large number of issues, and negotiating conferences were not well co-ordinated. UNCTAD IV did narrow down its agenda and group solidarity of the 77 was more pronounced and effective, but the very modest success of the Commodity negotiations may be a pointer to the fact that UNCTAD's negotiating role has not resulted in the formulation of acceptable negotiable positions on this issue.

Hypothesis 7: Distribution of posts within the Secretariat reflects the orientation of the organisation and the content of its substantive programme.

Table 9.2: *Regional distribution of highest UNCTAD posts, 1968 and 1976*

Region	1968a Number	Percentage	1976b number	Percentage
Group B	22	44.00	29	55.7
Group D	8	16.00	5	9.6
Group of 77	18	36.00	18	34.6
Africa	(7)	(14.00)	(2)	(3.8)
Asia	(6)	(12.00)	(10)	(19.2)
Latin America	(5)	(10.00)	(5)	(9.6)
Unknown	2	4.00		0
	50	100	52	100

Note: (a) From Nye 'UNCTAD: poor nations pressure group' in Cox, R. and Jacobson, H. *The Anatomy of Influences.* New Haven, (1973) p. 341.
(b) From A/C5/31/1.2 (31.8.76). The fifty-two posts include officers in the UN salary ranges USG, ASG, D2, D1 and P5.

Table 9.2 describes the regional distribution of posts within the UNCTAD Secretariat.

In 1968, according to Nye 'Western countries in general (were) heavily represented'.[25] Table 9.2 illustrates that Western representation increased from 44 per cent in 1968 to 56 per cent in 1976. Western state nationals accounted for as much as 68.3 per cent of all established posts in UNCTAD Secretariat in 1976—the UK's share being as high as 21 per cent of total established posts. LDC share of the major posts at UNCTAD dropped from 36 per cent in 1968 to 34.6 per cent in 1976, and they accounted for only 27.1 per cent of all established posts in UNCTAD in 1976. Of the 18 major posts occupied by LDC nationals within the UNCTAD Secretariat as many as 10 (55 per cent) came from Asian countries. Only 2 senior posts were allocated to African nationals. We may conclude therefore that the distribution of offices within the Secretariat is not significantly associated with the orientation of the organization or its work programme. It may be argued that the increasing proportion of Western representation corresponds to a change in the nature of UNCTAD work. It was a 'forum' organization in 1968, and is now more of a 'negotiating body'. However, there is little clear evidence that distribution of posts is related to national influence within the organization.

It is of course difficult to make firm generalizations on figures that are eight years old. But the UNCTAD Secretariat's refusal to publish a national breakdown of the 452 established posts that exist currently indicates that the distribution pattern has not changed and the Third World Secretariat representation has not increased.[26]

Hypothesis 8: Subgoals are more operational than the global task; subgoals are the main concern of the subunits.

The organizational structure of the UNCTAD Secretariat consists of the following units:

1. Office of the Secretary General.
2. Economic Policy Evaluation and Co-ordination Unit.
3. Offices of Administration.
4. ECE/UNCTAD Joint Reference Unit.
5. Division of Conference Affairs and External Relations.

6. Division for Money and Finance.
7. Division for Economic Co-operation among LDCs.
8. Division for Trade with Socialist Countries.
9. Commodities Division.
10. Manufactures.
11. Shipping.
12. Transfer of Technology Division.
13. Office of Technical Co-operation.
14. Special Programme for Least Developed Countries, Landlocked Countries and Island Countries.
15. Research Division.
16. The New York Office.
17. Assistance Unit for Palestinian People.

Seventy-eight per cent of the major posts are established in subunits dealing with substantive programmes. Reorganization and expansion have occurred through the creation of a division for economic co-operation among LDCs, a transfer of technology division and a special programme for the least developed, landlocked and island countries. UNCTAD's intention of becoming a negotiating body has naturally meant that the emphasis is on the reformation of the organizational ideology in terms of specific subgoals. Thus task expansion has largely occurred in areas of substantive policy making. After UNCTAD IV, the Secretary General requested a sum of US$5,767,000 for implementing the substantive components of the resolutions adopted. This money was used by divisions involved in the making of substantive policy. As against this, the UNCTAD Secretary General requested a sum of US$2,391,000 for an expansion of Conference services, that is, 70 per cent of the additional funds were requested to meet an expansion in substantive programmes. It can thus easily be concluded that the pursuit of specific subgoals represents the most operational part of the Secretariat's work. The subunits dealing with substantive programmes have their interest clearly defined, and their concerns are acutely focused. As time has gone on and the involvement in technical assistance has increased, it has become uncommon that the typical Secretariat official would be primarily concerned with the 'trade gap', 'convergent policies', 'the peripheral economy' and other themes contained within the Prebisch doctrine. He is much more directly involved in the conclusion of a commodity agreement, the provision of effective advice on export expansion or the establishment of a port. This is not to argue that the Prebisch ideology has consciously been abandoned, but as task expansion has proceeded in terms of the growth of the negotiating role of UNCTAD, this ideology and the global task as defined by it has receded into the background, and pursuit of subgoals constitutes the main activity of the Secretariat.

The relative lack of success in negotiations has meant that no new units were established after UNCTAD V. After UNCTAD VI a new unit to assist the Palestinian people was established, which accounts for three of the four new posts created in 1983. UNCTAD VI also called for the re-establishment of the Research Unit, which had been in slow decline since 1974 and had virtually ceased to exist by UNCTAD V. Corea insisted that the re-establishment of the Research Unit should depend on the attraction of outside funds. Thus while there is a systematic pressure for organizational changes to accommodate the renewed emphasis on UNCTAD's forum character, the Secretariat continued to resist this pressure until Corea's departure from UNCTAD in late 1984.

Hypothesis 9: Interest coalitions between subunits of UNCTAD and members emphasize the achievement of specific subgoals.

Hypothesis 10: Communications networks specific to subgoals have developed.

An emphasis on negotiation and technical assistance has meant that communication networks specific to defined issue areas have developed which link UNCTAD subunits to interest groups within these issue areas. Interaction between UNCTAD officials and Third World representatives in the field of technology transfer, insurance, export promotion and of course commodity negotiation has increased significantly over the years as UNCTAD's advice-giving role in these has grown. The increased emphasis on technical competence of UNCTAD staff has meant that an expanded area of shared norms and shared interests has developed between UNCTAD officials and technical experts employed by governments of the Third

World and multinational business. It is natural that this coincidence of interests and orientation has meant the emergence of loose *ententes* for task expansion for the achievement of specific subgoals, and since a large part of the technical experts employed by UNCTAD are on relatively short-term contracts it is unlikely that this form of task expansion will entail a forceful endorsement of the concepts contained in UNCTAD's organizational ideology.

A case of the development of interest coalition on specific issue areas involving the UNCTAD Secretariat has been investigated by Bhattacharya in the field of generalized preferences.[27] He argues that:

(a) Prebisch's doctrine—which formed the core of UNCTAD's organizational ideology—was derived from the needs and aspirations of the Latin American countries.

(b) However, Prebisch's attempt to win Latin American support for the GSP was strongly countered by a faction of Latin American statesmen led by Campos, the Planning Minister of Brazil, de Santamaria, Chairman of the Inter-American Committee on the Alliance for Progress, and Restropreo, President of Colombia, who supported 'vertical' preferences granted by the USA to the Latin American countries.

(c) Prebisch countered this threat by maintaining that 'vertical' preferences would increase US hegemony over Latin America. Prebisch used ECLA as a basis for winning Latin American opinion to the idea of the GSP. Prebisch developed personal contact with the President of Colombia and de Sanatamaria, and Latin American opposition to the GSP had been neutralized by 1967.

(d) Support for the GSP scheme came also from Anthony M. Solomon, Assistant Secretary of State for Economic Affairs in the United States. He succeeded in convincing President Johnson that the GSP would be used as a tool for furthering the 'Open Door' policy advocated by the US. This would counter EEC protection as well as the threat from the Left in Latin America, who would mobilize if vertical preferences were granted—alleging that this meant an increase in Latin American dependence on the US.

(e) Latin American pressure for changing US policy towards GSP was extended through GATT, the Alliance for Progress and the Inter-American Special Committee for Consultation and Negotiations (CECON). In GATT Prebisch's allies—particularly Martines of Argentina and Silveire of Brazil—attempted to convince US delegates that GSP was essential to offset the disappointing results of the Kennedy Round. Even after Johnson's statement that the US would support GSP 'in principle' the issue was by no means certain, as in 1969 the Nixon administration decided to reconsider the American position on this question. During 1969 Latin American diplomats and statesmen in the Central American Common Market, in the Organization of American States (OAS) and in ECLA kept stressing to the Nixon regime the importance of the GSP proposal in Latin American eyes. In recording America's decision to 'press for a liberal system of GSP (so as to) eliminate the discrimination against Latin American exports' Nixon in 1969 reveals the real basis for change in US policy on this question.

This instance of policy formulation indicates that the UNCTAD Secretary General did seek to mobilize 'resourceful' individuals for changing the policy of the country that was the most powerful opponent of the GSP in the first instance. An investigation into other areas of policy formulation may reveal that communication channels specific to particular issue areas have developed, and that informal sympathetic groups for UNCTAD task expansion in these areas have also developed.

Hypothesis 11: Subgoal persistence has hampered goal reformulation, but loyalty to UNCTAD facilitated it.

Loyalty to UNCTAD as an organization was, in the days of its inception, based upon an acceptance of the organizational ideology developed by Prebisch. The top officials in the Secretariat in 1964—and particularly those who enjoyed Prebisch's confidence— came from the UN Department of

Economic and Social Affairs. Their influence was, in the early stages, particularly significant as it was difficult to attract high professionals to UNCTAD from the West, and the Third World countries did not possess or could not spare such experts. The main members of this group were: P. Berthoud, D. Cardovez, S. Dell, C. Eckenstein, R. Krishnamurti, W.R. Malinovski, J. Stanovnik and J. Viteri. In these early days Western critics talked of the UNCTAD Secretariat as a 'Sectariat' of the Third World, and, as we have noted earlier, there was little systematic attempt to develop contact with the Western permanent representative by UNCTAD Secretariat officials. The Secretariat—and Prebisch personally—enjoyed the confidence of the Group of 77. It serviced Group of 77 meetings, helped draft resolutions, formulated negotiating positions, etc. Prebisch could (and did) mediate in intra Group of 77 disputes—particularly between Latin American and African delegations. Most members of the UNCTAD Secretariat in the 1960s had actively participated with the developing countries for many years. Moreover, as long as the research study remained the main tool for the Secretariat its identification with the Prebisch doctrine tended to be reinforced by the bulk of its operational activity.

By 1983 Prebisch himself and all his close associates had left UNCTAD, and the number of Asian senior officials had increased significantly. This reflected, perhaps, the preference of the Secretary General, Gamani Corea. Since the departure of Prebisch the main organizational task has been the conduct of negotiations. New subgoals emerged during the Prebisch era itself—the move to achieve participatory status within the UNDP in 1966, the initiative on transfer of technology in 1967. There is no evidence that such task expansion was resisted by any segment of the Secretariat. This is largely explained by the retention of existing goals as important activities. Such a reformulation creates least friction if it can be posited that the new goals are merely tactics or strategies to achieve the old aim; thus the SDR link proposals could be presented as a way to achieve the 1 per cent target, the Commodity Plan could be presented as a way to achieve trade expansion after GSP had failed. The Secretariat has not resisted goal reformulation. Indeed the fact that representation from Western countries in the Secretariat had increased over this period lends evidence to the fact that the Secretariat staff is not committed to the organizational ideology as contained in the Prebisch doctrine, but welcomes a reformulation of this ideology which permits substantial task expansion in a way which enhances the negotiating role of UNCTAD.

9.2 ORGANIZATIONAL LEADERSHIP-A SUMMARY

Briefly we may sum up the 'effectiveness' of the strategy outlined in the section above. The Secretariat has–albeit to a limited extent–succeeded in redefining UNCTAD's organizational objectives in the sense that, whereas the establishment of the organization was seen by most mainly in terms of providing a point of focus for debating international development issues and problems, adroit management of these debates allowed the Secretariat to convince LDCs, and more significantly the Western countries, that the assumption by UNCTAD of a negotiating and a service role was in the interests of the members of the organization. The LDCs had long accepted, indeed advocated UNCTAD's role in international negotiations, whereas the Western countries had, at least until the New Delhi Conference, kept insisting that UNCTAD was a 'forum' organization, and negotiations and the rendering of technical assistance were not in its domain. By 1976 there appeared to be a general consensus that UNCTAD's most useful function was in the conduct of negotiations. This was the reason behind accepting the Secretariat's recommendation for restricting the Agenda to those items in which meaningful negotiations were possible. However, UNCTAD has so far not succeeded in achieving a major breakthrough in international economic negotiations. Thus the '77' are not willing to sacrifice UNCTAD's forum role and the West has yet to make it a major instrument for policy articulation.

This reluctance of both '77' and 'B' nations to endorse wholeheartedly a negotiating role for UNCTAD reflects limitations of the organizational ideology. This ideology has in the main not proved capable of providing the basis for constructing and sustaining interest group coalitions which can effectively press for systemic transformation. The international development environment has not improved significantly since UNCTAD's inception. Whatever improvement has occurred for the OPEC developing countries or the newly industrializing countries (NICs) has had little to do with UNCTAD. UNCTAD's substantive initiatives have had, at best, only a marginal impact on the substance of North–South relations—witness, for example, the irrelevance of the GSP programmes in trade. The organizational ideology did inspire the Secretariat officials during Prebisch's era, but I think the evidence presented in the previous section has shown that the Secretariat of today is more pragmatically biased and would not 'on principle' oppose a revision of this ideology, if such a revision would entail substantial organizational growth in terms of international influence. Controversy generated within the organization has not been a source of threat to the existence of UNCTAD. Such controversy either has been 'positively' resolved, leading to organizational task expansion, or it has led to a reformulation of Secretariat initiatives and a reordering of goal priorities. Organizational interaction has, however, not resulted in the development of interest coalitions in specific issue areas powerful enough to support UNCTAD task expansion to the extent that it leads to a basic change of the level and form of transactions between North and South in any particular issue area. This reflects the fact that the organizational strategy has been basically conservative. It has been concerned primarily with survival and with the achievement of modest levels of organizational growth. New environmental developments—such as the expansion of international liquidity in 1971, the commodity price boom in 1974 and the growing threat of protectionism in 1978–9—have been seized upon, but Secretariat initiatives have failed to win new clients, particularly within the West. This has resulted in a political impasse which the Secretariat finds itself increasingly unable to circumvent. The type of research undertaken by the UNCTAD Secretariat has made it difficult to identify particular interests affected by international action in specific issue areas. Typically, research undertaken is of a macroeconomic type, seeking to demonstrate the generally positive impact of a proposed UNCTAD reform. Such work may enhance UNCTAD's respectability among academic economists. It cannot contribute to the construction of politically salient

interest coalitions which can press for a substantial transformation of UNCTAD's role within the international
economy.

9.3 MAJOR FINDINGS OF THE UNCTAD CASE STUDY
AND LIMITATIONS

Part II provides fairly detailed description of UNCTAD's
impact and processes. The kinds of inputs and outputs evident
in the UNCTAD sub-system are similar to those generated in
its environment. The participants of UNCTAD are almost
identical with the participants of the system as a whole.
Behaviour of these participants within UNCTAD reflects their
relationship within the system. However UNCTAD's organizational impact on the environment cannot *prove* anything about
systemic transformation. UNCTAD inputs and outputs are
comprehensible only as parts of a wider systemic output and
input range. We cannot claim that systemic transformation has
been 'caused' by UNCTAD. UNCTAD has been one factor
among many influencing systemic transformation. On the
other hand it is easier to measure the impact of environmental
change on UNCTAD. The movement towards increase in
organizational autonomy or authority for example can be
correlated with the evolution of an organizational task that
corresponds to changes in the pattern of environmental inputs.

Our neo-functionalist theoretical paradigm permitted us to
investigate both the impact of UNCTAD on the international
environment and the processes through which UNCTAD
responded to changes in its environment. UNCTAD's impact
was assessed primarily by using transaction data on commodity and factor flows between and within the developed and
developing world. An attempt was also made to assess changes
in the attitude of governments, international organizations
and interest groups. The impact of the environment on
UNCTAD was also studied in the chapter dealing with organizational development.

The main findings of the study may be briefly summarised.

The study begins by analyzing the relationship between
UNCTAD's organizational ideology and its environmental

characteristics. It was argued that the possibilities of an IO developing autonomously—and not merely reflecting the minimum consensus that permitted the creation of this organization—are determined by the characteristics of its environment and by the scope these characteristics offer for building interest group coalitions which can press effectively for a redefinition and extension of the international agency's organizational task. Unlike organizations such as the World Bank and the IMF, UNCTAD has had little to offer effective interest groups in the West. It has paid little attention to the task of mobilizing effective support in the West. This has meant that its organizational tasks has not expanded significantly despite an increase in the range of issues which have been debated in its forums.

The salience and impact of UNCTAD depend on the scope, that is the number and importance of interest groups to which its activities are relevant and the level and the degree of commitment of members to giving it an institutional problem–solving role in specific issue areas. Changes in scope and level are influenced by the organizational process. There is an inter–relationship between organizational development and environmental impact—although a highly complex one. An autonomous organization is by no means necessarily an effective one. To increase the effectiveness of an EIO its organizational development has to be attuned to the characteristics of the environment. Thus if the distribution of power in the environment is significantly different from the distribution of power within an EIO, there is not likely to be a positive relationship between the growth of organizational autonomy and the enhancement of organizational effectiveness. In the case of UNCTAD the growth of organisational autonomy and distinctiveness did not enhance its effectiveness because the rich countries who were environmentally powerful found UNCTAD's initiatives and decisions not reflecting their own perspectives and policies, and they denied it an enhanced role within the international system.

An important explanation of the relatively slow pace of growth of UNCTAD's environmental effectiveness lies in the organizational strategy of the Secretariat. The main concern of UNCTAD's leadership over the period 1964–83 has been with organizational growth and functional diversification. Relatively little attention has been placed on broadening the base of support for UNCTAD policies. This has meant that although UNCTAD has matured as an organization—its financial resources have increased, staffing levels have gone up, new functional units have sprung up, the organisation has become more autonomous, and so on—its environmental impact has not kept pace with its organizational growth. This suggests that an enhancement of UNCTAD's effectiveness and a redefinition of its global role requires a change in the leadership's strategy and a reinterpretation or modification of UNCTAD's organizational ideology.

But what of the relative importance of factors such as environmental characteristics, leadership and organizational processes of bargaining and decision–making as determinants of organizational development and effectiveness?

UNCTAD's environment was characterized by a relatively high degree of multi-polarity. The issue of development was of central concern to the hundred or so members of the Group of 77 throughout this period. The Western countries were not united in their response to the demands of the 77. The inherent stability of the system—the reluctance of the major actors to permit the escalation of local conflict into global military confrontation—meant that a high value was placed on international bargaining and negotiation. UNCTAD benefited from this environment. Its leadership developed an organizational ideology which made possible the institutionalization of a process of protracted negotiations centred on the development issue. The leadership was successful in convincing its main clientele that an increase in UNCTAD's organisational autonomy was in the interests of the Third World. It may also be legitimately claimed that the leadership played an important role in preventing a decline in the level of representation from the 'key' Group B countries in UNCTAD conferences and TDB meetings. A favourable international environment facilitated the development of a strategy which focused each UNCTAD conference on issues which could not be ignored by the West at least during the period 1964–76.

However the organizational ideology and the leadership strategy proved largely ineffective in enhancing UNCTAD's scope. Throughout the period under study UNCTAD's main concern was to increase the responsiveness of the West to its initiatives. But the environment was not conducive to the attainment of this objective. Economic transactions within the West were significantly more important to the West than transactions between the West and the Third World. A large proportion of trade between Group B and the Group of 77 countries was concentrated in industries such as textiles, leather manufacturing, food processing, and such like. In most Western countries these are declining industries and their international vulnerability is a matter of national industrial concern. Furthermore UNCTAD's organizational initiatives did not succeed in increasing the number of interest groups directly participating in negotiations between the North and the South on specific issues.

In the wake of the Ramadhan war of September 1973, the UNCTAD leadership perceived an opportunity for enhancing Western responsiveness. Commodity prices—not just the price of oil—were increasing and many in the Group of 77 showed an inclination to exercize 'producer power' by establishing commodity cartels. But the leadership misread both the extent to which the Western countries were willing to go in order to accommodate the demands of the Third World and the extent to which the Third World was willing to accept a reformulation of the organizational ideology in order to tranform UNCTAD into an effective international negotiating forum. The 'Common Fund' initiative, therefore, did not lead to a transformation of the character of UNCTAD and a significant enhancement of its systemic integrative potential. It served to strengthen UNCTAD's structure, diversify and extend its organizational tasks and increase its financial and human resource base. UNCTAD has thus been a beneficiary of the autonomous environmental change—the rise in the price of oil and other industrial raw material—since 1973. The growth that took place has led to a modification of the organizational ideology with increased emphasis being placed on the compatibility of UNCTAD's task expansion with the strength-ening of existing market structures in the field of international commodity trade.

UNCTAD's organizational ideology has made possible the

survival of the organization. The Group of 77 has identified with this ideology. The Secretariat's concern with organizational growth has led to a modification and partial reinterpretation of this ideology. UNCTAD has contributed to modest system change. However UNCTAD's organizational ideology did not provide an adequate basis for constructing stable and effective international interest coalitions for influencing the volume or structure of economic transactions between the West and the Third World. Decisionmaking procedures also sometimes reduced organizational effectiveness—many decisions were based on the 'maximum common denominator' of Third World interests and did not amount to an 'upgrading' of national objectives. Subgoals dominated the general organizational goal of system transformation. Programme planning did not feature consultation with clients in order to build variable issueoriented clienteles. The 'spill-over' effect of UNCTAD decisions remained modest and limited. the incidence of unintended consequences leading to new functions and tasks is less pronounced in the case of global economic agencies than it is at the regional level where there is a greater *symmetrical* heterogeneity implying the existence of a 'post industrial' society with roughly corresponding interest groups constituting the main actors. The existence of systemic heterosymmetry constitutes a powerful environmental barrier to IOs seeking systemic transformation. IOs can overcome this barrier by 'the conscious planning of consequences unintended by the national actors but compelling these elites to undertake new planning later in order to deal with the unintended consequences of their earlier purposes. The implication being that the purposes growing out of these consequences could be met only by an increased international task'.[28] UNCTAD did not perform this task particularly successfully and its integrative impact remained limited. In other words the UNCTAD leadership did not succeed in building the type of creative tension between organizational goals and systemic demands that could lead to systemic transformation. It could not promote 'integrative' compromises among combatants and transform their goal structure.

Systemic transformation depends both upon the organizational qualities of the transformation–seeking international agency and on the characteristics of the targets (the nation states) the international organization seeks to integrate. As noted earlier, the greater the similarity or symmetry between these states the greater the scope for integration at the international level. UNCTAD's environment contained states with widely different economic and political structures. Moreover the organizational leadership did not attempt to develop any durable links with the groups that could influence governmental policy in the Western countries. Cox has argued that in pluralist societies the leadership of a transformation-seeking international organization must have the ability to reach below the government into society. It must have access to influential social and political groups, a perception of their goals and an ability to manipulate international action so that these groups can perceive that the organizational leadership is pursuing their interests.[29] UNCTAD's leadership did not give priority to the task of building effective interest group coalitions. It did not succeed in reaching 'below the government into society' and it could not significantly offset the environmental barriers to systemic transformation.

Finally the impact of organizational processes on effectiveness must be noted. The neo-functionalist approach has allowed us to study the development of UNCTAD as an international organization in detail. We have seen that UNCTAD has achieved an impressive level of autonomy and organizational distinctiveness. It is capable of 'rewarding' those active within the organization. Office distribution is not solely determined by environmental pressures. Financial and manpower resources have increased. There has been an increasing trend towards functional diversification and new functional sub-units have sprung up. However, the distribution of influence and power within UNCTAD is different from the distribution of power within its environment. This has meant that the environmentally influential states have been reluctant to extend UNCTAD's mandate fearing that such an extension would be deterimental to their interests. Thus UNCTAD's organizational development has not been such that it can substantially enhance its integrative role or lead to environmental transformation in accordance with its organizational ideology.

The theoretical framework of this study has led to a concentration on the relationship of UNCTAD to the Group B countries and on an analysis of the organizational development of UNCTAD. In my view this has allowed an investigation of some important questions, and certain relevant trends and problems have been identified. However there are serious limitations to adopting this approach to the study of UNCTAD. In the present study this has meant that a thorough analysis of UNCTAD's interaction with the Third World could not be undertaken and the considerable achievement of the Secretariat in first binding, and then holding together the Group of 77 despite its many structural and policy dissimilarities, is somewhat obscured. Similarly, the political flavour of UNCTAD's major debates and conferences is only touched upon for study does not set out to discuss the politics of decision–making and negotiations within the UNCTAD forums.

The findings of this study are subject to all the limitations that apply to behaviouralist analysis since the major part of the present work has been conducted within a behaviouralist framework of enquiry. The limitations of the behaviouralist approach in the field of international politics are well known and documented.[30]

A behaviouralist approach has been adopted in investigating many aspects of UNCTAD's development and functioning because a primary reliance was placed on published and relatively easily accessible material for studying this organization. It is obvious that this type of analysis must be supplemented by what is sometimes regarded as the more 'traditional' approach to the study of international politics, based on historial evaluation and personal observation of organizational activities. Observation of organized events such as negotiations, the interviewing of delegates and secretariat officials can lead to a fuller appreciation of the inner life of an EIO and the political context within which its decisions are made and implemented. Such an appreciation can greatly enhance one's ability to assess the role an EIO is playing within a given issue area as well as in identifying the scope that exists for enhancing this role. But the use of these investigative methods depends crucially upon co–operation from the EIOs.

Whereas diplomatic considerations will necessarily circum-scribe the extent of scholarly observation that may be permissible in specific cases, a general encouragement of international organization-based investigations—involving for example internships for international economics and international relations doctoral candidates and lecturers in EIOs—and the adoption of an 'open door policy' vis-a-vis research scholars can prove to be of great value to the study of international organization.

NOTES

1. Described in detail in Cordovez, D. 'UNCTAD: institutional background and legislative history, *Journal of World Trade Law* (1967) Vol. 5, No. 8, pp. 243–328.
2. UNCTAD *Proceedings,* Nairobi, Vol. 1, (1976). Session on Com-modities.
3. Haquani, Z. *UNCTAD for a New Economic Order,* UN New York (1978) pp. 51–2.
4. UNCTAD *TOB Proceedings,* (1983).
5. Speech by President Johnson to American Chiefs of State at Ponta del Este, 14/4/67. Bulletin, US Dept. of State, 8/5/67, p. 709.
6. UNCTAD *Proceedings III*, Vol. 1, Santiago (1972).
7. *See* speech of UNCTAD Secretary General to UNCTAD IV and to the XVIth TDB. *Proceedings,* Nairobi, Vol. 1 (1976) and TDB *Records,* Geneva (1976).
8. TDB/INF/1462 p. 4.
9. TD/B/114 (30.1.67) p. 12.
10. For details on this *see* Curzon, G. 'The GATT: pressure and strategies for task expansion', in Cox, R. (ed.) *International Organization: World Politics*, Macmillan, London (1969) pp. 248–57.
11. Gosovic, B. *UNCTAD: Conflict and Compromise,* Sijthoff, Leiden (1972) p. 203.
12. TD/B/133 (3.8.67) paragraphs 43–6.
13. Commission of the European Communities—Preparation for UNCTAD (Meeting of TDB, March 1976) COM (76) 39. Final p. 3.
14. A/31/276 p. 4.
15. Statement of UNCITRAL's Chairman to TDB Committee on Shipping TD/B/240 24.7.66, and General Assembly Resolution 2421 (XXIII) December 1968.
16. TD/84 16.3.68.
17. Quoted and discussed in Hill, M. *The United Nations System: Co-ordinating Its Economic and Social Work,* Cambridge University Press, London (1978). p. 96.

18. UNCTAD *Monthly Bulletin* No. 180, p. 8.
19. UNCTAD: *The Main Issues for UNCTAD in the 1980s.* UNCTAD Seminar Programme Series No. 4 (July 1975).
20. Hill, M. *The United Nations System.* Cambridge University Press, Cambridge (1978) p. 18.
21. Hill, *op. cit.,* p. 83.
22. Gosovic, B. *UNCTAD: Conflict and Compromise,* Sijthoff, Leiden, p. 307.
23. Nye, J. 'UNCTAD: poor nations' pressure group', in Cox, R. and Jacobson, H. (ed.) *The Anatomy of Influence,* Yale, New Haven (1973) p. 49.
24. UNCTAD TA/INF/147/1983, p. 7.
25. Nye, *op. cit.* p. 341.
26. Similar figures are also provided by Rothstein, R., *Global Bargaining,* Princeton University Press, New Jersey (1979) pp. 183-4. Rothstein's figures are also for 1976.
27. Bhattacharya, A. 'The influence of the international Secretariat UNCTAD and GSP', *IO*, Vol. 29, No. 1, (1976), pp. 75-90.
28. Haas, E. *Beyond the Nation State*, Yale University Press, New Haven, Conn. (1964) p. 113.
29. Cox, R. 'The executive head' *IO*, Vol. 29, No. 1 (1969) pp. 205-30.
30. Riggs, W. (*et al.*) 'Behaviouralism in the study of the UN *World Politics* Vol. 23, No. 2 (1970) pp. 198-23.

Index

299; and GSP 250; relations with
Group of 77, 185, 300; relations
with Third World 197–205;
relations with UNCTAD 196, 234,
275, 281, 303; and restructuring
of economy 274;
voting in UNCTAD 198, 255, 257
Group D 254
'Group of 77' (formerly 'Group of
55'):
delegates to TDB 227, 231, 232;
delegates to UNCTAD 229, 234,
299; discipline within 194; and
GSP 250; and restructuring of
economy 274; role 126; trade with
Group B countries 300; and
UNCTAD 185, 252, 253, 255, 281,
301; and UNCTAD Secretariat
294, 303
GSP (General System/Scheme of
Preferences) 104, 209, 210, 211,
217, 249–51, 292, 293
Guatemala 245, 247
Guinea (Conakry) 246

Haas, Ernst 16, 22, 37, 38, 39, 40, 44,
50, 66, 67, 69, 77, 80, 104, 106, 157,
158, 178, 187
Haiti 246, 247
Hardin, R. 177
harmonization 11–13
Hart, J. 127
Hayter, Teresa 28
Hecksher-Ohlin model 60
Hill, Martin 284
Hnyilicza, E. 116, 117
Hobbes, T. 171
Hoffman, S. 33, 77
Holy See 247
Honduras 247
Hong Kong 207, 211, 215
Hoole, F.W. 81
Hopkins, R.F. 110, 111
Hufbawer 61
Hungary 245
Huq, Mahbub ul 160

IBRD (International Bank for

Reconstruction and
Development) 69, 189, 257, 279;
as 'co-operative' agency 28
ICCICA (UN Interim Co-
ordinating Committee for
International Commodity
Agreements) 280
Iceland 198
ICFTU (International
Confederation of Free Trade
Unions);
as regional EIO 30
IEA (International Energy Agency)
68, 119
ILO (International Labour
Organization) 12, 18, 29, 77, 169
IMC (International Meat Council)
282
IMF (International Monetary
Fund):
Articles of Agreement 114;
autonomy of 114–15; as economic
regulator 59; and international
liquidity 79; origins 257;
'orthodoxy' 61; relations with
commercial banks 164;
relations with private credit
clubs 114; reserves held by 48;
and rules to limit free riding 20;
as specific function
organization 26, 27; structure
109–10; as supernational
organization 14–15; and Third
World 46, 55, 113, 273; and
transgovernmental coalitions
120; voting power in 22, 189
IMO (International Marine
Organization) 280
import liberalization 79
India 15, 180, 234, 242, 244, 265, 266
Indonesia 242, 244, 245
Integrated Commodity Plan *see*
UNCTAD
Integrated Programme for
Commodities *see* IPC
integration 16–17, 37–8, 39
Inter American Bank 128
Inter American Committee on the